MW00833865

RELIGION IN
SECULAR ARCHIVES

RELIGION IN SECULAR ARCHIVES

Soviet Atheism and Historical Knowledge

SONJA LUEHRMANN

OXFORD
UNIVERSITY PRESS

OXFORD
UNIVERSITY PRESS

Oxford University Press is a department of the University of
Oxford. It furthers the University's objective of excellence in research,
scholarship, and education by publishing worldwide.

Oxford   New York
Auckland   Cape Town   Dar es Salaam   Hong Kong   Karachi
Kuala Lumpur   Madrid   Melbourne   Mexico City   Nairobi
New Delhi   Shanghai   Taipei   Toronto

With offices in
Argentina   Austria   Brazil   Chile   Czech Republic   France   Greece
Guatemala   Hungary   Italy   Japan   Poland   Portugal   Singapore
South Korea   Switzerland   Thailand   Turkey   Ukraine   Vietnam

Oxford is a registered trademark of Oxford University Press
in the UK and certain other countries.

Published in the United States of America by
Oxford University Press
198 Madison Avenue, New York, NY 10016

© Oxford University Press 2015

All rights reserved. No part of this publication may be reproduced, stored in
a retrieval system, or transmitted, in any form or by any means, without the prior
permission in writing of Oxford University Press, or as expressly permitted by law,
by license, or under terms agreed with the appropriate reproduction rights organization.
Inquiries concerning reproduction outside the scope of the above should be sent to the
Rights Department, Oxford University Press, at the address above.

You must not circulate this work in any other form
and you must impose this same condition on any acquirer.

Library of Congress Cataloging-in-Publication Data
Luehrmann, Sonja.
Religion in secular archives : Soviet atheism and historical knowledge /
Sonja Luehrmann. — 1st [edition].
   pages cm. — (Oxford series on history and archives)
Includes bibliographical references.
ISBN 978–0–19–994362–3 (hardback : alk. paper)
1. Atheism—Soviet Union.   2. Soviet Union—Religion.   I. Title.
BL2747.3.L74 2015
200.947'0904—dc23
2014047220

9 8 7 6 5 4 3 2 1
Printed in the United States of America
on acid-free paper

Contents

Acknowledgments

As an anthropologist, I am accustomed to thanking key hosts and conversation partners who helped me during field research. During research for this book, such guides and facilitators were archivists who made the institutions they worked in not only more transparent but also more hospitable. In particular, I am grateful to Valentina Pavlovna Shomina and Valentina Ivanovna Orekhovskaia (Ioshkar-Ola), Dina Nikolaevna Nokhotovich and Liudmila Gennad'evna Kiseleva (Moscow), Lialia Zaudatovna Khasanshina (Kazan), Larisa Seago (Keston Archive, Baylor University), and the staff of the Archive of Audiovisual Documentation, Nizhnii Novgorod. For facilitating archival access and entry into the intellectual worlds of their cities, I thank Marina Kopylova, Rustem Tsiunchuk, Marina Mogilner, Ilya Gerasimov, and Olga Shimanskaia.

This book draws on archival research that was carried out in conjunction with several years' worth of research projects, funded by the German Academic Exchange Service, the Wenner-Gren Foundation, IREX (with funds provided by the US Department of State) and the President's office and the Faculty of Arts and Social Sciences at Simon Fraser University. Generous visa and logistical support was provided by the international departments of Mari State University and Kazan Federal University. Special thanks to Aleksei Fominykh and Farit Khaidarov.

Francis Blouin and William Rosenberg are another pair of key facilitators, without whom this book would not exist. They invited me to submit a proposal to the series edited by them and provided much valuable advice. Bill Rosenberg in particular has been a steadfast mentor and support, whose enthusiasm for archives and atheism motivated me to keep coming back to these documents. Nancy Toff was an astute editor at Oxford University Press, and I am grateful for her patience in waiting for the completion of the manuscript. It is difficult to imagine that my father, Dieter Lührmann, is no longer there to read through the book before most other people are even aware that it is out, but his love of detective work and close reading is certainly present in these pages.

This book bears the imprint of conversations and exchanges with Alexander Agadjanian, Julie de Graffenried, Paul Hebbard, Jeanne Kormina, Alaina Lemon, Rudolf Mrázek, Richard Nance, Vlad Naumescu, Kimberley Powers, John Schoeberlein, Natalia Shlikhta, Victoria Smolkin-Rothrock, Viktor Solov'ev, Ann Stoler, Raufa Urazmanova, Katherine Verdery, Ilya Vinkovetsky, and Catherine Wanner. Special thanks are due to the reviewers for Oxford University Press for their helpful and incisive comments. Participants in the 2012/13 ReSET seminar on Anthropological Approaches to Religion and Secularism, sponsored by the Open Society Institute, engaged in a stimulating discussion on reading archival documents from the Council of Religious Affairs. Anastasia Rogova edited references and compiled the bibliography.

Parts of Chapter 2 previously appeared in Russian as "Chto my mozhem znat' o sovetskoi religioznosti? Sopostavlenie arkhivnykh i ustnykh istochnikov iz poslevoennogo Povolzh'ia," *Gosudarstvo, Religiia, Tserkov' v Rossii i za rubezhom* 30:3–4 (2012): 485–504. I appreciate the opportunity to use them here.

Finally, I thank Dr. Gudrun Westphal, history teacher extraordinaire, who encouraged me to stop worrying about the imposing staircase and learn to love the archive when I was in twelfth grade. I was fortunate to be able to sustain this love in a history-friendly anthropology department at the University of Frankfurt and in the joint Doctoral Program in Anthropology and History at the University of Michigan. Joining me along the way, Ilya, Philipp, and Vera Vinkovetsky became part of my travels to Russian archives and made sure that I took plenty of breaks from writing about them, for which I am doubly grateful.

Note on Transcription, Translation, and Archival Citation

With a few exceptions, the archival documents analyzed in this book originated from the Russian Soviet Federal Socialist Republic (RSFSR), one of fifteen republics that made up the Soviet Union. The predominant language of archival documentation in the RSFSR was Russian, even in regions where significant parts of the population spoke other languages (such as the Turkic and Finno-Ugric languages of the Volga region). In transcribing Russian Cyrillic script, I followed the Library of Congress system, omitting diacritics. I usually encountered Tatar names in their Russianized versions, so that my Latin renderings of these names follow the conventions for transcribing Russian rather than Tatar. All translations from archival and published sources are my own.

In Russian, as in English, capitalization of nouns often denotes respect. Aware of this, Soviet authors intentionally used small initials in words such as *bog* (god), *bibliia* (bible), or *koran* (qur'an). I follow the original capitalization choices in translated quotes to show how atheist perspectives permeate printed and handwritten texts through modified standards of spelling.

Citations of material from Russian archives follow the standard format: archival acronym, f[ond]—fonds or collection, op[is']—register or series, d[elo]—file, l[ist]—numbered page in the file. The Keston Archive at Baylor University uses its own system, explained in Chapter 4. Since I use recent documents dealing with issues that still resonate in Russian society, I sometimes omit the names of private individuals where sensitive information is involved.

RELIGION IN
SECULAR ARCHIVES

Introduction

Secular Archives, Religious Trouble?

In January 1956, loyal Soviet citizens had every reason to think that history was on their side. Nikita Khrushchev had succeeded Joseph Stalin in 1953 and would soon denounce his predecessor's "cult of personality" in his secret speech at the twentieth congress of the Communist Party. His early policy initiatives already demonstrated that far from collapsing after the death of its feared and imposing leader, the Soviet Union could take on ambitious new targets for production of food, consumer goods, and housing construction. Socialism seemed about to deliver on its promises of a better life, and volunteers had mobilized to help bring this about. They participated in the Virgin Lands campaign to make the Kazakh steppe arable and began to form people's patrols that called on fellow workers and neighbors to take responsibility for social order. Another aspect of such populist mobilizations were new waves of humiliation and harassment directed against religious communities, who were cast as anachronisms with no place in the forward-moving country.[1] The scholars and atheist propagandists who gathered in Moscow for one of the first all-Russian seminars on atheist propaganda since the beginning of the Second World War were once again encouraged to equate being Soviet with being secular, and both with freedom from any constraints of the past.

Participants at the seminar reported on activities in their region, and repeatedly debated the question of how much one needed to know in order to be an effective atheist. Should propagandists have access to religious scriptures in order to debate believers? Where could they find the latest scientific theories on the origins of the universe and human beings in order to contest religious narratives? Which bits of scientific and political information were most likely to sway believers and keep atheists focused on the importance of their task? As a participant from Novosibirsk noted with dismay:

> Since the church no longer takes up a counter-revolutionary position in our country, but calls for peace, since priests in their sermons support a healthy life style and preach against drunkenness, many draw the mistaken conclusion that we need the church and that religion is not harmful.[2]

At the same time as producing a renewed emphasis on the incompatibility of religion and socialism, the years after Stalin's death marked the emergence of new standards for the observation and analysis of religious life in the Soviet Union. Intrigued by the riddle of why religion was not disappearing as fast as material life was progressing, Soviet bureaucrats, activists, and scholars embarked on a quest to understand this phenomenon. They proposed new explanations for what religion was and how it functioned, and they also spoke to religious believers about their motivations, sometimes in the context of administrative or court proceedings, sometimes as part of a scholarly study. The result is a large number of texts that describe religious practices and communities and their development under socialism. After the demise of the Soviet Union, these texts—some stored in archives, some published—have become historical sources on the dynamic contours of religious life in a society that no longer exists. But when it comes to using these sources, their hostile perspective and our retrospective knowledge of the failure of the atheist project stand in the way of any simple reading that takes their content at face value.

Working with the wealth of documents on religion in Soviet archives, I often found myself pulled in two directions at once. I tried to pierce through the obligatory rhetoric and standard formulae and filter out the facts about religious life that might hide behind them. But I also felt the charm emanating from the archival forms themselves: the tone of collegiality or defensiveness between letter writers and addressees; the unexpected linkages or distances between documents created by the filing system; and the orthographic errors, wrong salutations, and garbled references to religious narratives that showed how alien both religious and bureaucratic discourses were to some authors. The visual aesthetics of typed reports marked up in blue and red pencil by a succession of skeptical or triumphant readers cast documents as crucial nodes in nets of social relations that could not be reduced to the truth value of their content. Inspired by a growing body of scholarship that takes just such material and stylistic features as points of entry into thick histories of writing, power, and bureaucratic knowledge, I decided to allow myself to linger on style, texture, and archival classification systems.[3] At the same time, I remained interested in the content of Soviet observations of religious life and was dissatisfied with the idea that the stacks of paper waiting for me in various archival reading rooms spoke only of the internal workings of Soviet state bureaucracies. This book is an attempt to show how awareness of "archival ecologies"[4] can open up documents as richer and more multi-faceted historical sources, especially in cases where the good faith and expertise of the authors in relation to the phenomena described must be questioned.

Looking at some of the most commonly accessible types of Soviet-era sources on religion, I consider their materiality and placement in the archives as traces of the social relationships from which they emerged and that continue to shape them: the relationships between believers, administrators, and occupants of various bureaucratic hierarchies from which texts originated; the rules about bureaucratic classification and inter-office communication that determined where and how documents were filed; and the changing stances of archival researchers toward Soviet society after the collapse of the USSR. In his work on colonial history in Haiti, Michel-Rolph Trouillot distinguishes four levels of silencing that affect archival research: "the moment of fact creation (the making of *sources*); the moment of fact assembly (the making of *archives*); the moment of fact retrieval (the making of *narratives*); and the moment of retrospective significance (the making of *history*)."[5] By analogy, one could say that documents can be made to speak at all these different levels, and an analysis that makes connections between levels can open up new opportunities for understanding.

Knowing the constraints under which Soviet observers operated when creating sources on religion provides a deeper appreciation of the insights they came up with as well as a better-founded caution of the limits of such insights. Attention to archival filing systems that foreground and contextualize certain sources while omitting or marginalizing others can open a window on the bureaucratic logics of classification that shaped the lives of all Soviet citizens, including religious believers. Equally important are the levels of fact retrieval and changing retrospective relationships with sources, closely linked in the Soviet case because possibilities of archival access expanded dramatically at the same time that socialist state-promoted secularization ceased to be a living political project. Being aware of how scholarly concepts of modernity, secularization, and religious persistence have shifted globally in the wake of sweeping political changes casts doubt on any certainty that twenty-first-century academics are inherently better positioned to understand religious subjectivities than twentieth-century atheists. Like Soviet atheists in the 1950s and '60s, contemporary scholars are still trying to grasp what happens to religion in modern and postmodern societies.

Exploring the insights and blind spots of institutionally hostile observers can help us re-evaluate where accurate understanding of social worlds comes from.

Optimism and Doubt in the Archives

One aspect that separates our retrospective readings of Soviet atheist sources from those of their intended contemporary readers is also a source of their peculiar charm: the optimism about social progress expressed in predictions that religion was destined to disappear eventually, along with all other forces of social backwardness. Especially in the early Khrushchev years, this expectation was part of a general sense of history moving in the right direction, giving atheist speeches a pathos familiar from situations of economic growth and accelerated social change elsewhere in the world. "The main reason for the growth of mass godlessness in our country is the victory of socialism . . ., the consolidation of the socialist order, the development of culture, and the active participation of the masses in the building of communism," affirmed Chairman Khudakov of the atheist section of the All-Union Knowledge Society, which hosted the 1956 seminar. In a country that felt itself moving rapidly into the future, religion needed to disappear because it represented "one of the most tenacious and vibrant survivals of the past."[6] In particular, groups whose demands on the everyday lives of their members set them apart from Soviet norms were vilified as fanatical.[7]

The notion of religion as a survival based in ignorance was fueled by Marxist teachings about evolutionary stages of human history, but it took on a special salience in the post-war decades through the institutional placement of anti-religious work. The Knowledge Society's full original name was All-Union Society for the Dissemination of Political and Scientific Knowledge, and its mandate was to bring "knowledge to the people" through lectures by scholars in front of popular audiences. Founded in 1947, it inherited the task of promoting atheism from the more specialized pre-war League of the Militant Godless, which ceased to operate during the war.[8] For the pre-war and post-war periods respectively, the reports, correspondence, and meeting minutes of both organizations represent major sources on Soviet efforts to promote atheism. Complementing state and party memoranda, they also contain important clues about new and old forms of religious life in the state of workers and peasants.[9] But compared to the League, the Knowledge Society embraced a wider scope of activities, ranging from lectures on evolutionary biology and direct contestations of religious narratives to presentations on literature and art. The assumption was that religious decline would result from the spread of knowledge about the advances of Soviet science. Like its counterparts in other socialist countries, the Society pitted science against religion in a rhetoric of "knowledge" versus "faith" familiar from North American controversies about evolution and creationism.[10]

Because Soviet documents place religion in the larger narrative of overcoming backwardness, information about it is clothed in a tone of confidence in the social benefits of scientific advances. As cosmonauts explored space, agronomists opened new lands for cultivation, and mathematicians applied their knowledge to new fields of processing information and simulating economic models, Soviet citizens were not only expected to become more knowledgeable but also better and happier people.[11] In the age of climate change, this optimism has become difficult to understand. In the aftermath of the Second World War, however, it had analogues in many other parts of the world, including the uranium-producing regions of the American West, whose residents traded immense health risks for participation in a Cold-War version of manifest destiny.[12] In both contexts, science came to stand for a desired future, while communities that represented alternative paths of historical development (Native American and Mexican communities

"What people still believe" is the title of a display at Staryi Tor"ial rural library, Mari ASSR, about 1972. In this rare image of locally made atheist propaganda, a quotation from the early anti-religious activist Emelian Iaroslavskii (1878–1943) illustrates the view of religion as false knowledge that prevents scientific progress: "Religion is a blindfold on a person's eyes that keeps him from seeing the world as it is." *Courtesy of Novyi Tor'ial District Museum, Republic of Marii El, Russia.*

in the United States, religious communities in the Soviet Union) were relegated to the margins.

Specific to the socialist version of progress, the expectation of the imminent disappearance of religion was fueled by readings of Marx and Engels that treated religious belief as a kind of human adaptation to unjust and incomprehensible social relationships. As "inverted world consciousness" produced by an "inverted world," religion might be expected to fade away on its own with the creation of a classless society built on principles of social equality. But from the beginning the Bolshevik government did not entirely trust the historical process to do this work on its own, as vicious persecution of clergy and lay believers in the 1920s and '30s showed .[13] Under the impact of the Second World War, the Soviet Union switched to a more conciliatory course and developed a specialized bureaucracy to monitor religious affairs, the twin Council for Russian Orthodox Church Affairs and Council for Religious Cult Affairs. As commissioners for both councils started to collect statistics on ritual observance and attendance at worship, it became clear that circumcising and baptizing children, observing religious holidays, and praying for dead and sick relatives remained very much a part of Soviet life, often carried out alongside participation in socialist construction.[14]

The awareness that so-called survivals of the past were not disappearing as expected increased after Stalin's death, at a time of new interest in building communism through voluntary commitment rather than fear and command. Urging Soviet citizens to take responsibility for their own social problems, Khrushchev warned that almost forty years after the Bolshevik Revolution, there was no reason to "keep blaming [Tsar] Nicholas II" for everything that went wrong.[15] Along with religion, such uncanny "survivals of the past" that were perhaps not survivals at all included alcoholism, interpersonal violence, and small-scale, unauthorized trade.[16] Late Soviet archives confront researchers with the boredom and predictability of bureaucratic procedures, but also with striking moments where self-identified agents of progress reflect on the limits of their own transformative work. Different from other socially troubling phenomena, religious practices were supported by full-fledged institutions, many of whom operated legally within the Soviet Union, while others appeared in unexpected places. For this reason, reports of their occurrence and effects are not just expressions of moral panics but also show how Soviet bureaucracies acknowledged the limits of their own administrative and ideological reach.

Religion in Lenin's City

The question of whether ongoing religious practices were survivals of the past or consequences of the internal contradictions of socialism was raised most pointedly in towns that were founded during the Soviet period. Different from older cities that had to be reconstructed to fit the requirements of socialism,[17] Soviet-founded cities had no houses of worship and pre-revolutionary traditions of processions, shrines, or other localized ways of engaging the sacred. The transcript of the January 1956 seminar of atheist propagandists records the presentation of a lecturer from Shatura, an industrial settlement east of Moscow famous for the role of its peat-fueled power plant in Lenin's drive to build socialism through the electrification of the entire country.[18] The lecturer contrasts this historical fame to the challenges posed by persisting religious practices:

> Shatura, Lenin's Shatura. The town grew up beside the power station. The station recently celebrated its thirtieth anniversary, which means that the town is of the same age—thirty years. A young socialist city. There is not a single church there, not a single house of prayer, and in the vicinity of Shatura in a radius of 15 km churches stopped functioning in the 1920s, they were turned into schools.[19]

In spite of these promisingly secular environs, the lecturer recounted that factory workers refused to attend atheist lectures, announcing "I am a religious believer, and am not going to listen to nonsense about religion."[20] Seventh-day Adventists and Baptists were active in the city, and the sole remaining Russian Orthodox church ten miles away was such a popular destination for Easter and other holidays that the railway administration put in additional trains to transport Shatura residents there. As Easter approached bakeries sold *kulich*, a sweet bread that the faithful took to church to be blessed on Holy Saturday. The bread was labeled "spring cake" in the stores, "but we all know what it really is."[21]

Throughout the post-war decades of developed socialism, reports from various parts of the Soviet Union add to this picture of religion cropping up in places where it was not supposed to be. The low-level officials who wrote such reports and the more centrally placed functionaries who read them often attempted to explain the discrepancy, pointing to the enduring religious monopoly on alleviating the fear of death[22] or the uneven exposure of the population to Soviet cultural offerings.[23] Many such explanations implied that religious persistence challenged cherished assumptions about Soviet society—that it was a society without fear, for example, or one in which all citizens were equally included. But by acknowledging religious persistence, observers also reaffirmed the narrative framework of socialist construction, showing that it was strong enough to name problematic phenomena and address their causes. When the lecturer from Shatura described his encounters with religiosity in a quintessentially Soviet city for an audience of fellow lecturers, he appealed to shared expectations about the eventual triumph of communism and demise of religion. These would also be shared by the intended readership of the typed transcript of the seminar proceedings, including Knowledge Society officers and members of the Communist Party nomenklatura in charge of cultural policy.

Archives in Retrospect

When I read the conference transcript almost half a century later, during a fall season of research in Moscow archives in 2005, I came to the thick, cloth-bound volume of typewritten pages with different sets of questions and assumptions. Now stored in the building that housed the part of the collections of the State Archive of the Russian Federation that were generated by "Russian" (as opposed to USSR-level) institutions, the file came from the *fond* (collection) of the Russian branch of the Knowledge Society. I was looking through the Society's records as part of a research project on secularization and atheist propaganda in the Soviet Union under Khrushchev and Brezhnev and their impact on post-Soviet religious life.[24] Because the Russian Federation had signed on to the international standard of barring access to archival documents for thirty years after they were generated, the temporal distance that separated me from the year 1956 was accentuated by the fact that the closest I could work toward my own present using documents from the same archive was 1975.

But more than time separated me from the meeting of atheist activists. In 1991, the state they had served had collapsed and the twin projects of building communism and promoting atheism had been disavowed. Although the Knowledge Society continues to exist as an organization dedicated to popularizing scientific discoveries, the aims and contents of its activities have shifted. It is no longer tied to the Communist Party (which oversaw all so-called mass organizations in the Soviet Union) and is no longer considered to be doing work of vital importance to the state. Outside of archival opening hours, I was spending my time interviewing religious activists, most of whom had recently converted and were eager to disavow the value of Soviet-era knowledge.[25]

The political and economic upheavals of the early 1990s have made the records of the Knowledge Society accessible to foreign researchers, but they also dramatically shifted the "horizons of expectation"[26] of potential readers. At the same time as these documents have become accessible, their value as historical sources has been thrown open to question. How should one read a document generated in the service of an abandoned project whose underlying assumptions about historical development have turned out to be largely mistaken? Can it still serve as evidence of the phenomena of religious persistence and incomplete secularization it discusses? In Trouillot's terminology, the job of

creating facts about religious life in the Soviet Union was over-
whelmingly in the hands of organizations dedicated to its control and eradication. Given the deep silences and loud polemics
that shape the available sources, what can we tell about the way
these sources were created, assembled, and read by others that
helps them speak in new registers?

This is the question this book grapples with, and one of the
reasons it matters is a third kind of gulf that lay between me as
a reader and the reports filed by Soviet atheists. Not only had
decades passed and political orders changed, but academic ori-
entations had shifted as well. Questions about religious decline
and persistence continue to provoke public debate, but the basic
assumptions that ground the debate have changed. From this
altered perspective, we now bring questions to Soviet-era documents that their authors did not anticipate, precisely because
the results of twentieth-century socialist attempts at speedy,
state-enforced secularization continue to have comparative and
theoretical importance for studies of religion and modernity.

Imagining Secularization

In the 1950s and '60s, committed Soviet atheists would not have
been alone in their surprise to discover evidence of religiosity in
modern cities. The idea that religion would disappear, or at least
lose public significance, in industrial modernity was at that time
well accepted among Western historians and social scientists. In
fact, by international comparison, Soviet atheists may have been
unusually attentive to the presence of religious practices among
industrial working populations. As social history in Western
Europe and North America focused on the living conditions,
labor struggles, and emerging forms of collective consciousness of
workers, evidence that religion played a role in these processes
was often treated as an embarrassment by those who noticed it.[27]
In 1963, for instance, the British labor historian E. P. Thompson
published his seminal study *The Making of the English Working*

Class, in which he grudgingly acknowledged the popularity of Methodism among nineteenth-century English workers, only to call it "the desolate inner landscape of Utilitarianism" and "a ritualised form of psychic masturbation."[28] His expectation that the working class should be a force for progress, and that progress involves the disappearance of religion made Thompson unable to conceptualize the social importance of working-class religious institutions. Instead, he inadvertently echoed the perspective of nineteenth-century Anglican and Catholic clergy who saw such low-church religiosity as a temporary veneer that hid the underlying disintegration of established churches.[29]

A similar tendency to overlook or belittle religious phenomena was evident among non-Marxist scholars of modernizing societies: for example, many scholars of the Muslim world discussed Islam primarily from the perspective of how much it impeded economic development or could be made compatible with it.[30] Although there were social historians who started looking at religious institutions from the 1970s onward, these scholars often saw themselves as pioneering new ground and testing the limits of their field.[31] Had a translated transcript of the debates among Knowledge Society activists made its way west during the heydays of the Society's work, the sense of incongruity and surprise at finding religion in Lenin's city would have been easily intelligible to readers from all sides of the political spectrum.

For a scholar coming upon the archival transcript in the early twenty-first century, the relationship between religion and modern life presents itself in a different light. Inspired in part by a post–Cold War world in which religious allegiances emerge as major political factors, in part by an ongoing shift of attention to all things "cultural" and away from harder "economics" and "social facts," interest in religion has returned to the mainstream of the humanities and social sciences.[32] An ever-growing number of books presents religious commitments and practices as integral aspects of all periods of human history, including industrial and post-industrial societies. Some scholars have even demanded that the so-called secularization paradigm should be abandoned, at least if it is understood as the idea of an inevitable decline of the role of religion in public life under conditions of modernization.[33]

Others—many of them historians and sociologists working with quantitative data on observance of religious rites and statements of belief and unbelief—insist that the second half of the twentieth century has seen a dramatic decline of many indicators of religiosity, at least in Europe, North America, and parts of the Pacific Rim such as Australia and Japan. These scholars argue that there is indeed a link between modernization and secularization, but that technological change alone does not explain it. Rather, people modify or abandon religious commitments in the context of changed gender relations, political and economic prospects, and models of successful life courses in an increasingly differentiated society where social norms and human relationships are in flux.[34] In socialist Eastern Europe and the Soviet Union, government efforts to promote atheism led to a "forced" or "accelerated" secularity whose consequences are still palpable in such places as East Germany, the Czech Republic, and Bulgaria, where populations show low levels of liturgical participation and assent to religious dogmas.[35] At the same time, social transformations in East and West also provoked those who remained religious to intensify their practice. In many European countries, revivalist reform movements, new strategies of proselytizing, and searches for alternative religiosity exist alongside declining trends of overall religious adherence.[36]

While the jury is still out on the secularization thesis, most twenty-first-century scholars agree that they live and work in a world shared among religious and non-religious people, and that this will remain so for the foreseeable future. In post-Soviet Russia, surveys show that the percentage of declared atheists and unbelievers declined from 42 percent of the population in 1991 to 20 percent in 2004, a number that has remained constant in more recent surveys.[37] At the same time as one fifth of the population continues to profess no religious belief, confessional adherence remains an important aspect of collective identity. In a 2003 survey of Russian citizens, 71 percent of respondents claimed to be Orthodox Christian (*pravoslavnyi*), while only 62 percent said that they believed in God.[38] In other parts of the industrialized world, the numbers of people who claim no religious affiliation are also growing at the same time that migration and changing roles of religious institutions create new landscapes of religious diversity.[39]

Such pluralism of worldviews is at the heart of the philosopher Charles Taylor's definition of late modern societies as "secular." Religion has not vanished, but even religious people must recognize that not everyone shares their convictions, which are therefore subject to personal choice and negotiation.[40] For their part, committed secularists have to acknowledge the persistence of religiously inspired forms of social action, a challenge quite comparable to the one faced by Soviet atheists seeking to come to terms with the religious aspects of life in 1950s Shatura. In the early twenty-first century, the expectation of inevitable secularization has itself become an object of historical study. What were the larger assumptions about rationality, social class, education, and historical causality that made the idea that modernization and industrialization led to religious decline so convincing to scholars, clergy, and politicians? What stories of struggle, strategic decisions, and unintended consequences did historians overlook when they thought of secularization as an automatic process?[41]

In the course of such self-critical questioning, some scholars have suggested that normative expectations of secularization have led academics to adopt distorted views of religious communities. The perception that religion and modern life are incompatible led to portrayals of religion as oppressive and irrational and discouraged explorations of theological models of agency and embodied ways of knowing.[42] According to this line of argument, a kind of crypto-atheism prevents historians and social scientists from doing full justice to religious subjectivities.[43] Soviet atheism presents an interesting test case because scholars and activists linked to the Knowledge Society and the Communist Party were open and unapologetic about their secularist perspective, and yet they claimed to be producing valid knowledge about religious life. In some cases, publicly endorsing atheism may have been the only way to realize an academic interest in religion.[44] It is difficult to reconstruct personal motivations in hindsight, but no matter what a researcher's personal attitude may have been, the only way religion could be discussed in Soviet-era writings was within the horizon of expectation of its eventual disappearance. How did such an antagonistic stance toward the subject of research affect possible knowledge about it?

Religious Others in the Archives

An excerpt from the transcript of another Knowledge Society seminar shows the range of questions raised by documents of antagonistic inquiry. The seminar was held in May 1959 and dealt with "questions of theology and Russian Orthodoxy." One of the speakers was a researcher at the Institute of Ethnography of the Soviet Academy of Sciences, L. A. Pushkareva, who reported on research among collective farm workers in Kalinin region (a part of northwest Russia whose capital is now again known by its pre-revolutionary name of Tver'). Using generation and gender as key characteristics that determined someone's relationship to "religious survivals," the ethnographer presented a narrative that acknowledged the persistence of religiosity and legitimized its study while reaffirming an overall trend of secularization. Only the old generation of collective farm workers has knowledge of "religious ideology," such as "ideas about god, about judgment day and the saints." This is the generation that was brought up "in the patriarchal school" before the revolution, "where they studied catechism."[45]

Members of the next generation, people in their forties, "have only fragmented (*otryvochnye*) ideas about religion. These are people who went through the harsh school of the Great Patriotic War. It is safe to say that all men of this age do not believe in god and are free of religious prejudice." There are also atheists among the women of that generation, but more typically such women claim that "there is something higher that stands above people, in accordance with the authority of the elders[.] They carry out traditional religious rituals and require the same of young people." Although women of this generation tend to have no knowledge of religious dogmas, they hold on to ritual traditions because of their "low level of education and comparatively closed way of life in the family."[46]

Whereas for men, according to Pushkareva, fighting in the war was a reason to abandon religious faith, wartime losses made women more religious: "Many women lost their husbands, fathers, and brothers during the war, and became more religious as a result. If before they never crossed the threshold of a church, now they've all started to pray."[47] In this account, gendered experiences of violence and loss frame religion as an irrational consolation that true soldiers reject but that appeals to a generation of bereaved widows. Religiosity among younger women is treated as a consequence of being cut off from social life and subjected to the authority of older women in the household:

> Young married women are most easily subjected to [religious] influence. These women are burdened by domestic duties, [although] many of them are former activists. Now they stop attending clubs, cinemas, libraries, are sucked in by daily chores (*zasasyvaiutsia bytom*). As a result, their spiritual world is impoverished and they cannot resist the old people . . . . This is apparent from the fact that in many villages of Kalinin region almost all children born after the war have been baptized, while children born in the 1920s remained mostly unbaptized. Now the elders insist on baptizing the children. When they cannot convince the

young people with words, they refuse to baby-sit and thereby force them to baptize the children. Women who do not wish to have their children baptized face condemnation.[48]

This sketch of rural power relations is typical of Soviet ethnographic research on religion, discussed in more detail in Chapter 3. It acknowledges worrisome trends such as high rates of infant baptism but argues that they do not indicate a vibrant religiosity among the generation that counts most: the young workers preparing for positions of responsibility in enterprises and communities. For the historian it is hard to know how much credence to give to this account of the state of religiosity in rural Russia in the 1950s. Blaming old people and housewives for ongoing religious expression was a common way to demonstrate the continuing threat posed by religion (thus justifying resources devoted to atheist propaganda) while protecting officials from having to take steps against any individuals whose career might have suffered if they were found to be involved in religious practices.[49] The idea that pressure from grandmothers forced young parents to have their children baptized was common in Soviet literature, but there is some evidence that not even Soviet bureaucrats entirely believed it. Regulations prohibiting churches from baptizing minors unless both parents signed the baptismal registry indicate that policymakers were well aware how tempting it was for a parent who was a teacher or party official to disavow responsibility by sending a spouse, mother, or mother-in-law to request the baptism.[50]

This example shows that the same archival collections can contain officially sanctioned narratives about a religious phenomenon and evidence of practices indicating lack of trust in these narratives. Archival documents can provide the grounds for their own critical deconstruction, if read against one another and with questions about the author's institutional and personal interests in mind. It was through such practices of reading against the grain that historians and anthropologists of colonialism first

sought to make "'hostile' documents"[51] fruitful for their inquiries. In many encounters between groups with unequal access to
literacy or technologies of documentation, the records of agencies dedicated to eradicating or reforming popular practices furnish the principal source for learning about them. The "prose
of counter-insurgency" with which colonial officials described
anti-colonial resistance is one example; reports about magic
compiled by the Catholic inquisition are another.[52] Scholars
working with such sources have defined their task as reversing
the authors' antagonistic perspectives and constructing sympathetic portraits of the phenomena described, be they resistance
movements in colonial India or popular religiosity in early modern Europe.

One way to accomplish such a reversal is to analyze the narrative structures that made an account convincing and that were
often in some way co-constructed between bureaucratic scribes
and the people whose deeds and voices they conveyed. Natalie
Zemon Davis argues that the petitions submitted by convicted
murderers in sixteenth-century France give us no direct access
to patterns of crime and psychological motivation in that society
but provide insights into the ideas about honor, responsibility,
and credibility that supplicants and court scribes appealed to in
their quest to receive a pardon.[53] Seeking to be sympathetic to
the marginalized voices of those who are only indirectly represented in written accounts, the historian attends to the cultural
resources they muster in the struggle be heard by an unc
nial audience.

Analyzing Pushkareva's account of rural religiosity in this
vein, one might ask about her position in academic and political
organizations, and how this may have shaped what collective
farm workers told her, what they preferred to hide, and how she
passed on her findings to various audiences. As an ethnographer
speaking before an assembly of atheist propagandists, Pushkareva
may have been tempted to exaggerate the continued importance
of religion in rural life while providing ideologically acceptable

explanations. This made combining commitments to studying and combating religion a serious but not entirely hopeless task. By reiterating common Soviet assumptions about the links between gender, age, and religiosity, the ethnographer supports other speakers' calls for more attention to rural residents, housewives, and pensioners in the struggle against unwanted "survivals." She also presents the collective farm workers in a largely positive light, emphasizing their contributions to the war against Nazi Germany and their capacity to accept atheist insights if given the necessary opportunities and freedom from the social control of older generations. As a narrative strategy, Pushkareva's portrayal of rural religiosity places the collective farmers on a developmental trajectory pointing toward full integration into socialist life while simultaneously justifying the Knowledge Society's demand for state resources to support its work.

Such an interpretation reads between the lines of an archival account to decode the intentions and political strategies of the author and those whose experiences she describes. Post-colonial readings of archival and literary accounts, for example, have helped us appreciate the ways in which political goals and narrative conventions shape what people can and cannot say, what projects can be formulated and carried forward and which ones remain inarticulate, though sometimes active at the level of fear, fantasy, or rumor.[54] Schooled in this literature, historians who traveled to newly accessible Soviet archives in the 1990s were well aware that these collections could not be expected to tell the literal truth about their subjects. Trial and interrogation records, secret police reports, industrial statistics, and the minutes of political and organizational meetings all needed to be read with questions in mind about the strategic interests, fears, and organizational constraints of those who wrote and compiled them.[55]

But the parallel to colonial and early modern archives also has its limits. If the reports of Soviet state authorities often represented a "prose of counter-insurgency" comparable to that of colonial administrations, Soviet educational policy meant that ever larger parts of the population were able to express themselves in writing.[56] Citizens of increasingly varied social and ethnic backgrounds left behind personally authored documents such as diaries, letters to newspapers, and letters of denunciation or complaint to the authorities. Many of these documents speak of a complex relationship between citizens and the state apparatus, from whom they expected benevolent or antagonistic responses, reprisals or rewards.[57] Historians of the Soviet period encounter a broader diversity of identifiable authors in the archives than historians of early modern Europe and many parts of the colonized world. Twentieth-century technologies of audio recording even bring transcripts of oral utterances into the archival record, making parts of the records of the Knowledge Society and other mass organizations read like plays. The voices are more diverse, but the demands of genre and appropriate frames of interaction weigh as heavily on them as on the scribe who transforms an illiterate person's tale into a legal document.

As a good example of the multivocality of Soviet archives, the transcripts of Knowledge Society seminars contain verbatim quotes attributed to scholars and propagandists from many parts of the Soviet Union. Trained in the skills of reading against the grain and between the lines, a historian might mine these documents for insights into the ways in which low- to mid-level activists understood and appropriated anti-religious and scientific rhetoric. The same tradition of critical reading would predispose the researcher to be highly suspicious of the content of activists' statements. When Pushkareva describes intergenerational pressures to perpetuate religious traditions, it is hard to overlook how conveniently her account reinforces Soviet equations of religiosity with age and rural backwardness while protecting younger women and cultural activists from blame. In an approach to archival documents broadly inspired by the work of Michel Foucault, such a reading moves us away from focusing on the truth value of the documents, raising questions such as those Katherine Verdery has asked of the Romanian secret police files: "What regime of truth or knowledge do they assume and attempt to serve, and how is it connected with power?"[58]

Where this discursive approach can fall short is that it does not allow us to consider Soviet critiques of rural social hierarchies as containing valid insights that do more than simply perpetuate an existing regime of power. In fact, there is quite a bit of affinity between Western feminist critiques of power and gender in intimate settings and the complicated stance toward tradition taken by late Soviet social scientists.[59] Focusing solely on ideological truth-claims can also lead us to exaggerate the social distance between those who created records and those described in them, or the difference between the persona someone adopted in a letter to the authorities and in family or friendship relationships. Bureaucratic and scholarly knowledge were not created in isolation from the lives of Soviet citizens but were simultaneously products of complex social interactions and constituted environments for such interactions. Reading strategies that incorporate critical discourse analysis, but also move beyond the texts can yield insights into the workings of the Soviet state *and* the changing forms and possibilities for religious practice that existed within it.

Documentation as Action

One way to look at atheist sources as permeated by regimes of truth and power, but also connected to a reality outside of themselves, is to understand practices of studying, documenting, and explaining religious life as actions in an ongoing struggle about the place of religion in society. This struggle did not just take place at the level of interpretation. Rather, it affected the possible forms of religious practice for Soviet citizens. Official documentation played a key role in this struggle, because files were the places where the voices of different sides—religious adherents as well as atheist critics—were collected, preserved, categorized, and made available for further study and administrative decisions. Long before post-Soviet historians gained access to them, files with transcriptions of Knowledge Society seminars circulated among various levels of the Society's leadership and were mined for reports to Communist Party functionaries. Once deposited in the archives, some of them became available to Soviet scholars entrusted with writing current history. Many transcripts and reports bear the traces of such journeys in the shape of underscores and handwritten notes in the margins of typed pages. Thinking about documentation as a practice with social effects opens the way to reading "along the archival grain" and studying the ways in which decisions about compilation, destruction, and preservation are part and parcel of larger struggles about knowledge and its practical impact in a particular historical situation.[60]

Looking at archival files as active records means that they do not simply contain true or false descriptions of historical circumstances but are evidence of crucial processes of documentation that Soviet citizens had to reckon with, whether they were religious believers or not. Understanding documentation as "doing things with texts" in analogy to speech acts, I see the creation and circulation of documents as important ways in which states and citizens pursue their goals in relation to each other.[61] From this perspective, gauging the influence of normative atheism on the quality of archival information on religion is not just a matter of counting the blind spots and measuring the silences. Rather than just talking about religion in more or less accurate ways, the bodies of documents now housed in archives are the results of dynamic encounters between a state that wanted to eradicate religion but also needed to govern religious believers, and citizens who lived in ways disapproved of by the state but also needed its services and support. In the words of Miriam Dobson and Benjamin Ziemann, documents have "reality effects."[62]

In order to take such a view of documentation as action, I focus not only on individual documents but also on the way they are classified and put together in files and larger series and collections. Moving from the level of source creation to the level of assembly, it becomes easier to see the multi-faceted (and often deliberately obfuscating and confusing) way in which the state presented itself to believers, requiring them to participate in its symbolic orders and modes of political expression rather than remaining completely separate from them.[63] On the part of the state, the overall hostile stance toward religion as a social phenomenon created particular slots for collecting and preserving voices of religious practitioners—for example, in letters of complaint or notes on conversations. At times, the files of Soviet religion bureaucracies make it seem as if what citizens most cared about was where to pray, how to bury their dead according to religious traditions, and when and where to go on pilgrimage. The ubiquity of believers' voices and other forms of documented religious expression in the archives is sometimes treated as evidence of religious revivals at certain periods of Soviet history, notably during the 1970s and 80s.[64] Attention to archival logics of documentation helps us see that officials could over- as well as underestimate the strength of Soviet-era religiosity. Within this logic, evidence of ongoing religious expression sometimes created embarrassment for the officials who recorded them, but could also count as proof of their diligence.

A number of scholars have pointed to the inevitable polyphony and multiple authorship of records that document alien social worlds.[65] A file is often a heterogeneous compilation whose overall narrative is constructed through letters, notes, and depositions from inspectors, witnesses, experts, petitioners, and minutes of meetings and conversations. Some voices may be muted, others amplified through their placement in relation to other documents. Voices of religious believers have been present in Soviet archival collections from the beginning, and not always with the exclusive intention of debunking religious

Staff members of the State Archive of Gorkii Region assemble at their workplace for an excursion to Moscow in 1960. Being an archivist in the Soviet Union was a highly feminized profession. These were the people who accessioned and cataloged the files deposited by various bureaucracies. *Photo by B. A. Alekseev, courtesy of State Archive of Audio Visual Documentation, Nizhnii Novgorod, Russia, sn. 29975.*

views. Vladimir Bonch-Bruevich collected documents on sectarian groups that were illegal before the revolution to document tsarist oppression, and generations of pre- and post-war Soviet archeographers scoured Old Believer villages for manuscripts for the purpose of preserving authentic folk voices as well as withdrawing these books from religious use.[66] In these situations, there was a certain amount of overlap between the Bolshevik project of seizing control of history and older efforts of religious minorities to represent themselves to the state apparatus and to posterity.[67]

The aims of recording contemporary religious voices under advanced socialism were different from these earlier efforts to preserve evidence of popular resistance to the tsar. In the Soviet Union, documenting social reality was always done for the purpose of being able to change it, and the documentation of religious life tended to intensify during times of heightened struggle against it. But closer examination of archival collections shows that the roles ascribed to religious subjects and adopted by them varied over time and by documentary genre. Understanding choices of inclusion and exclusion and following the bureaucratic trajectories of particular statements makes it harder to count them as quantifiable evidence for the prevalence or scarcity of religious practice at particular periods in Soviet history. But it can reveal much about the scope for action available to those Soviet citizens who identified as religious.

Archives as Moving Targets

Once deposited in archives, records are not frozen in time but continue to have a history. Like public archives the world over, Russian federal and regional archives are organized according to the principle of bureaucratic provenance, grouping together records originating from a particular office or agency. As a researcher interested in religion, one learns to ask for particular *fondy* (archival fonds or collections). Of central importance are the records of the regional commissioners (*upolnomochennye*) of the two councils that were created in 1943 to deal with the ongoing reality of actually existing religion under socialism, and which merged into one Council of Religious Affairs in 1965 (*Sovet po delam religii*). Files of the Communist Party department of propaganda and agitation and the Knowledge Society also contain information on religious activity and atheist propaganda, as do those of educational institutions and court and custody records.

The files of the secret police (KGB) are currently largely inaccessible in Russia, and published collections relate mainly to

the Stalin era. Accessibility can be better in some other former
Soviet republics, such as Ukraine or the Baltic States.[68] Given
their links to surveillance, intimidation, and arrest, KGB files
have even stronger reality effects than those of the Council of
Religious Affairs. Otherwise both kinds of files raise similar
problems of interpretation, where an undesirable phenomenon
is subjected to very detailed scrutiny, but it is ultimately hard to
say if its importance is exaggerated or downplayed in notes and
reports.[69]

The basic logic of where religion is filed remains the same in
different archival locations across the former Soviet Union. But
differences between available bodies of records show how strategies of acquisition, attrition and loss, and changing regimes of
access shape and reshape what will be available to researchers at
any given moment. Much of this book draws on research conducted between 2005 and 2012 in archival collections related
to Marii El and Tatarstan, two ethnically autonomous regions
on the Middle Volga. Like many parts of the Soviet Union, the
Middle Volga region was an area where adherents of different religions (in this case, Muslims, Orthodox Christians, and
adherents of indigenous, land-based rituals) had lived together
for centuries.[70] Records from this region best reflect the fact that
governing and combating religion in the USSR always meant
dealing with *religions* in the plural, something that is easily over-
looked in studies that focus on the relationship between the
Soviet state and single denominations.[71]

The State Archive of the Republic of Marii El (GARME)
in Ioshkar-Ola and the National Archive of the Republic of
Tatarstan (NART) in Kazan contain well-preserved collections
of the commissioners of the Council of Religious Affairs and the
Knowledge Society. In the fall of 2005, I traveled to Moscow to
look at records related to the Volga region and to broader atheist
work in the State Archive of the Russian Federation (GARF).
Everywhere my research focused on the period between the
1950s and the mid- to late 1970s. The upper limit of this time

frame was determined by the restrictions on archival access to a file within thirty years after its creation; the lower limit reflects my interest in the post-war and post-Stalinist reconceptualizations of religion.

The tone and classificatory approach toward religion was similar in all three archives, but they differed in terms of what was available and accessible. In Ioshkar-Ola, I also worked with Communist Party documents, which were administered by the same archival institution but physically housed in a separate depository and reading room located in the basement of the municipal administration building (previously the city committee of the Communist Party). In Kazan and Moscow, the party archives are separate institutions with their own protocols for access, which time constraints did not allow me to pursue. However, directives from the Central Committee and the department of propaganda and agitation were included in the files of the council, making it possible to trace at least some of the flow of ideological guidance between party and state institutions.[72]

Because of the centralized nature of Soviet governance, one can theoretically find reports from any part of the Soviet Union in the collection of the Council of Religious Affairs in Moscow's GARF (*fond* R-6991), and duplicates of the same reports in regional archives. In practice, the bureaucratic tendency to reduplicate efforts can work to the advantage of a researcher against the vicissitudes of attrition and restricted access. In GARF, I found semesterly reports from the commissioner of religious affairs in the Mari republic from the 1960s and '70s that were listed as missing (*utracheno*) in Ioshkar-Ola. As GARME archivists had explained, a commissioner who served in the 1970s took the local copies home and then retired and died without bringing them back. When I worked in GARF, on the other hand, the fourth register of the council's files, representing the Khrushchev years, was still classified and inaccessible, whereas documents from the same period had been freely available in Ioshkar-Ola, minus the missing reports. In Kazan, the records of the commissioner were preserved in unusual detail, including not only the commissioner's correspondence with superiors in Moscow, the regional party committee, and local religious organizations, but also with lower-level authorities such as the police and tax agencies, and with commissioners in other parts of the Volga-Urals region. The contrast in tone and content between the correspondence with Moscow and with local authorities allowed for rich insights into the separate paper trails that made it possible for late Soviet dealings with religion to govern existing communities at the same time as trying to reduce their numbers.

In a previous book, I drew on the archives in Ioshkar-Ola and Moscow to describe Soviet efforts to promote atheism in the Mari republic and their legacies in post-Soviet religiosity.[73] In the present study, informed by new archival research in Kazan and in a counter-archive of religious dissident writing in Waco, Texas, I focus on materials that document Soviet-era religious life and ask how the interested perspectives of these documents can become an additional source of insight rather than a distortion to be eliminated from the reading. My inclination to take Soviet atheist perspectives on religion seriously is shaped in part by ongoing ethnographic research among post-Soviet Christians, Muslims, and Pagans in Marii El, Tatarstan, and elsewhere in Russia. The ideas, sensibilities, and ways of getting things done of these religious activists often have much in common with those of more secular neighbors and with approaches I read about in the archives. The habit of moving back and forth between reading archival documents and observing the practices of my contemporaries also makes me conscious of all the details of real-time interactions that never make it into the written accounts. Keeping in mind that the past is always "a scarce resource"[74] and we cannot afford to waste much evidence, this book aims to give students of Soviet-era religion insight into the range of archival, oral, and published sources available, and some ideas for navigating the hostility and partiality that pervade many of them.

As shown by the anecdote about the commissioner who took home records, one thing to know about Soviet archives is that they were compiled for continuous but always restricted use. The rule of keeping documents closed to users for thirty years was adopted by Russian archives only in the 1990s, so Soviet documents were never locked away and frozen until a date when their content would have no immediate connection to the present. Rather, each file transitioned gradually from its status as working bureaucratic record to historical evidence. The originating agency often retained claims to a file even after it was incorporated into state archives.[75] What is more, the "user sheet" (*list pol'zovatelei*), included to this day in the inner cover of every Russian archival file, shows its gradual transformation from a document of current affairs to a record of the past. On this sheet, every user is expected to record the date, purpose, and precise nature of use (which pages were looked at, which excerpted or copied). In the Communist Party archives in Ioshkar-Ola, for example, many files from the 1950s and '60s were consulted repeatedly throughout the late Soviet period. I was struck by the rich use that had been made of the minutes of district and city committee meetings almost from the moment of their accession, often for theses and dissertations that dealt with various aspects of socialist construction.

Rather than opening up previously closed depositories, the post-Soviet "archival revolution" reordered access, away from a regime that privileged institutional affiliation and politically opportune projects to one based on the age of the records and a user's ability to demonstrate a need to see them. As elsewhere in the world, most users of post-Soviet archives are not professional historians but people examining records for personal and practical reasons. In North America I have shared archival reading rooms with people engaged in genealogical research. Russian archives are full of retirees looking for proof that they worked in a particular enterprise (often one that has long since gone out of business) in order to substantiate pension or disability claims. Other common visitors include the employees of churches, mosques, or synagogues in search of old construction plans needed for restoration work or property claims. Most Russian Orthodox dioceses also have canonization commissions, whose members search the archives for records on executed clergy and laypeople.[76] Trustworthy or not, Soviet state records have reality effects even for post-Soviet religious life.

State Archives and Their Alternatives

This book does not offer a systematic overview of archival depositories that contain sources on Soviet religious life. Instead, it starts from a few archives I have come to know well and explores different avenues of inquiry into how they work, simultaneously looking "inside" and "outside" the state archive. The marvelous diversity of files from Kazan shows the variety of documentary genres and correspondence partners through which the commissioner of religious affairs conducted his work, helping me develop the theme of documentation as action. Going on from there, I investigate various constellations of evidence that combine official archival documents with oral history, published sources, or alternative counter-archives. None of these "outsides" of the Soviet state archive presents an autonomous discourse untainted by the political narrative of secularization. Rather, we find elements of that narrative in the reminiscences and writings of Soviet citizens who identified with a religious tradition and in archives established by their western sympathizers. At the same time, words attributed to religious believers were essential to the ways in which official documents and Soviet-era publications achieved their desired effects of documenting the successes and ongoing need for atheist work.

Like other scholars who combine archival, oral, and published sources for research on socialist societies, I find that the richest narratives emerge when we allow these different sources to complement and challenge one another.[77] A crucial step in creating such unsettling dialogues is to consider what each type of source was meant to do in a particular context. These contexts might be as different as an interview about memories of persecution in the 1990s, a meticulously documented inspection by the tax police in 1960, or a research publication in the 1970s that kept a difficult balance between demonstrating political usefulness and investigating unpleasant truths.

How does a study of documents and bits of information that move in and out of archives and develop different kinds of agency equip us to better use hostile as well as friendly documents as historical sources? For one thing, a focus on the material aspects of circulating, compiling, and cataloging documents reminds us that the aims and conceptions of the original author are not all that matters in a document's career. The uses of a document may fail to fulfill its original purpose but still have practical effects, as in the case of a misquoted article or a letter of introduction used by the wrong person. At the moment of assembly of documents into an archive, the values and logics inscribed in the text may be at odds with those of the filing system and finding aids, and the conceptual apparatus with which a researcher navigates these layers of information in retrospect may be different still. In the case of Soviet documents, their relationship to what one might think of as social reality is further complicated by the fact that documentation of life in the USSR was never intended to be neutral or objective but to participate in transforming the reality it described. Whereas colonial reports might try to disguise their "affinity with policy"[78] behind a rhetoric of objectivity, the mandate to transform and eliminate was part of the stated purpose of Soviet writings about religion, and it takes little critical energy to uncover it. More work is required to see how the production and circulation of documents were embedded in the social relations they sought to describe, and what role the documents fulfilled, or failed to fulfill, in bringing about the desired transformations.

Controversial Readings

For historians who seek to be faithful to the people whose voices they find in the archives, documents that are designed to serve a quest for transformation pose a methodological and ethical challenge. Rather than providing evidence of the past as it was, they are indexical traces of practices that were meant to push social life toward a different future, desired by some, treated with cynicism or fear by others. In the face of partial sources that show us society on the move, do we try to reconstruct and possibly even celebrate who the authors and objects of archival descriptions were at a given point in time, or do we affirm the efforts some of them were making to become something else?[79]

The topic of anti-religious struggle in particular evokes controversies to which it is hard to remain indifferent because they touch on long-standing contradictions in Western political thought, where religion is both the ultimate sphere of freedom and tolerance and a source of (sometimes voluntarily chosen) constraint.[80] Under socialism, a hostile stance was the condition of ideological admissibility for any consideration of religion because it was deemed a dangerous public force, whereas Anglophone readers may be used to thinking of it as a benign private choice. At the same time, the demands that religious traditions place on adherents continue to provoke public debate in many parts of the world.[81] Moving targets in an enduring controversy, archival descriptions of Soviet religion are simultaneously artifacts of a time when religion remained a mundane part of Soviet life and agents of bureaucracies whose purpose was to move the country toward a more secular future. In today's Russia, religion rather than atheism appears to be winning the day, and many current users are interested in the descriptive value of Council of Religious Affairs documents while being suspicious of their performative role in the service of secularization. In the effort to recover a religious past that was not allowed expression on its own terms, it can be tempting to turn to state documents for the facts that they were never meant to provide in a neutral way. Understanding the social interactions, bureaucratic conventions, and multiple authorships that went into creating archival sources and collections can help us read documents more critically but also let them speak in a richer array of voices. Meanwhile, contemporary controversies about the place of religion in public life remind us that Soviet atheists were not the only people who found it hard to remain impartial with regard to religious phenomena.

CHAPTER 1

Documentary Acts

Archival Genres in Anti-Religious Struggle

In 1964, the director of the library of Kazan State University wrote to the commissioner of religious affairs of the Tatar Autonomous Soviet Socialist Republic, Faizulla Mangutkin, with the request to authorize "the unremunerated transfer of manuscripts and books kept in the Mardzhani mosque of Kazan." A handwritten note on the letter records Mangutkin's response: "By agreement with the executive committee of Privolzhskii municipal district, I am directing the leaders of the religious community to transfer all books kept in the mosque to the research library."[1]

This letter, kept in the files of the commissioner of religious affairs in Tatarstan's national archive, represents a moment of unusual openness about the intricate links between documentation, custody of historical memory, and the exercise of power. As many analysts of literacy and statecraft have noted, the drive to document has been a crucial part of political and economic governance since the invention of writing systems. Administrative archives originated as authoritative sites that vouched for the authentic power of the documents placed in them.[2]

Few historians would dispute this fact, but most would also be left dissatisfied by attempts to see archives as nothing but storehouses of acts of power. For historians of Soviet religious life, the exchange between Mangutkin and the university library must be seen as a key moment in the forced expropriation of a religious community's historical treasures by a government agency. But the same correspondence also provides a glimpse of the central role played by religious institutions in local practices of knowledge transmission well into the Soviet period. An earlier letter from the republic's archival administration states that the mosque held "valuable and unique manuscripts and books in Arabic, Persian, and other eastern languages."[3] In addition to bearing witness to a wanton exercise of power, the letter can stimulate a reader to go to the library and look at the manuscripts and books expropriated from the mosque as evidence of the literacy practices and transregional ties of Russian and Soviet Muslims, whose importance and vitality as a form of indigenous cosmopolitanism was denied by anti-religious policy.

Archival researchers often find that documents have such a dual character. They bear witness to the interests of those who demanded they be kept and those who wrote, compiled, and assembled them, but they are also fascinating windows onto past times to which we would otherwise have no access.[4] A central argument of this book is that instead of ignoring one of these aspects at the expense of the other, we can gain a richer reading of past lives *and* a deeper understanding of how documentation sustains systems of power if we do not see archival documents as passive traces of actions and interests that played out "in real life." Rather, processes of producing, exchanging, and compiling documents were integral to the ways in which administrative apparatuses acted on populations and in which historical change unfolded.

In the case of the expropriation of the mosque's library, it was not enough that the books were physically moved, but a selection of the written and oral communications around this event had to be preserved to make the transfer permanent and define the proper authorities who had to be consulted in similar cases.

Notably, these proper authorities did not include the lay leadership or clergy of the religious community. The document also made the transfer "reportable" to central agencies in Moscow as proof of the contribution of local officials to the struggle to break religion's hold on people's lives. Finally, as an unintended consequence of the intended permanence of paper documents, such records of transfers could become the basis of claims for the return of religious objects and books after the collapse of the Soviet Union changed the balance of power between groups of archival users. What was written as a legitimizing act and preserved as evidence of the historical struggle of the forces of science and progress against religion could later turn into evidence of injustice.[5]

Among the actors who made such changing historical fortunes possible were archivists who sorted through stacks of paper and made decisions about what to discard, what to keep, and what order to impose on documents.[6] Other actors included staff of various offices and institutions who made decisions about what transactions to document in writing, what to leave out (such as the methods of persuasion used to convince mosque representatives to relinquish their library), and what to do with a document after it was filed. In the words of one ethnographer of bureaucratic procedure, "The quiet return of a case file to the (perhaps temporary) oblivion of the record room can settle an issue as much as the signature on a decision."[7] Bureaucratic actions and decisions were not simply recorded in documents but depended on the flow (or immobility) of pieces of paper between offices and agencies.

New Bureaucracies, New Documentary Practices

While discrediting religious institutions as custodians of social memory and expropriating their historical documents, the Soviet leadership set up new bodies that generated and collected knowledge of religious life.[8] During the first decades of the Soviet Union's existence, several organizations exercised bureaucratic oversight over religious activity. A commission of the People's Commissariat of Justice oversaw the implementation of the decree on the separation of church and state between 1918 and 1924; from 1922 onward, the secret police were in charge of supervising religious institutions, while a division of the party's department of agitation and propaganda promoted atheism and mobilized the population for anti-religious events.[9] Starting in 1943, the Moscow-based councils of Orthodox Church and Religious Cult Affairs and their commissioners in individual republics and regions became the central government locus for supervising and regulating religious activity. The councils' merger in 1965 created a unified organization whose name is usually translated into English as Council for Religious Affairs, obscuring an important grammatical detail that shows official awareness of the multi-religious nature of the Soviet population. In Russian, the council was called *Sovet po delam religiĭ*, an institution dealing with "religions" in the plural, not a generalized "religion."

The files of these councils that are collected in regional and central archives constitute a major source of information on religious life in the Soviet Union, from the mid-1940s until the council's dissolution in 1991. Scholars using these documents tend to have an ambivalent relationship to them. On the one hand, it is impossible to write a history of Soviet religious life without them; on the other, it is hard to ignore the distorted understanding of the agents of an atheist state regarding the religious lives of those they supervised. Historians of church-state relations point out that many commissioners came from the ranks of the KGB.[10] In the introduction to his book on the religious history of Crimea between 1945 and 1961, Boris Kolymagin writes with some regret that the local commissioner's "style, intonation, and gait are noticeable on every page" to the point that he "became equal to an author." Acknowledging that the tone, style, and content of archival quotations leave their imprint on the monograph, the historian, whose obvious sympathies are with religious believers in general and the Russian Orthodox Church in particular, expresses his discomfort at having allowed someone into "coauthorship" who was "a real enemy of the Church."[11] And yet these tainted sources, complemented by the published works and sermons of the charismatic Orthodox bishop Luka (Voino-Iasenetskii, canonized in 2000), allow the author to paint a picture of a fascinating multi-religious region where religious denominations adopted a variety of strategies for working out relationships with a hostile state whose agents had to come to terms with the persistence and vitality of their "enemies."

A common strategy for reading the archives of the council is to focus on interactions between the state and religious institutions, leaving aside the question of actually existing religious practices.[12] Another is to adopt a lens of distrust and try to identify the inaccuracies in reporting that may have occurred because of the administrative position of the council's officials, their relative lack of theological training, and the inherent conflict between their political mandate and the interests of religious groups. For example, some scholars argue that the council's statistics of reported attendance at religious services or numbers of active religious groups are necessarily deflated and need to be corrected upward.[13] Because there are few other figures besides those kept by the council, such assumptions are necessarily based on more or less educated guesswork. It seems sensible to assume that individual citizens, religious institutions, and Soviet bureaucracies would all have had a tendency to underreport actually occurring religious activity. But local commissioners reporting to their superiors could also have an interest in overemphasizing the presence of religious phenomena so as not to seem as if they were overlooking something.[14] In archives organized by bureaucratic provenance, the council's intense attention to phenomena it recognized as "religious" acts as a magnifying glass: council files separate religious practices from the rest of Soviet life and also make it difficult to gauge their relative scale.

Doing Things with Documents

In practice, most researchers interested in Soviet-era religious life acknowledge the limitations of the archival source base but adopt a third strategy, one of attempting to read between the lines. In order to make use of archival documents with unpleasant ideological overtones, authors may give a privileged place to the vignettes and anecdotal observations that were incorporated into official reports and that appear to represent a more unfiltered view of everyday life. Put in conjunction with other available sources, such as memories, published studies by Soviet scholars, or visual evidence, the Soviet prose of counter-insurgency becomes a source of unintended information.[15]

My approach is sympathetic to the third strategy and its attempt to make the best possible use of the sources we have. Of necessity, I am also interested in the relationship between state and religious institutions. At the same time, I am inspired by work in post-colonial studies and historical anthropology that argues that to read the archives in a richer and more persuasive way, we need to take into account the logic of documentation according to which files were written, circulated, and compiled.[16]

These logics of documentation shaped not only the archives we find today but also allowed judicial and administrative bureaucracies to constitute themselves as collective or composite agents, with consequences that often reached beyond the bounds of a single institution. To stay with the Soviet example, Cristina Vatulescu has argued that the conventions of observation and suspicion associated with the genre of the police file and other surveillance records had a deep impact on the aesthetics of early Soviet literature and film. Historians who looked at letters of complaint sent to newspapers and bureaucratic offices

СССР Министрлар Советы янындагы
рус православия чиркэүе эшлэре буенча
Советныӊ Татарстан АССР дагы
В Ә К И Л Е

УПОЛНОМОЧЕННЫЙ
Совета по делам русской православной
церкви при Совете Министров СССР
по Татарской АССР

г. Казань, Кремль. Совет Министров ТАССР

телефон № 2—80—08

№ _____ " 10 " января 196 6 г.

Секр. ОК КПСС Табееву
Зав. отд. Андрианову,
Секр. ГК КПСС Морозову

Осенью 1965 года ко мне обратился заведующий литературной
частью Казанского драматического театра им. Качалова тов. ИНГВАР
с просьбой о консультации по вопросам современного старообрядчества
так как театр собирался ставить пьесу "На горах". Мной была предло-
жена кандидатура тов. Соколова П.П.,который,как член комиссии содей
ствия Бауманского райисполкома,изучал работу казанской общины старо
обрядцев.

18 декабря 1965 года тов. ИНГВАР пригласил меня на генеральную
репетицию пьесы "На горах". После окончания представления обсужде-
ния работы не было сделано,или может быть оно было,но мне не было
предложено в нем участвовать.

Однако считая своим долгом сообщить свою точку зрения по
этой работе театра я вынужден изложить ее в прилагаемой рецензии.

ПРИЛОЖЕНИЕ -упомянутое на 4-х листах.

Уполномоченный Совета
по Татарской АССР   /И. Михалев/

A letter from the Commissioner of Religious Affairs for the Tatar ASSR Mikhalev to Communist Party and government officials, January 10, 1966. Signed and written on the bilingual letterhead of the commissioner, this is a copy of correspondence that stayed in the records of the Council of Religious Affairs. The names of three addressees of outgoing copies are noted by hand near the top. The letter comments on the production of a play dealing with Old Believers, for which the municipal theater consulted with the commissioner. *Courtesy of the National Archive of the Republic of Tatarstan (NART), Kazan, Russia, f. R-873, op. 1, d. 17, l. 1.*

have pointed out how quickly Soviet citizens adopted genres of bureaucratic writing and manipulated them for their own ends.[17] When we read archives for the requirements of genre and for evidence of how the dynamics of internal bureaucratic proceedings affected the course of events, the question of whether a document is a truthful account of an independent social reality gets partially displaced by another question: What role did this document and the documentary practices that produced it play in making particular events happen? Instead of thinking of documentation as a passive record of events, one can think of it as a form of action.

Such an approach should not be confused with the claim in some fields of postmodern literary studies that there is nothing outside the text. Rather, a serious interest in practices and conventions of documentation breaks down the division between social life and what gets written about it that both radical constructivists and positivists seem to take for granted.[18] When calling documentation a form of action, I have in mind something akin to the idea of a speech act. In John Austin's terms, the latter means utterances that "do" something rather than describing a reality that already exists without them. One of Austin's examples is the marriage ceremony, where statements such as "I do" and "I now pronounce you man and wife" change the legal and social status of the two people concerned. But as Austin acknowledges, saying the words correctly is not enough. The person conducting the ceremony has to be authorized to do so according to some system of state or religious law, and the newlyweds have to be qualified to marry by the standards of that system. If it becomes known later that one or both lied about their age or marital status, or if they are found to be more closely related than was assumed, the marriage might be invalid.[19]

Though Austin acknowledges that there can be written speech acts (or "inscriptions") that take force through an act of signing,[20] he does not discuss the documentation of a speech act as something that helps it take effect. But for practical purposes, being properly documented is an important "felicity condition" of many speech acts that rely on institutional authority.[21] Depending on the laws of their country of residence, two people who marry but fail to obtain a marriage certificate may later find that they cannot qualify for shared health benefits or tax credits. They may also encounter difficulties registering a child's birth or applying to emigrate together. A similar dilemma applies to an examinee who is told by the properly authorized instructor "you passed" but forgets to file the necessary paperwork to obtain an official diploma. In modern bureaucracies, speech acts are often embedded in larger processes of documentation whose results—paper or electronic documents—give the words lasting force and make them portable and valid across time and space. To preserve the analogy to speech acts, I use the term "documentary acts" to refer to the production of documents that were meant to initiate, change, accelerate, or slow down a course of action.

In many Soviet life cycle ceremonies, the importance of documentary acts was recognized by putting special ritual emphasis on the signing or distribution of papers. The crowning moment of the civil wedding ceremony was when the couple and the presiding official signed their names in the registration book, often using an unusually large, decorative pen. The colloquial term for concluding a civil marriage in contemporary Russian is *raspisat'sia* (to sign), referring to that same moment. Other rituals in a Soviet citizen's life revolved entirely around receiving particular documents, such as the ceremonial handing out of first passports to sixteen-year-olds that served as a coming-of-age ceremony, or the ceremonies of acceptance into the Communist Youth League or the Communist Party, in which great emphasis was placed on membership cards and the need to handle and store them carefully.[22] As "accomplices"[23] and catalysts of bureaucratic action, documents are bearers of textual information but also material things that tell us something about the social practices of which they were a part.

Secularizing the Past

In the Soviet Union, there was little doubt that the establishment and maintenance of state archives was not a passive process of depositing materials but an active struggle for control over information and historical memory. Among the key adversaries in that struggle were religious institutions that had been important record keepers in imperial Russia, creating and storing information on births, marriages, and deaths.[24] In one of the earliest decrees of the Bolshevik government, passed on December 18, 1917, state offices were set up to administer the so-called acts of civil status (*akty grazhdanskogo sostoianiia*), and churches, mosques, synagogues, and temples were required to turn over their registers to organs of local government. Starting in June 1918, a series of decrees followed to centralize existing imperial archives into a Unified State Archival Fonds and add to it collections held by the army, noble families, commercial enterprises, museums, and other non-state bodies.[25] The decree on the separation of church and state made the state sole proprietor of all religious paraphernalia, making it necessary to compile detailed inventories of objects kept in cult buildings. Once inventoried, buildings as well as objects could be loaned to religious communities for their use or destroyed or diverted to other purposes at the whim of local authorities.[26] During the early years of Soviet power, many books and other valuable documents held by Russian Orthodox churches came into the possession of state archives and museums through campaigns to exhume and expose relics (1918–20) and to expropriate church valuables in aid of the victims of the famine of 1921–22. When religious organizations re-established administrative structures after the Second World War, many lacked access to such basic records as personnel files and records of economic and ritual activity.[27]

A letter from the Soviet Far East that is preserved in the files of the Tatar commissioner of religious affairs shows the real-life consequences of these shifts in property regimes and documentary authority at a time of tumultuous social change. Written on thin paper and sent in an airmail envelope by registered mail, the letter from far-away Khabarovsk is addressed to "the commissioner of the council for the affairs of religious cults, Kazan, Tatar ASSR." The sender, Khanema Karymova, states her connection to the Tatar Republic in bold letters directly under her return address: "Nationality: TATAR."[28]

The letter, dated September 3, 1962, describes the troubles of an aging woman whose documented biography did not coincide with her biological age. Born in 1907 in Blagoveshchensk on the Amur River into a Tatar family, Karymova's birth was recorded at the city mosque under her Tatar name, "Khanifa Mikaelevna." The books, she specifies, were kept in Arabic letters.[29] In 1925, her father "obtained papers" (*dobyl spravku*) stating that she was "born significantly later" to enable her to become a trainee at a local pharmacy. The implied background of this story is that new opportunities for education opened up after the Bolshevik Revolution and Civil War, and in a general situation of turmoil and widespread displacement, many citizens of the new state used forged papers to meet specific age or class criteria.[30]

In 1932–33 Karymova received a passport also stating her false date of birth. In 1962, at the biological age of fifty-five and having "been employed for thirty-three years and six months," Karymova would have qualified for retirement under Soviet law had it not been for the later birthdate in her official papers. The mosque in Blagoveshchensk had been destroyed decades earlier. According to the memories of elderly residents, the imams had left for Kazan or Ufa, the spiritual centers for Muslims in Soviet Russia. In her quest for an accurate record of her birth, the ailing worker had already written to the civil registration offices in a number of Far Eastern and Siberian cities as well as to Kazan, Leningrad, and Moscow, only to receive negative answers from all of them.

Karymova had decided to write to Commissioner Mangutkin to ask if the "mosques or their governing bodies" in Kazan had perhaps received the registration books from the closed mosque thousands of miles away. "After all it is not my fault that the EXECUTIVE ORGANS did not preserve such important documents, and thereby put us in unbearable circumstance IN OLD AGE."[31] Judging from his handwritten note on the letter, "answer 13/IX 62," Mangutkin replied to this inquiry, but the file contains no copy of his response. One can presume that it was negative: the importance of books filled with Arabic writing for uses other than fire starters or food wrappers may easily have escaped those who closed down the mosque.

Though it probably failed to achieve the desired result for its author, this letter shows that changes in documentary practices were part and parcel of broader processes of social change in twentieth-century Russia. The resulting ambiguities and loss of traceable information were beneficial for citizens who tried to pass as younger or older than they really were or to conceal an undesirable class background, but they could also backfire. The papers (*spravka*) obtained by Karymova's father became the reality of her life for the purpose of interaction with state bureaucracies because the religious institutions whose records could have provided an alternative documentary source had been discredited and lost or destroyed.

Genres and Rules

Karymova's letter shows what can happen when there is a change in the institutions authorized to perform documentary acts. There are other self-referential moments in the archives where the rules of proper performance under the new authorities are made explicit, often because they have been breached. Especially up to Stalin's death in 1953, secrecy was an important goal of government documentation, and a number of rules and procedures were meant to protect it. In 1951 the commissioner of religious cult affairs for the Tatar republic was rebuked by two staff members of the council in Moscow for having "broken the rules of secret recordkeeping (*sekretnogo deloproizvodstva*)." The two women who opened the "secret package No 17-c" drew up a record (*akt*) to show that the package contained typed materials without noting how many copies of these materials existed, to whom they had been sent, and under what number the typist's office that had handled them was registered. As if meant to be a didactic demonstration of best practices in secret recordkeeping, the text ends with the line: "The current act was drawn up in 2 copies. Signed: [signatures]."[32]

One of the copies was sent to Kazan as a rebuke and ended up in the archives there, along with the "explanatory note" (*ob"iasnitel'naia zapiska*) with which the commissioner responded. In it he explained that every report was typed in four copies: one was sent to the council in Moscow, one went to the regional party committee, one was forwarded to the Council of Ministers of the Tatar ASSR, and one remained in the files of the commissioner. The other copy of the "act" probably traveled higher up to the council's leadership, protecting the two employees from possible charges of having stolen or misplaced any of the contents of the secret package. Throughout, there is no reference to the subject matter of the materials included in the package. It seems that the trigger for secrecy is not so much the need to protect specific facts from outside readers but to underscore the relationship of subordination between the commissioner and those to whom he was obliged to report. The rules also safeguarded the boundaries of institutional channels of communication in a situation where important information had to pass through the hands of relative outsiders, such as typists.[33]

As this reflexive moment in the chain of documentation reminds us, files collected in Soviet archives are products of documentary acts that effected changes in the mutual relationships of offices and institutions and in the social and legal standing of individuals (and sometimes, as in the case of police and trial records, made the difference between life and death). Even when it is hard to tell whether a report on religious life in a particular region depicts the inner workings of a religious group in good faith and if the author was well informed, it can be worth trying to reconstruct the chain of documentary acts of which the report was a part, and ask what this chain tells us about the conditions of possibility for religious practice.

The genre of archival documents is an important clue for understanding what these papers were meant to "do."[34] Genre designations such as *"akt,"* "explanatory note," "report" (*otchët*), "order" (*prikaz*), "certificate" (*spravka*), or "petition" (*zaiavlenie*) are often explicitly stated in the heading of a document and predetermine the reader's expectations. Many genres also invoke other kinds of documents and forms of bureaucratic action. An *akt*, for example, is a record of proceedings in which several signatories confirm that a particular action has taken place, and it thus serves as proof of that moment in the case of an official investigation. This method of creating written proof for an embodied action exemplifies the point that in many bureaucratic contexts a speech act only becomes effective once it is recorded in writing. It also implies the expectation that someone might call into doubt that an event actually happened, or that competing accounts of it might emerge from the memories of participants. The documentary act repeats its performative force every time the document is presented in a later verification or dispute.

An explanatory note, innocuous though its name sounds, often responds to a written rebuke from a superior. The note acknowledges that the author has made a mistake and forms part of the monitoring procedures to assure that the mistake is corrected. By being asked to explain why a mistake occured and what will be done to avoid it in the future, the author is made to acknowledge his or her inferior place in a chain of command, and his or her beginner status in a chain of personal development. Just like speech and literary genres, documentary genres thus come with their specific emotional tone that reflects an awareness of social relationships.[35]

Genre designations also help to clarify the direction in which a given document traveled within the administrative structure—reports and petitions move upward and inward, from peripheries to centers, while orders and circulars move downward and outward, from centers to their peripheral subordinates. Copies were usually retained by both sender and addressee, so that central and local archives are now linked by the presence of duplicate documents in their collections. A "certificate" (*spravka* or sometimes simply *informatsiia*) is often the record of a double movement that creates vertical and horizontal connections: a citizen obtains a piece of paper from one agency that needs to be presented to another; or an official travels outward from center to periphery, inspects conditions there, and forwards a record of the inspections to his own superiors or another agency. Documents that travel in a centrifugal direction are often prompts for action by subordinates that will be taken outside of the world of paperwork; reports that travel toward the center and upward on an administrative ladder transform that activity back into paperwork as a means of keeping local officials in good standing.

In addition to their genre designations, documents contain other clues to their trajectories. These clues include marginal notes, sets of approval signatures, or patterns of forwarding. For example, any researcher working with collections of commissioners of religious affairs will encounter letters of complaint written by local believers to various offices in Moscow—the Council of Ministers, the secretary general of the Communist Party, or the Council of Religious Affairs. These were routinely forwarded back to the local commissioner and by him to municipal and district governments, even if the complaint concerned abuses committed by these authorities.[36] A cover letter or a note written on the forwarded letter itself usually instructs the local commissioner to "investigate" (*razobrat'sia*), a process that often generated considerable local correspondence before it was summarized and validated by a new report back to Moscow.

These overlapping circuits of paperwork placed religious communities in a real double bind. Their local commissioner of religious affairs was both a central agent in a network determined to undermine their existence and the sole addressee for possible claims for redress in the name of Soviet legality. The ability to separate and coordinate different streams of documents was crucial to his ability to play both roles at once.

From Files to Archive

If bureaucratic practices of filing and documentation were an important interface between officials and citizens, how much can we infer about these practices from today's archival collections? The files in Kazan's archive were sewn together into folders after accessioning the documents and do not automatically correspond to the filing practices of the individual offices that deposited them. But the archival principle of provenance requires that archival classifications reflect the way the creator of the records sorted them, or at least respect categories of correspondence already somehow marked in the body of deposited records.[37]

The files of the commissioner in Kazan include some information on his role as temporary custodian of records. On February 14, 1945, the newly appointed Commissioner for Religious Cult Affairs Bagaev received documents relating to closed mosques and churches from a staff member of the information statistics department of the Supreme Soviet of the Tatar ASSR, and the two signed an act to confirm the transfer.[38] Four years later, Bagaev and his successor Safin signed a longer inventory listing everything the incoming commissioner received from the departing one. The first two items are the stamp and seal of the commissioner, important tools of authentication that empowered the bearer to give force to written documents. There follow thirteen items of active bureaucratic files and registration books for correspondence, dealing with currently active religious groups and substantive and financial reports to Moscow. Eight "archival files" contain minutes of meetings and rejected petitions from religious organizations (sorted into "rejected" and "rejected orally"). The new commissioner also received blank forms for reporting on incoming petitions for the opening of places of worship (thirteen copies) and for creating statistical overviews of active worship places (ten copies).[39]

Although the purpose and criteria of preservation of such an internal working depository were different from those of historical archives operated by the state, the distinction between the current records of an institution and a permanent archival collection was quite fluid in the Soviet Union. It was only in 1962 that the commissioner in the Tatar ASSR was asked to transfer his archival files to the republic's archive.[40] We may recall that his Mari counterpart was taking already deposited files home in the 1970s, indicating that the transfer of custody did not preclude an ongoing sense of authority over the records. As the council became defunct in the early 1990s, its staff members and their successors again played active roles in deciding what records made it into archives. Vladimir Pudov, a former staff member of the Council of Religious Affairs in Moscow, recalls that many of his colleagues destroyed personal notes on conversations and research prior to the liquidation of the council in 1991. The Orthodox priest and historian Aleksandr Balyberdin, who served as advisor on matters of freedom of conscience to the government of Kirov region from 1996 to 1999, inherited 130 active files from the apparatus of the commissioner of religious affairs, about half of which dealt with the persecutions of the Khrushchev era. It was his initiative to add them to the collection of Kirov's regional archive.[41] Such anecdotes show that what we find in central and regional archives today does not preserve all aspects of the recordkeeping practices of the council. Comparing the archives in Tatarstan and Marii El, for example, one finds extensive correspondence between the commissioner and local authorities in Kazan that never seems to have made it into the archive in Ioshkar-Ola. The correspondence with Moscow and registration files of religious communities and clergy seem to be treated everywhere as representing the core activities of the council. The survival of local correspondence and personal notes is more uneven, but presents an invaluable view of the many faces the state took on as it interacted with religious communities.

Not only archivists treated the reports to Moscow as the representative core of the council's activities. Local commissioners were well aware that their reports might be scoured for quotes and illustrative examples for public reports, and they were careful to frame their actions in the language of Soviet legality. Contrary to what researchers may hope for, this part of the internal correspondence of the council is not necessarily any more open and frank than published materials. Reports and circulars that were exchanged between Moscow and the regions do contain information that was not available to the general public in the Soviet Union, such as the precise numbers and locations of functioning houses of worship. But even internally, it was important to maintain an image of procedural correctness, making the records problematic representations of the officials' own actions as well as of those of religious believers.[42]

Instead of uncensored openness, the internal records of the council show its efforts to juggle the dual role of maintaining the legal standing of religious communities while also undermining their existence. The documentary acts of commissioners set in motion chains of events that often impacted religious life in the most interventionist way, while the separation of content between different recipients helped ensure that the reports that went to Moscow always presented evidence that the council worked within the legal framework of the separation of church and state and freedom of conscience. Archival filing practices maintain this separation but also allow researchers to make connections between different circuits of correspondence.

Documenting Correctness: Kazan's New Imam

For understanding how the Council of Religious Affairs managed its dual role in supporting and undermining the existence of religious communities, the commissioner's records in the National Archive of the Republic of Tatarstan present an impressively varied and relatively complete collection. In addition to the correspondence with the council in Moscow, there are files for almost all post-war years containing "correspondence with commissioners of religious affairs in other regions," "correspondence with local authorities," and "petitions and complaints by believers and related correspondence." Different genres of documents predominate in different files: reports in the correspondence with the council, letters and short notes on conversations in the correspondence with religious believers, telegrams in the correspondence with commissioners in other regions. By noting the separation between the files but also reading across them, one can picture the limbo between legal incorporation and administrative exclusion that was the ground on which religious communities in the USSR existed. Distributed across different files, the archival traces of the conflict that ensued in 1963 after the death of Kazan's only officially registered imam are an instructive case in point. I follow this case through the different files, starting with the reports to Moscow, which are first in the order of cataloging and among those council materials most often consulted by historians. Moving from them to correspondence with other partners requires some chronological jumps backward and forward, but these will help readers see the deliberately disjointed narrative and distribution of administrative responsibility created by the principle of sorting files by correspondence partner.

An imam is a man in charge of leading prayers and preaching at a mosque, usually referred to as *mulla* (mullah) in Russian. In commissioner Mangutkin's correspondence with the council in Moscow, his handling of the succession reads like a model of

Mardzhani mosque, Kazan, 1954. Built in the late eighteenth century by special permission from Empress Catherine the Great and named after the prominent Tatar scholar and educator Shigabutdin Mardzhani (1818–1889), this was the only functioning mosque in Kazan from the late 1930s to 1991. Still preserving its minaret and half-moon emblems, it was an obligatory destination for delegations from Muslim countries that visited the Soviet Union during the Khrushchev and Brezhnev years. *Courtesy of the National Archive of the Republic of Tatarstan (NART), Kazan, Russia, f. R-1499, op. 1-4, d. 44.*

procedural correctness and restraint. In response to complaints from believers received in Moscow and forwarded back to him in the usual fashion, Mangutkin explains to his superiors that the previous imam of Mardzhani Mosque had died in the summer of 1962.[43] "After his death, Mufti Khialetdinov [of Ufa] temporarily entrusted the muezzin of the mosque, Gizatullin, with carrying out the duties of the mullah." But the muezzin, whose normal duties only involved intoning the call to prayer, "does not satisfy the standards of Kazan's Muslims" in his level of education, and they began to look for another candidate. Officially, such appointments were made by the mufti of Ufa, the religious leader responsible for Muslim communities in European Russia and Siberia. Mufti Shakir Khialetdinov recommended a certain Shangareev, recently arrived from the southern city of Rostov where he had worked as imam. Mangutkin allowed him to practice temporarily but made inquiries to the KGB and the commissioner of religious cult affairs of Rostov region. At the KGB, Mangutkin "was advised not to register him," and his counterpart in Rostov confirmed this opinion. After receiving the *spravka* (informational certificate) from Rostov, Mangutkin "notified the leadership of the mosque of my refusal to register Shangareev as mullah of the religious organization."

In March 1963, "DUMS [the Spiritual Directorate of Muslims of Siberia][44] designated the mosque's former accountant Almanov as mullah of the Kazan religious community. Against whom we raised no objections." However, when the mufti arrived from Ufa to proclaim the accountant imam, "the majority of believers categorically refused to accept Almanov." At the time of writing, the muezzin Gizatullin again carried out the duties of imam, making the complaints of the believers groundless. "No one is forcing Almanov on them. Almanov has long since quit his work in the mosque."

In this report, the agency of the commissioner of religious affairs is downplayed in favor of that of the mufti and other state organs such as the KGB, the commissioner of another region, and the branch of municipal government under whose authority a financial audit of the mosque had been conducted. Where references to the decisions of the mufti create the impression that Muslim organizations are regulating their own affairs, references to other state organs demonstrate that Mangutkin has placed his actions within the proper chain of command and consultation. He uses passive and indirect constructions for his own decisions ("was advised not to register," "raised no objections") and active verbs for DUMS and the mufti ("temporarily entrusted," "designated," "categorically refused to accept"). In this way, Mangutkin engages in a strategy of "distributing responsibility" that is a common way of self-protection of bureaucrats who make weighty decisions in the name of institutions and collectives.[45] In the context of Soviet religious policy, displacing and denying agency also serves to uphold the legal fiction of the division between church and state. The letter itself calls this fiction into question through the short but decisive appearance of the KGB, whose staff already possess information about a potential imam while Mangutkin is still waiting for an opinion from his counterpart in another city. Moreover, records in other files relating to the same case illuminate the very active role played by Mangutkin and his strategically distributed patterns of correspondence in steering the case toward the desired outcome.

A thin file entitled "Correspondence of the Commissioner of Religious Cult Affairs with Council commissioners from other regions on questions of religion"[46] contains the original letter from Rostov, a copy of which is included in Mangutkin's report. The letter confirms that Karim Shangareev served as imam at the mosque of Rostov but lost his registration "for gross violations of the law on [religious] cults." Unhappy with the recent expropriation of the mosque building and the removal of the congregation to a smaller space, Shangareev began to "interfere with the personal family affairs of believers and their family members" and was accused of taking more money than noted on official receipts when visiting believers at home. The Rostov commissioner recommends refusing Shangareev registration in Kazan for at least six months.[47]

Under Soviet law, religious organizations employed clergy, but such employment contracts were valid only if the commissioner of religious affairs registered the candidate as a legitimate "minister of the cult." Inquiries from commissioner to commissioner regarding the conduct of newly arrived or visiting clergy routinely appear in the council's records. Such transregional correspondence ensured that a bad relationship with the commissioner in one region would follow a priest, imam, rabbi, or pastor even if he moved somewhere else, sometimes leaving him in a desperate financial situation.

A common accusation that could lead to loss of registration for a member of the clergy was that he charged more than the permitted rates for ritual services. According to Marxist anti-clerical narratives, this meant exploiting gullible laypeople. Given the low official prices for ritual services and high rates of taxation, it is likely that many priests and imams accepted extra "gifts" or received additional payments for the services of spouses and assistants. According to the Rostov commissioner, Shangareev asked believers to give extra money to his wife who accompanied him on his visits, ostensibly "to hide his participation in extortion." It may well be that the wife served as *abistai*, reading from the Qur'an to the women gathered in a separate room.[48] The Soviet registration scheme, which recognized only male imams, left no place for such female practitioners to be officially remunerated as "ministers of the cult."

By soliciting this negative opinion and forwarding a copy of it to his superiors in Moscow, Mangutkin further distributes agency and responsibility between himself and other council officials, presenting all commissioners as arbiters looking to protect ordinary believers. But correspondence with Ufa preserved in the same file presents a very different picture. Since the official religious authority for Muslims in the Tatar ASSR was the mufti in Ufa (the capital of the neighboring Bashkir ASSR), the commissioners in Kazan and Ufa frequently had to coordinate travel of religious dignitaries and questions of clergy registration. To accomplish this, the commissioner in Kazan often asked his colleague in Ufa to suggest (*podskazat'*) a particular decision to the mufti, obviously assuming that neither the Ufa commissioner nor the mufti were in a position to refuse.

In an undated copy of a letter probably sent in the spring of 1963, Mangutkin makes such a suggestion regarding the search for a new imam.[49] Based on "the advice of appropriate organs" (a euphemism for the KGB), he had refused to register two previous candidates suggested by the mufti, one of whom was Karim Shangareev from Rostov. Instead, "we agreed to nominate for the position of mullah of the Kazan mosque a local believer and active member of the congregation, the accountant of the mosque Islam Almanov." The unspecified "we" may refer to an agreement between the commissioner and the same "appropriate organs," or with parts of the mosque community.

Almanov, the letter goes on to explain, had been accountant for a long time, had served as delegate to an Islamic conference in Tashkent, and he "understands our expectations well, is knowledgeable (*gramoten*) in spiritual matters and quite tactful. I ask you, comrade Arduanov, to suggest to Khialetdinov that he nominate Islam Almanov as mullah of the Kazan mosque." From Mangutkin's point of view, Almanov's qualifications lay in his experience as intermediary between a community of believers and state authorities. The mufti's active support would be necessary because members of the congregation were looking for different qualities in their spiritual leader: "He never worked as minister of the cult before, and in order to raise his authority it would be quite helpful if Khialetdinov himself recommended Almanov . . . . This is required by the situation in the congregation in Kazan."

This letter shows the careful management by the commissioners of the "autonomous" decisions of religious dignitaries, whose authority in their own community had to be maintained. One may read the direct correspondence between colleagues in this file as revealing "the truth" that the vertical report to Moscow obscured under the language of correct procedure. But the degree of control over the situation that is suggested in these letters may also be an exaggeration, as indicated by the ominous reference to "the situation in the congregation in Kazan." The next file in the collection, containing "Complaints and petitions from believers and related correspondence" paints a far more chaotic picture.[50]

Following several other complaints and petitions to open houses of worship in various cities, the second half of the file consists almost exclusively of letters relating to the search for a new imam. With one exception (a letter authored by the mufti), all letters come from Kazan residents who worshiped at the mosque. One of these letters, sent to the council in Moscow and to the Tatar Council of Ministers in April 1963 (both copies were promptly forwarded to Mangutkin) probably provided the trigger for Mangutkin's explanations to the council with which I began this story.[51] In these complaints, it becomes clear that groups of parishioners had been asking for the removal of Almanov as accountant and were outraged when they heard that he was being elevated to the post of imam. There are also accusations of intimidation against Mangutkin: when members of the mosque congregation asked the commissioner to organize a financial audit and review of the mosque's leadership, he "yelled at us and proclaimed: 'You are nobody to me, don't go anywhere with your complaints, don't come to me. If you get on my nerves I will close your mosque down.'"[52]

In January 1964, some of the letter writers report having been called in to see the vice chairwoman of the Council of Ministers of the Tatar republic, who threatened to put them on trial for libel (*kleveta*) if they continued to write letters to the central daily *Pravda* and other places.[53] Adding to the embarrassment of the officials who backed Almanov, parishioners agitating against him managed to place an article in the journal *Molodezh' Tatarii/Tatarstan iashlare* (Youth of Tatarstan) under the standard anti-religious title "Crooks in turbans."[54] All these materials returned to Mangutkin from Moscow in April 1964, with a cover letter asking him to "sort out this matter and provide detailed information on measures taken." In a handwritten note on the cover letter, Mangutkin notes that "during the meeting of June 27 I explained the circumstances to the council orally."[55]

The publication of the article in particular reveals that matters in Kazan had gotten out of hand. The editors of the bilingual Tatar and Russian journal may have accepted the submission in good faith as anti-religious propaganda, or they may have sympathized with the group that wanted to remove Almanov. The forms of oral communication mentioned in the complaint letters and in Mangutkin's notes also suggest that the tone of bureaucratic correctness that the written records strained to maintain had become a very thin veneer. We read of intimidating yelling and threats, and can imagine a tense discussion between Mangutkin and his superiors. A number of historians have pointed to the deliberate use of oral communication as a less traceable alternative to written forms, from Stalin's oft-discussed telephone calls to later informal problem solving between bureaucratic offices.[56] That this preference was not absolute but restricted to specific contexts is shown by the fact that oral interactions in the council's files are often documented in writing, especially when they relate to vertical interactions between subordinates and superiors. In other cases oral prompts may have preceded the creation of a written document for a specific purpose—for example, to create a counter-narrative to the writings of complaining believers. A striking example of this is an earlier letter in the file, headed simply "Complaint" and written by the mufti Shakir Khialetdinov.

In this letter, dated before the complaint letters from members of the mosque community, Khialetdinov gives his account of what happened when he came to Kazan to proclaim Almanov the new imam during Friday prayers: "from some places in the first room of the mosque there arose voices against Islam [Almanov], wanting to remove him from the rank of imam: offending and exposing him in every way, they swore at him with abhorrent words." The mufti himself also became the object of "angry speeches." At the end of the prayers Khialetdinov felt that some people were planning to raise their hands against the new imam, which was averted "only by my judging gaze. I was shocked to encounter such savagery and roughness and even was in danger myself." Calling into question the "religiosity of these idiots," Khialetdinov concludes with a paragraph that affirms both his Soviet and his Volga Muslim loyalties, while insisting on the autonomy of his decision to report the incident to the commissioner:

> To see such a pitiful incident in the mosque named for Shigabutdin Mardzhani in Kazan, in the center of cultured Soviet Tatarstan, was completely unexpected. I consider it my duty to present my impressions for your consideration.[57]

This assertion of independent motivation implies the possibility that Mangutkin had asked the mufti to write this letter (or at least "suggested" he do it). While the story behind this document must remain a matter of conjecture, the file as an overall composition shows the power of the commissioner to craft a narrative of the event, despite his attempts to emphasize the agency of religious dignitaries through grammar and content.[58] All the complaints and counter-complaints came together in the commissioner's office, no matter where the complainers tried to turn. Because the letter from the mufti is placed first, anyone perusing the file is primed to see the conflict as simply a matter of internal disagreement among the Muslim faithful, glossing over a complex story about an internally divided religious community under severe strain from government interference. But through preserving the sheer number of complaints and demands for explanation, the file also belies any efforts to create a sense of coherence and control.

Correctness and Collusion: Sorting the Files

So far, we have seen the effort to sustain a narrative of bureau-cratic correctness and respect for the division of state and religion in those files that contain communications along the vertical chain of command with the council in Moscow. In the horizon-tal correspondence between colleagues (commissioners in differ-ent republics) and the incoming messages of religious believers, that narrative is cast into doubt through evidence of much more active (though not always successful) work by the commissioner to control the situation. A fourth file presents more evidence of the resources at the disposal of the commissioner: collabora-tion with local administrative organs.[59] In March 1963, as he was corresponding with his counterpart in Ufa about having Almanov proclaimed imam, Mangutkin also protested to the administrative staff of the republic's Council of Ministers against the actions of an auditing committee sent to the mosque by the city district, at the request of the group that opposed Almanov. The committee had sealed storage spaces and documents of the mosque, and Mangutkin denounced these actions as "gross vio-lation of the Soviet legislation on cults and administrative inter-ference into the activity of a religious community."[60]

The same file contains a list of people nominated for pilgrim-age to Mecca for that year, to be sponsored by funds from the mosque. It includes Almanov's name, probably in an effort to bolster his spiritual authority.[61] Correspondence with the city district authorities shows another part of the commissioner's efforts to enforce the appointment of the new imam. In April, the district police chief assured Mangutkin that police patrols around the Mardzhani mosque had been reinforced.[62] Later that summer, Mangutkin wrote to the chairman of the district executive committee with a request to "hold accountable" five men whom he considered to be the organizers of unauthorized meetings at the mosque, where "believers discuss the actions of government organs, and question the right of state organs to control the activities of religious organizations and clergy."[63]

Later in the year, Mangutkin writes to another branch of municipal government on behalf of a second appointee, Ismagil Rakhmatullin from Cheliabinsk region, who needed permission to purchase a house in Kazan.[64] However, believers continue to complain about Almanov until the following year and never mention another imam. Perhaps Rakhmatullin's appointment was short-lived, or it was a formal concession while Almanov continued to have authority in the mosque. As is common with archival documents concerning social or political problems, the resolution of the case is not recorded in the files, because a dispute only generates investigative reports as long as it remains active.[65]

Reading these four files together, we can appreciate that a commissioner's power lay in his ability to coordinate lower-level agencies to put pressure on religious communities while presenting a picture of legal order and control in his reports to Moscow. The question arises whom Mangutkin was trying to fool with the insistence on correct procedure and denial of agency. Presumably, none of his superiors really expected him to give free rein to the mosque community in the choice of a new imam. So why did he have to insist that no one was forcing an unwanted candidate on them? In a secret recordkeeping regime, why do some elements of the paper trail deny practices that are clearly demonstrated in others? The answer may lie in an awareness of the further uses to which particular documents could be put. Commissioners' reports to Moscow were secret but also provided materials for the council's public statements about the situation of religious believers in the Soviet Union. As Yaacov Ro'i puts it, they were "intended *a priori* as part of the input on which policy-making was based" and had to provide correct phrasing that could be used in further documents in addition to fulfilling the practical expectations of the organization.[66]

One of these expectations was that the documentation provided by commissioners should support the domestic and international image of the Soviet Union as a state where believers and nonbelievers enjoyed the same rights of freedom of conscience.[67] Another important expectation was that commissioners keep religious expression in their regions under control. By reassuring his superiors that he was avoiding open breaches of legal procedure while also consulting with all the relevant administrative organs to ensure that the new imam would be loyal to state interests, Mangutkin was casting himself as a reliable administrator capable of fulfilling both the letter and the spirit of Soviet laws on religion. Unfortunately for him, he was not the only person writing to Moscow on this matter. The widespread literacy of the Soviet population allows us a glimpse of the bitter and drawn-out dispute that his reporting and filing practices tried to gloss over.

Dealing with the State

What do these documentary practices tell us about the lives of religious believers? There is much that remains outside the purview of the archives—for example, the formal and informal qualifications that mosque attendees would have looked for in their imam had they been given an opportunity to deliberate about it without state interference. One aspect that existing records illustrate well is the participation of religious communities in bureaucratic processes. Through such participation, we catch a glimpse of religiously inspired ways of life that were simultaneously forced to the margins of Soviet society and fully a part of its development.

As citizens, religious believers had to submit to the same logic of documentation as everyone else and needed to harness bureaucratic forms of action to achieve their aims, such as securing lease rights to a house of worship, replacing a deceased or retired cleric, or making a pilgrimage to holy sites abroad. As members of communities that constituted one of the few legal alternatives to communist forms of sociality and that recognized a supreme authority other than the Communist Party, they could assume that most mechanisms of bureaucratic action would be primed against them. A telling example from the years immediately preceding the conflict about the imam's succession is the long effort by a group of Kazan Muslims to construct a building for ritual washing of the dead at the municipal cemetery. The group collected the necessary funds and secured the cooperation of a nearby factory for providing access to the water and sewage system. After many petitions, they were told that they could not go ahead with construction because standard blueprints for cemetery design used throughout the Soviet Union contained no provision for such a building.[68]

In addition to architecture and urban planning, bookkeeping was another area where socialist norms directly impacted the economic and ritual life of a congregation. Keeping accounts for enterprises and collective farms was always a creative practice in a planned economy, where holding back resources for hoarding and bartering was common and managers wanted to avoid appearing either too successful or too unsuccessful at meeting their production targets.[69] Every registered religious organization had to have an accountant, and this position was often conflict-laden because commissioners of religious affairs and religious communities had different expectations of good bookkeeping. For members of the religious community, an accountant was honest if he or she did not divert any money for personal use and was willing not to record a baptism or circumcision upon request. For the commissioner, an accountant was honest if he or she recorded all rituals with the full amounts of payments and the names and signatures of participants.

Constant reminders that proper receipts had to be issued for all life-cycle rituals and both parents had to sign the register for rituals performed on children attest to the way in which accounting standards served as a form of intimidation. Believers, by contrast, reportedly used written consent statements—sometimes notarized with the seal of their village administration—to persuade clergy and church accountants to record baptisms in the absence of one or both parents, showing their capacity to invent new kinds of documentary acts.[70]

As the case of imam Shangareev's loss of his registration shows, members of the clergy were almost forced to participate in the semi-legal second economy by low salaries, high tax rates, and strict licensing requirements. Under Khrushchev, citizens were recruited to participate in the surveillance of economic practices through "committees for the observation and control over the activity of religious organizations." In 1964, such a committee reported proudly that as a result of stricter financial control, the salary of the priest at Kazan's St. Nicholas Cathedral had fallen considerably and the number of choir members had shrunk.[71] Later that same year, the leadership of the cathedral, obviously feeling the tighter control and afraid to engage in unofficial purchases, testified in an *akt* that a psalm reader and his wife from a remote village had tried to sell thirty-five hand-made funerary shrouds at the price of 2 rubles each. The couple explained that they "urgently needed money."[72]

The pattern of accepting extra gifts and unscheduled payments as a matter of economic survival links clergy to other low-paid Soviet service professions such as teachers and doctors. Members of these very secular and respected professions regularly supplemented their incomes through monetary and in-kind payments from patients and students, a feature of the pervasive "second economy"[73] that was likely well known to the commissioners who denounced similar practices in the ritual economy. The fact that there were no special committees to investigate how gifts given to medical personnel were accounted for shows that clergy could not expect the same state lenience toward such free-market supplements as other citizens in low-paid service occupations. The ultimate purpose of surveillance through account books and inventories was not so much maximizing state revenue but reducing the viability and social influence of ritual activity. For example, Orthodox congregations were forbidden from redistributing in-kind gifts of food, fabrics, and clothing received from believers under the pretext that these were property of the state, but also with the consideration that such charitable activity would "support the strengthening of religious moods among the population."[74]

Being excluded from legal trade and distribution and disadvantaged as providers of a service whose usefulness was not recognized by the state, religious organizations were forced to engage in illegal economic practices. Accountants thus held a vulnerable, but potentially powerful position between congregations and the state because cleverly kept books were crucial to a congregation's economic survival, but a financial audit by state organs could easily turn up desired evidence of the parasitical and dishonest nature of ritual specialists. Another ubiquitous form of documentation, the official reference letter (*kharakteristika*), had a similar effect of simultaneously normalizing religious belief and relegating it to the margins of Soviet modernity while impacting the possibility of living out religious vocations.

As the name implies, a *kharakteristika* is a reference letter attesting to a person's character. It was often issued from a place of employment or residence, and was necessary for such diverse purposes as entering a university, finding a new job, joining the Communist Party, or receiving authorization to travel abroad. In the files of the Council for Religious Affairs, such reference letters are provided to or submitted by religious believers applying to go on the hajj to Mecca, receive theological training, or enter a monastery. The biographical narratives they tell share standard features with *kharakteristiki* written and submitted for secular purposes, but they are organized around the suspicion that something must have gone wrong in a person's life in order to turn him or her into a religious believer. For example, when the twenty-year-old Tatar Gabdel'khamit Zinatullin applied to study at the *medrese* Mir-Arab in Bukhara in 1974, assistant commissioner Akhmetshin penned a summary of a conversation with the young factory worker, which resulted in a positive recommendation. Akhmetshin notes that the worker, who had a middle school education, was respected by his colleagues and conducted volunteer work as an agitator and member of the sports team, although he had refused to join the Communist Youth League "with reference to his religious views." He had engaged in religious practices since childhood, learning from his father and mother.

> "He says *namaz* [Muslim daily prayers] at home and visits the mosque on Sundays. He is
> studying Arabic using a college text book . . . . It is his personal wish to perfect his knowledge and serve in the name of religion."[75]

Mir-Arab was one of just two functioning institutions of higher Islamic learning in the Soviet Union, and few imams had a *medrese* education, access to which was as tightly controlled as seminary training for Christian priests.[76] What motivated the positive decision here was the candidate's working-class background, evidence of a positive attitude toward Soviet social life, and the affirmation that his motivation was personal and came from a private religiosity inculcated in the family, not through contact with proselytizers. The deviation from a normative Soviet biography was minor and could be explained by a tradition that had been handed down in the kin group without breeding open resistance to Soviet life.

In the case of a young Orthodox Christian woman who had tried to join a convent in Riga eight years earlier, commissioner Mikhalev was less convinced of healthy connections to Soviet society. Instead of approving the request, he arranged for changes to the applicant's personal and work environment. During the year after the death of her mother and brother, the twenty-eight-year-old Matveeva, who worked in the heating plant of a clock factory, came to know old women at church who suggested she join the monastery. Personally, Mikhalev found that she was "not a religious fanatic, knows very little about problems of religion." To help her out of the "desperation" that led her to request admission to the monastery, the commissioner arranged for her to move from the now-empty family apartment to the factory dormitory, "where she can live with young workers of the enterprise." He had also secured a promise from her employers to move her to another position that would provide better pay. After a personal conversation with atheist propagandists, "she withdrew her application to join the monastery."[77]

By writing a letter of reference, commissioners of religious affairs opened or closed pathways to religious vocations, providing one of the most striking examples of a secular documentary act that impacted religious communities. Part of the reason one petition was accepted and the other was rejected may have lain in the political climate of the time. 1965–66 was a time of a final flare-up of anti-religious campaigning under Khrushchev's successor Leonid Brezhnev. By the mid-1970s, officials in many regions seem to have tacitly accepted that religious traditions were there to stay and did not necessarily pose a threat, especially if they were part of local ethnic or national traditions that mature socialism regarded with increasingly nostalgic eyes.[78] But another reason may lie in the relationship of each case to narratives of exemplary Soviet or stereotypically religious biographies.

Like the pardon-tales analyzed by Natalie Zemon Davis, *kharakteristiki* construct normative biographies for Soviet citizens, from which believers deviate to varying degrees. In the case of the successful applicant for study in the *medrese*, the only deviation lay in the religious tradition practiced in an otherwise well-integrated working-class family. It provided no hold for the common atheist critique that religiosity led to a voluntary separation from socialist solidarity. Because of her loneliness and the connection of intensified religious practice to recent bereavement, the woman who wanted to become a nun conformed more closely to the image of the religious believer as a temporarily afflicted person who needed to be cured by human solidarity. Her application to join a convent, forwarded back to her local authorities, triggered a mechanism by which the state tried to outdo the religious institution in fulfilling the role of able caretaker.

In addition to showing how paperwork helped the Soviet state assert claims to custody over people, the two letters suggest two different ways of being a religious believer in the Soviet Union. In Zinatullin's case, religious practice seems to blend in with being part of a particular subgroup within the larger society (a Tatar family observant of religious traditions). As a nested form of identity, his Islamic observance is perfectly compatible with being a productive and socially active member of the secular work collective. In Matveeva's case, religion becomes newly attractive to a young adult in the context of a crisis where previous social bonds are destroyed. Stereotypical as they are, these two positions reflect structural possibilities for religion to persist as a marginalized practice in a secularizing society. As the only legally existing institutions that were separate from the party state, religious communities could attract people whose needs were not being met by official structures. Conversely, pursuit of a religious vocation could become an additional compartment in a life that otherwise took place within those structures.[79] What distinguished the Soviet Union from secular liberal democracies was the insistence with which the state claimed the role of arbiter even for aspirations that deviated from official norms. In their sheer volume and elaborate emphasis on correct procedure, Council of Religious Affairs documents begin to tell us about the formatting challenges faced by believers and bureaucrats alike. In the face of a bureaucracy whose dual task was to curate and curtail the existence of religious communities, the problem for believers was not so much exclusion from normal Soviet life but rather the requirement to always articulate their activities and aspirations within the framework of that normality.

CHAPTER 2

Mirrored Fragments

Archives and Memory

In the summer of 2005 I visited a village about thirty miles outside of Ioshkar-Ola, the capital of the republic of Marii El in Russia's Volga region. To take me back home, my hosts had arranged a ride with the chairman of the agricultural collective, who was returning to his house in a suburb of Ioshkar-Ola. This man had been chairman of the Soviet-era collective farm since the early 1980s, and as we sat in the farm's large black Volga—he in the front next to the driver, I in the back—he recalled that it was thanks to his labors and influence that the road we were traveling on had been paved. The family of teachers with whom I had been staying had also stressed how much the chairman had done for the village and that he was continuing to act as an advocate with the republic's government to address the needs of rural Maris.

But to my surprise, the memories of this successful champion of socialist modernization were not limited to the challenges of paving roads and making technical improvements. Keeping correct documentation was another difficult part of heading a Soviet collective farm, especially when it came to reporting losses of livestock. For example, when a particular milkmaid was too successful in meeting and exceeding production targets, the other milkmaids "had ways" to make her cows get sick and die. The chairman knew that the cause was witchcraft. But for the purpose of bookkeeping, he needed to devise another reason that would be acceptable to his superiors in the district and republican government. Sickness and death among dairy cows could make the collective farm look bad, and as a chairman he was caught between his own understanding that harmful magic was an unavoidable expression of the envy caused by socialist competition and the bio-medical framework required by official reports.

This anecdote illustrates once again the ironies of the imperative to document: written records of the Soviet period abound, but they present a highly selective picture of events. What is edited out of this picture is not just the perspective of the milkmaids and other ordinary Soviet citizens for whom divine and magical forces constituted possible realities. As the chairman's reminiscence shows, the contents of a document may not fully convey the author's own interpretation of events, even when that author was a loyal servant of the Soviet state.[1]

The challenge of reading records in state archives is not just to reckon with the limited understanding and potential ideological biases of those who created them. One also has to ask what such officials thought their superiors, or the superiors of their superiors, wanted to hear. As an escape from the seemingly endless spiral of such feedback loops, the oral commentary of the chairman, made in hindsight, appears to offer an attractively clear intimacy: believe what I say now, not what I wrote back then. If archival records reflect the self-referential imperatives of a bureaucracy that enacted documentation for documentation's sake, the memories of eyewitnesses might seem to offer more direct access to the lived experience of Soviet citizens, especially when it comes to practices that lay outside the standard Soviet biography.

Oral history can indeed provide rich insight, especially for the late Soviet period whose living witnesses are readily available, while archival access is only beginning to open up.[2] What is more problematic is when the turn to oral history is motivated by a view of personal "memory" as a morally pure alternative to official, ideologically biased "history."[3] If the archives won't tell us anything about milkmaids who bewitched their competitors or about the suffering endured by many convinced religious believers, it is tempting to turn to interviews as independent correctives to official silences.

Social memory studies provide the best warnings against a sharp contrast between official history and popular memory. Researchers who solicited memories of life in colonial societies, for example, have found that oral accounts often reproduced official narratives of happy and grateful colonial subjects, while discordant or ambivalent experiences remained more difficult to express.[4] One reason for this is that most people come up with a "scripted" way of telling their life story, influenced in part by the constructions of official history that they learn about at school, through the media, and through participation in public events. In any given telling, a life narrative may draw on different discourses to emphasize different aspects of a person's identity, depending on the political and interpersonal circumstances of the telling.[5] If I had met him in 1982, the collective farm chairman might not have been as eager to present himself as someone who saw through and subverted the guises of modern Soviet recordkeeping, at least not to a stranger with whom he was speaking in the presence of his driver.

If the memories recounted in oral history cannot fill in all blanks left by archives-based histories, this is in part for the obvious reason that all citizens of the Soviet Union, including religious believers, were constantly exposed to versions of official ideological discourse and could not completely remain outside of its influence. Another reason lies in the fact that the person who tells a story in 2005 is no longer the same person who experienced an event in 1982, especially when she has since lived through the collapse of an entire economic and political system. Orally narrated memory is always the result of a complex exchange between a present self, a remembered past, and immediately present and imagined audiences. Written records can open up a gap between the remembering self and a remembered past, some aspects of which may not fit the preferred narrative of the day.[6] In this sense, written archives can do as much to challenge present orthodoxies as oral histories can challenge established images of the past.

For example, anyone who has done research on post-Soviet religious communities will know that the percentage of adult members who have been continuously religious throughout their life is small, while many current religious activists were at some time in their lives convinced members of Soviet organizations. Some even describe themselves as former atheists.[7] In the multi-religious Volga region I often found that people who had taken up religious practice during and after perestroika tended to reject atheist perspectives on their own denomination but reproduced stereotypes about other religious groups that they had learned during their Soviet-era education. Pagan and Lutheran Maris talked about the Russian Orthodox Church as an instrument of colonization and ethnic discrimination. Adherents of denominations with a long local history (i.e., Orthodox Christians, Muslims, and traditionalist Mari "pagans") reproduced stories according to which newer groups, including Protestant Baptists, Lutherans, and Pentecostals but also the stricter school of Salafi Muslims, compromised the mental and physical health of their members or followed foreign missionaries in search of material gain. Far from presenting a critique of Soviet power, the oral accounts of current religious believers often contained echoes of Soviet-era textbooks and reports.[8]

In contemporary Russia as in other socialist and post-socialist societies, the line between "enforced historical orthodoxies" and informal practices of "unsanctioned remembrance"[9] is not a neat distinction of written versus oral accounts. In the case of the collective farm chairman, a major difference between his reports and his later recollections is how the event of a cow dying is emplotted in a larger narrative.[10] Paper forms required the identification of a chain of cause and effect that ends with the animal's death, whereas the oral reminiscence follows a plot familiar from witchcraft accusations around the world, where an unfortunate event is placed in an ongoing web of relationships among people living and working together.[11] Both plots contain familiar Soviet tropes: the absolute truth of science and the envy of the lazy toward the industrious. Being able to emplot each trope in the appropriate narrative genre for use with administrative or village audiences was probably a basis for the chairman's success as a rural politician.

This does not mean that telling history is just a matter of constructing narratives, one of which is just as good as any other. Rather, it means that the best insights are unlikely to emerge from oppositional readings, where archival documents represent official scripts and oral memory gives access to "hidden transcripts" of resistance.[12] Neither do they come from simply placing different accounts side by side as complementary pieces of the same puzzle. If different oral and written genres place specific narrative demands on an author or teller, sources can ask questions of each other in a productive dialogue that may never be resolved into a single finished image of what happened.[13] Clarifying how sources differ in terms of expected plotlines, strategies of reporting and incorporating alternative voices, and criteria for what constitutes an event worth telling makes it possible to let one type of source to speak on questions raised by another.

Adversarial Voices

One of the reasons scholars turn to oral histories is to put the voices of religious believers center stage. A closer look at the archives, however, shows that such voices constituted important ingredients in Soviet knowledge about religion as well, as sources of authority as well as proof of the ongoing necessity of atheist work. In commissioners' reports from the late Soviet period, quotes and detailed descriptions help convince the reader of the diligence of the author and enable him to call attention to gaps and delays in the expected course of socialist development. In august 1967, Viktor Ivanovich Savel'ev, commissioner of religious affairs for the Mari Autonomous Soviet Socialist Republic (ASSR), visited Zvenigovo district in the southern part of the republic.[14] The itinerary included settlements along the railway line that linked Ioshkar-Ola to Kazan' and Moscow. Similar to Lenin's Shatura, these settlements had emerged during the early decades of Soviet rule, had multi-ethnic populations, and lacked officially recognized houses of worship of any denomination. According to official Marxist narratives of historical progress, there should have been no signs of religious life in these villages and small towns. However, secular Soviet institutions and social imaginaries were not the only ones present: Savel'ev prefaces his account by acknowledging that throughout the district, "sectarianism develops without inhibition."[15]

"Sectarianism" is a very wide term in the commissioner's usage and includes any form of unsanctioned religiosity that is not carried out by state-licensed clergy in registered houses of worship.[16] In the settlement of Mochalishche there is a community of Seventh-day Adventists. Muslims gather in private homes. There are frequent appearances of "a woman of 50–60 years in black vestments and dark glasses, she is referred to as a presbyter, but her identity could not be confirmed."[17] Presbyter (Russian *presviter*) is a term for a priest or elder in a variety of Christian denominations. In Suslonger, Savel'ev counts three Adventist women with their children and six Pentecostals, as well as adherents of the underground "True Orthodox Christians," and a number of unregistered imams and priests. Though named in his report, they remain hazy figures, their actions reported from hearsay:

> In the same settlement lives the itinerant mullah Shakir Suleimanov, aged 75. In order to draw people into religion Muslims at Suslonger Station organized the beautification (*blagoustroistvo*) of the cemetery, while the village council remained passive. In the same settlement Badanov, Mazanov, Bichurov and Nikitin are organizing collective worship services [of unidentified denominations].[18]

Savel'ev devotes more attention to the unregistered community of Seventh-day Adventists, colloquially known as *subbotniki*, from the Russian word for Saturday (*subbota*). They represent the kind of sectarian who raised political concern in the 1960s and '70s: Protestant splinter groups that had split off from legal organizations because they refused to give up pacifist commitments, insisted on baptizing children and adolescents, and rejected other restrictions imposed by the Soviet state.[19] Painting such denial of the benefits of socialism as far out of touch with reality even in a remote rural region, the report places the group in a normal Soviet village full of representatives of secular culture and knowledge:

> The freest and fastest development of sectarianism is occurring on the territory of the Shelanger rural council. Take, for example, the Spartak village. It has only 32 households. Among the inhabitants of the village are: 2 teachers . . ., the director of the library of Shelanger Middle School, the chairman of the executive committee of the rural council, and in the same village there are four party members. Nonetheless, the *subbotniki* have put down firm roots in the village.

Focusing in on one Adventist family, Savel'ev performs a shift in narrative perspective, from relaying hearsay to incorporating reported speech from a direct encounter with believers. At a time when circulars from the Council of Religious Affairs were directing all local commissioners to struggle against sects, the passage emphasizes the seriousness of his investigative efforts while retaining rapport with intended readers in Moscow.[20]

> On August 7, 1967, Ivanov [a forty-year-old villager] went through the rite of baptism. He goes from house to house and agitates among the collective farm workers to have them join the sect. To confirm his agitation he tries to prove that he was sick and disabled, and thanks to joining the sect was completely healed. According to the brigadier of [the collective farm] Ul'ianov, this *subbotnik* calls communists antichrists and claims they have sold their souls to satan.
>
> His daughter Galina declared during an interview: supposedly (*iakoby*) everything that is good, it all comes from god. And now supposedly the end of the world is coming near, to confirm this she points to earthquakes, floods, and wars. The fact that chicks hatch from eggs happens, she says, all thanks to god. Galina considers herself to be a sincere believer.
>
> Ivanov stated during an interview with the correspondent of the newspaper *Marii Kommuna* that god had introduced two work-free days before the Soviet government did, and his daughter confirms the same.[21]

In this report, the indirect speech of selected Adventists makes them real to readers and simultaneously sets them apart from the background of a thriving Soviet village. The sense of surprise at hearing sectarians deny achievements of socialism and ascribe them to divine help is a standard feature of Soviet language about them, and reporting such denials as the words of actual believers helps distance both the author and the intended readers from the views expressed. At the same time, Savel'ev reassures readers that the teachers, librarians, party members, and brigadiers are not involved in religious practice. His sectarians are sufficiently realistic to show that the commissioner dug beneath the surface of the settlements he visited. At the same time, they remain sufficiently marginal that their words reveal ridiculous misrecognition of Soviet achievements rather than a serious critique.

By mixing evidence of having talked to believers with commentary by more respectable Soviet citizens and expressions indicating his own critical stance, Savel'ev shows his awareness of the ideological and polemical character of words, where meaning is inseparable from evaluation and readers will infer political loyalties from the phrasing used. As the Soviet linguists Valentin Voloshinov and Mikhail Bakhtin pointed out, there is a potential in written language for reported and authorial voices to leak into each other, so that a quotation can determine the tone in which the narrative text will be read or vice versa.[22] In reported dialogues in the records of the Council of Religious Affairs, this potential for discursive leakage is always carefully managed through scene-setting, selection of quotes, and stylistic and grammatical devices creating distance. Nonetheless, they should not be read as pure works of fiction, but as reflecting a practical predicament in which the commissioners found themselves once post-Stalinist policy shifts called for them to monitor and combat not just religious institutions but popular religiosity.[23] This required them to talk to and seek out believers, and to be in contact with unregistered as well as registered groups. In the process, they were bound to have encounters and conversations that challenged the stock assumptions underlying late Soviet ideological language. For example, Savel'ev uses the term "agitation" not only to cast the speech of believers in a negative light but also to portray them as parasitical upon Soviet approaches to political education. What is meant as a distancing device actually shows the uncanny resemblances which lay behind the Soviet government's harsh reaction to proselytizing sects.[24]

Член колхоза «Октябрь» Советского района комсомолка Таисия Рябчикова в марте приняла крещение, а во время весеннего сева ее поймали с краденым семенным горохом.

ПОП: Рабе божьей Таисии заранее прощаю все грехи.

Рис. В. Яковлева.

A cartoonist's view of baptism in the Mari republic. The priest says, "I grant the servant of God Taisiia advance absolution from all her sins." The text above the image explains that the collective farm worker and Communist Youth League member Taisiia had been baptized in March, but during the following spring sowing she was caught stealing seed peas. Accusations of hypocrisy and economic carelessness were typical of campaigns against rural religious practice in the 1960s and must have set a tense tone for the commissioner of religious affairs' conversations with believers. Drawing by V. Iakovlev. *Mariiskaia Pravda*, June 25, 1960.

Throughout the report, the commissioner works to keep his own voice separate from the words of religious believers, aided by the assurance that his readers are as certain as he is that people and not divinities are the agents of social progress. The distancing devices used to prevent discursive leakage indicate aspects of believers' speech that were especially troubling to Soviet secularist certainties. At a time when there were few rhetorical positions from which developed socialism could be challenged, the imperative to seek out and report on religion reintroduces dialogical and polemical elements into bureaucratic language.

Of all his religious and secular interlocutors, the one person whose words Savel'ev reports at some length is Galina, the daughter of the recently baptized Adventist. As a representative of a young generation of believers that should not exist according to the proper historical narratives of Marxism, Galina's voice supports Savel'ev's claim to having exercised due diligence in locating believers in unlikely places. It also adds a risky dose of ideological ambiguity, as when he reports Galina's claim that work-free Saturdays had been provided by God (to those who kept Saturday as the Sabbath) before the Communist Party introduced them in the 1960s. The particle *iakoby* (as if, supposedly) and such verbs as "declares" and "says" create a boundary between Savel'ev's speech and this blatant inversion of Soviet claims to progress. As tools of "assimilation" of another's utterance,[25] they assign a different degree of trustworthiness to each speaker, devaluing the voices of religious believers, but also making it possible to include them.

These framing verbs and particles mark shifts between descriptive account and ideological commentary, demonstrating to the intended readers that the author knows how to draw the boundary between them. As an unforeseen reader coming upon this reported dialogue in the archive, I am reminded of the inherent instability of the atheist enterprise. The believers whose voices were needed to demonstrate the continuing relevance of atheist work were also the only citizens of the Soviet Union who had an ideological reference point outside the late Soviet version of Marxism-Leninism that was supported by institutional

structures. Whereas late Soviet ideological language is often analyzed as having been "hypernormalized" to the point that there
was no outside standpoint from which to argue against it,[26] reports
by commissioners of religious affairs routinely quote ideological
critics. They thereby face the risk inherent in all reported speech
that it might "become more forceful and more active than the
authorial context" and infiltrate it with their points of view.[27]

By reporting her ideologically most outrageous statements,
Savel'ev perhaps makes Galina and other Adventists sound more
alien than they were, but he provides the flavor of a direct
encounter with ideological disagreement that was hardly a practical possibility for most citizens of mature socialism. Quoted
dialogues in council records stand out as islands of ideological
variation that are not to be found in more monologic genres
such as the financial reports of collective farms. When juxtaposed with other sources, such as oral accounts, those voices that
are in a weaker position in a report may be supported and amplified, while the perspective of the authorial voice is relativized or
marginalized. Often such alternative readings can work because
there is already an internal polyphony to archival documents.

Complementarity: Interpreting One Source
through the Lens of Another

If Soviet officials needed believers' voices to establish verisimili-
tude and demonstrate diligence, contemporary researchers often
use oral history to understand how people negotiated ideological teachings and the effects of official policies on everyday life.
As Marianne Kamp points out, archives emphasize the plans and
perceptions of party and state officials and may "compress" the
struggles and internal disagreements of those who became the
objects of communist transformations.[28] From her interviews with
elderly Uzbek women who lived through the transformations of
the Stalin era, she shows the selective uptake of Soviet ideas by
individuals who enthusiastically embraced education and, to some

extent, unveiling while rejecting the focus on companionate marriage and the nuclear family that was supposed to go along with
Soviet-style women's liberation. In her findings, Soviet ways of
doing things appear completely new and foreign to Central Asian
societies, and are accepted or rejected in discrete pieces.

Studies conducted in other settings find a more densely
woven interdependence between Soviet ideology and everyday life. Perhaps because the interviewees are of a later generation, perhaps because they are mainly ethnic Russians who
perceive less cultural distance between themselves and those in
power, Donald Raleigh's oral history of Soviet baby boomers
from Moscow and the Volga city of Saratov emphasizes a basic
acceptance of the legitimacy of the Soviet state and satisfaction
with growing up a Soviet citizen among the generation born in
1949–50. Archival accounts of school life in the 1960s might go
no further than showing that sense of conformity. But the personal memories collected by Raleigh between 2001 and 2008
bring out the wide range of interests and ideas that occupied
loyal Soviet citizens, although official ideologues would have
found them internally contradictory.

When it comes to views on religion, for example, members
of the post-war generation who affirmed that "back then we
were all atheists" also recalled coloring eggs for Easter and enter-
taining a vague sense of a higher power.[29] Some interviewees
remembered themselves as atheists and still found it important to
mention the presence of older, religious relatives, such as an Old
Believer grandmother about whom "the other children in my
class [didn't] know." [30] While not detracting from the felt absence
of religion in family life, these relatives constituted a reserve
of religious sensibilities and continuity with pre-revolutionary
Russia that had acquired renewed importance by the time the
interviews were conducted.

Different from Soviet sociological publications, which
argued that an atheist was someone who actively opposed religion and considered it to be incompatible with human progress,

calling oneself atheist in these memories had a more flexible range of meanings. It could refer to the absence of any practical relevance of religion in everyday life, sometimes quite compatible with acknowledging "that there's a God" or a higher power that is "the essence of all the best that humankind has lived through."[31] Being an atheist could also encompass practicing cultural traditions without ascribing deeper meaning to them. Official definitions of atheism would hardly have allowed for such a range of nuances.

Oral accounts and archival records from the Volga region confirm this picture of atheist and religious sensibilities being closely intertwined in a complex Soviet present. But in combination they also draw attention to an important distinction between historically established and often ethnically based "traditional" religions and relative newcomers to the area, such as the Adventists and other Protestant groups. Official and lay understandings of this distinction often overlapped. In Commissioner Savel'ev's report, the Adventist school girl reads Soviet newspapers and concludes from them that the end of the world is near. For his part, Savel'ev integrates the Adventist community into a broader narrative of religious practice that fulfills a common function but is hierarchically ordered into more or less legitimate expressions. If wandering mullahs, mysterious nun-like women, and preaching Adventists are treated under the common rubric of "sectarianism," this only partially reflects Soviet ignorance or indifference regarding theological distinctions. It also shows that a Soviet official's view of religious parallelism in this multi-religious region was not so different from that attested in nineteenth-century and post-Soviet sources.

In the understanding of the official as well as in local religious debates that originated long before his time and outlasted him, differences between religious groups existed, but were softened by an overall equivalence.[32] One itinerant holy person would be recognizable as addressing similar needs as another, but people would choose whom to approach and consult with according to the ethnic and religious origin of their family. By singling out the Adventists, who appeared in the region during the Second World War, as particularly threatening and misguided, Savel'ev echoes the widespread idea, going back to before the revolution, that "traditional" religions were more trustworthy than those that spread to an area through recent proselytizing.[33] Like atheist youth in Saratov, this commissioner worked from intuitions about the place of religion in social life that were not radically separate from those of his contemporaries who were religious believers. For both groups, religion was a field of practice that was not simply a matter of individual assent to dogmas, but of community membership.

When it comes to oral accounts from post-Soviet hindsight, it turns out that integration or separation from Soviet life was remembered differently depending on the religious tradition. All the members of Protestant churches I interviewed in the Mari republic were converts from the 1990s, when these churches experienced strong growth. But those that remembered meetings with "old-time believers" spoke about their courage and suffering in the face of state repression, with the paradigmatic case being a trial of unregistered Baptists that had taken place in Ioshkar-Ola in the early 1980s. Mirroring the exclusionary rhetoric about "sectarians" in Soviet and post-Soviet writings, community memory in Protestant congregations tended to focus on experiences of discrimination and strategies to cope with them.[34] "No matter where we worship now, we know that we all come from Brick Street," as the pastor of a moderately thriving Baptist church said in 2005 during a gathering in the small house on the outskirts of town that had served as an unofficial but commonly known place of prayer meetings since the 1970s.

In the memories of those residents whose ritual practice was relatively well known and accepted as traditional to the region, there was less emphasis on heroic resistance to atheist society. Rather, their stories emphasized the kind of everyday coexistence that speaks from the efforts of Suslonger's Muslims to restore the graveyard as a communal good, quite possibly with the tacit approval of the rural council. Many older residents of Mari villages recalled that traditional sacrificial ceremonies in sacred groves continued throughout the Soviet period, especially in the eastern parts of the Mari republic. Such ceremonies were officially forbidden as religious acts taking place outside of registered cult buildings. They are rarely mentioned in the reports of commissioners of religious affairs after the mid-1950s, when the frequency of reports shifts from quarterly to annual or semi-annual, and their content becomes more closely attuned to areas of special political concern.[35] Residents remember that many local officials looked the other way unless there happened to be an inspection from the district center, or there was a new and zealous party secretary or head of the police department. In other places, rituals in the sacred groves ceased for lack of specialists but were conducted at home. People in vulnerable positions such as teachers and postal workers had elderly or female relatives conduct rituals for them.

As the British anthropologist Caroline Humphrey describes based on her visit to a collective farm in southern Siberia in 1967, such ritual observances were understood to be disapproved of by higher authorities but were well integrated into the local institutional landscape, often receiving moral or practical support from collective farms and rural administrations. In Humphrey's interpretation, the support of local authorities for these activities grew from the fact that the optimism about progress embedded in Soviet ideology provided no answer to the problems it fostered, including the uncertainties of changing economic policy and growing environmental degradation.[36] Oral and written accounts of ongoing ritual practice in the Volga region also indicate how the new social units created by the socialist economic administration—collective farm brigades, groups of villages under one rural council, and rural districts, for example—became ritual units rather than remaining alien to them.

As shown by the case of the collective farm chairman and his reminiscences about witchcraft, the memories of officials in charge of producing administrative records can be important connecting pieces for understanding what records do and do not talk about. Several locally born former party officials remembered being aware of ritual activity but striving to save everyone trouble by not giving official notice. One long-term communist activist, born in 1953, remembered religious activity as a way of expressing care for the community. "No one came, no one chased people away," explained the former party secretary and club director of a village in the Morki region, recalling the regular summer ceremonies in the sacred grove near his native village:

> As a member of the party committee, for seven years, I went there every year in July, stood there, listened. After all, they prayed for the common good [*na obshchee delo*], so that people might have happiness, they asked on behalf of the people, not for themselves. That the harvest combines might work in the collective farm, that there might be grain.

The district headquarters of the Communist Party also knew about the yearly summer ceremonies in the village but only interfered "when one of the secretaries of the district committee had changed or someone transferred from another sector and said to tear the whole thing down."[37]

In the light of such recollections, police records and party meeting minutes that talk about disrupted ceremonies or punishments for participation in them appear not as routine parts of the repression of religion but as extraordinary events with additional causes, such as local shifts in leadership or policy changes in Moscow. One example that shows the ebb and flow of interest in religious practice are sporadic mentions of Mari religious practice on the territory of the collective farm "Avantgarde" in the meeting minutes of the Novo-Tor"ial district committee in the northeast of the Mari republic. In November 1960, the committee cancelled the strict warning and probation that had been imposed six years before on a party member of Mari nationality, born in 1912, "for carrying out religious rituals with sacrifices."[38] The year 1960 was as much a time of heightened anti-religious struggle as 1954 had been, so perhaps six years was a standard time of expiration of such warnings, or there might have been a more personal reason this party member came back into good standing. In 1973, the same collective farm came under scrutiny because on August 2, the day of the Prophet Elijah, residents of three villages "came to the Shokshem cemetery in Sernur district to commemorate the dead, which involved drinking and desecration of the graves."[39] Elijah's Day (Il'in den') is a day of commemorating the dead in many villages that observe a mix of Mari and Russian Orthodox traditions. On such a day, families come to feast on their deceased relatives' graves. These practices of drinking and food consumption would look like desecration (oskvernenie) to someone who thinks of a cemetery as an orderly, park-like place, but the activities were anticipated by the way cemeteries are set up across Russia. Benches and sometimes tables next to the graves mark feasting by the living as a crucial part of remembering the dead. The real offense was probably the loss of a workday, and the blame was put on the party organization and management of the collective farm for not taking anti-religious work seriously enough.

Since it seems that the Avantgarde collective farm had a reputation for being a place of Mari ritual observance, perhaps its residents were a convenient target whenever the district administration needed to demonstrate effective engagement in the fight against religion, either because of signals from above or because of a new or overzealous member. Or the point may have been to discredit specific people through accusations of being involved in religious practice. In dealing with such possibilities, it is less interesting to try to find out what really happened than to recognize that both written records and personal memories respond to shifting social and political currents in which religious phenomena gain and lose significance over time. To learn about such rhythms, the reminiscences of state and collective farm officials can be testimony that is as important as the memories of religious believers.[40] Different kinds of sources can complement one another and suggest better ways to read, listen, and ask. But ultimately they also point to the way in which the past retains its own integrity to which no source affords unobscured access.

Convergence: Cemeteries as Default Religious Sites

There are cases where archival and oral sources compensate for each other's blind spots, as when memory treats ritual observances in Soviet villages as commonplace, everyday, and uncontroversial occurrences and documents treat them as a periodically returning social ill that set in motion chains of official action. But there are also cases of convergence, where different types of sources point to the importance of a particular phenomenon while illuminating different aspects. In the Volga region and beyond, references to cemeteries taking on new roles as sites of ritual observance represent such a convergence. The group of Muslims who entered into negotiations with the local administration over the upkeep and use of the graveyard in Suslonger was far from unique in its solicitude.

Starting in the late 1940s, archival documents from the Mari ASSR mention cemeteries as sites of public worship, especially for Muslims. The only officially functioning mosque in the republic was located in a village far away from the main centers of the Tatar population, so people gathered at cemeteries in Ioshkar-Ola and other towns to pray during Islamic holidays.[41] In the neighboring Tatar ASSR, a group of Muslim villagers from the Bondiuga district wrote to the Central Committee of the Communist Party in Moscow in 1961, asking for permission "to hold Tatar religious prayers . . . not at home, but at the cemetery." They explained that they gathered regularly "to read prayers at the cemetery, somewhat like commemoration of the deceased. During the reading one of us acts as an elder [i.e., recites the prayers] and each of us gives him 10 kopecks in new currency. No one is getting rich through black labor."[42]

The use of graveyards for prayer gatherings during Muslim holidays and for other collective prayers was partly motivated by a loophole in Soviet laws about religion, which exempted graveyards from the general prohibition on conducting religious rituals outside of registered cult buildings. A letter from I. A. Mikhalev, Commissioner of Religious Affairs in the Tatar ASSR, asked his superiors in 1972 to clarify the status of graveyards as sites of religious ritual. Although he assumed that the law was intended to reserve the right to hold religious ceremonies at graveyards for officially registered religious communities, the commissioner found that local officials often interpreted it in a broader fashion and permitted unregistered groups to conduct a variety of ceremonies there.[43] In response to the request from Bondiuga, Mikhalev's predecessor Mangutkin felt compelled to venture into Islamic theology:

> According to Muslim custom a believer can read the qur'an on the grave of a close relative, [but] not as part of a group gathering. The collective commemoration of the deceased on the cemetery contradicts sharia law.[44]

Although not all commissioners were ready to make pronouncements on the matter of Islamic law, the common commitment to the care of cemeteries created constant points of contact between religious believers and Soviet power. Another letter from the Tatar ASSR asks the local district council to help provide a new fence for the Tatar graveyard in a village; another time Mangutkin had to respond to a complaint about an unknown traveler who had allegedly been buried in a Tatar village cemetery with a cross on the grave, provoking protests from Muslim families.[45] These pieces of archival evidence point to the role of cemeteries and other burial sites, such as Muslim and Christian shrines, as refuge spaces of religious practice.[46] Since their use for death rituals could not be entirely eliminated, there was a potential to expand from there to other rites.

In oral accounts of Soviet life, cemeteries likewise emerge as sites of irrepressible and sometimes unexpected encounters with the supernatural. When I asked a retired collective farm worker from the Morki district born in 1927 if she observed Mari rituals in her youth, she answered laconically that she had worked in logging from the age of fourteen: "we brought the logs back with horses, it was hard work." There was little time for religious traditions, but the old woman remembered three days each year when it was time to "commemorate the ancient ones": in springtime during the *sorta* festival (coinciding with Orthodox Maundy Thursday), one day in summer, and in the fall.

Rural-urban migrants who had moved away from their native village paid respect to the village cemetery on their return visits, maintaining this link to ritual traditions whose details they were increasingly unaware of. A woman born in 1945 who had left the remote Morki district to work as a schoolteacher remembered visits home to her mother: "And I also didn't know how to behave on the cemetery. I came from the city, mom and I went, let's go to the cemetery. But it turns out you also need to know the right order there. . . . In our village they go on *semik* [seven weeks after Easter]. Where my husband is buried they go on the feast of the Protection of Our Lady." She had only realized this after the Soviet period, when knowledge about Mari customs became more available and her generation started to feel responsible for maintaining religious traditions. A neighbor of similar age had a dream in which her deceased mother and other dead relatives stood at the cemetery gate, waiting on *semik*. "This means, they chose this day for some reason. We should only go on that particular day." But the ritual moment of visiting ancestors' graves, although not carried out on the traditional date, had been a constant even during her secular youth.

For urban residents, cemeteries could also become sites of unexpected encounters. Several graveyards close to Ioshkar-Ola are known to contain mass graves where victims of the repressions of the 1920s and '30s were buried. There are stories about certain graves from which light emanates and where people were healed after praying. The Russian Orthodox believers who told me about these graves in 2005–6 interpreted the light as evidence that priests who were executed for their faith were buried there.

In cities with more elaborate pre-revolutionary traditions of grave sculpture, depictions of saintly and divine figures opened up even more possibilities for symbolic reassignment. On the graveyard of Novodevichii convent in Saint Petersburg, there is a bronze statue of Jesus Christ wearing a long gown, erected on the grave of Anna Akimovna Vershinina (1858–1914), wife of a cavalry general. Part of a composition where Jesus stands under the horizontal beam of a large upright cross, the statue is designed to be a little shorter than life-size, and for that reason it looks as if the legs were sawed off below the knees. The story I heard in 2010 from a laywoman in her forties who worshipped at the convent church explained this odd look by reference to the well-known Soviet hunger for scrap metal. The statue, this post-Soviet convert had heard, was slated to be melted during the period of War Communism in the 1920s. A worker sawed off the legs below the knees and went off to finish his work the next day. But on the way home he was run over by a street car, and his legs were severed at the same place where he had cut off the legs of Christ. After that no one dared touch the remainder of the statue, and it became a site of popular veneration.

Based on correlating photographic evidence and archival records with the oral reminiscences of people who visited the convent during Soviet times, the historians Mikhail Shkarovskii and Elena Isakova construct a less dramatic story that nonetheless highlights the importance of graves as refuge spaces where religious practice could continue and even develop new forms. They conclude that people began to pray and light candles in front of the statue after the nearby cemetery chapel, dedicated to the Prophet Elijah, was torn down in the 1930s. During the post-war years, vandals threw the statue off the pedestal and almost stole it, but believers and citizens interested in the historical value of the cemetery prevented the theft. The memory of this incident may have merged with the urge to over-explain the statue's unusual bodily proportions and produced the story of the severed legs.[47]

Statues are not part of the standard repertoire of venerable images in the Russian Orthodox tradition, and the idea of using bronze and stone sculptures instead of wooden crosses as grave monuments came to Saint Petersburg elites from western Europe. But this particular grave monument became a place of unofficial veneration by virtue of its shape and location, and remains so today. When I visited in 2010, visitors to the cemetery still lined up to climb on the pedestal, touch the statue, and offer candles or a silent prayer, much as they might do with a miracle-working icon inside a church.

Although different sources may offer conflicting accounts of what went on at a particular cemetery, both archival and oral accounts point to graves and graveyards as sites of religious persistence and innovation. In addition to the officially condoned private commemoration of dead loved ones, these places were used for individual and collective rituals that were not always connected to particular dead people but offered access to divine powers. This development from the graveyard as a point of contact with particular dead ancestors to a place of collective religious observance, which is evident in sources from Muslim and Orthodox Christian populations, shows how the Soviet period could spur religious innovation even as religious traditions were under pressure.[48]

Contradictions: Events and Situations

Although written and oral sources both speak of graveyards as sites of innovative religious practice, stories about light emanating from tombs and city workers who died after trying to dismantle a grave monument were unlikely to make it into the Soviet state archives except in the carefully marked form of reported rumors. In general, narratives about the destruction of sacred sites and objects and the effects of such measures represent an area of stark divergence between archival sources and oral accounts. Official documents treat the closing and destruction of cult buildings and the prevention of popular pilgrimages to sacred sites as "events" in the sense of the *Annales* school of history, condensed turning points in the flow of time that change the possibilities for further action.[49] Especially under Khrushchev, there is extensive documentation of the process of decision making that led up to such an event, often involving a deliberate mobilization of public opinion through meetings of villages or work collectives.[50] The question of what happened after a building was closed or destroyed is of little interest in these records, perhaps because their purpose is to construct the decision to eliminate a place of worship as a definitive step along the way to declining religiosity. Too close an investigation of what actually happened over the coming years might have called the decisive nature of this moment into question.

In 1964, for example, a local district committee in the Tatar republic petitioned the Council of Ministers to transfer use rights for an old church building to the local collective farm, "which will be instructed: to take off the bells and deposit them as scrap metal and to transform the building into a storehouse."[51] The question of how those who used to worship in the church and those who removed the bells and repurposed the building continued to live together afterward matters little in the council's vertical communication. Only local-level correspondence between the commissioner for religious affairs and resident officials and activists acknowledges that there were religious buildings that had officially been closed but continued to be used or treated as sacred. In one case, an atheist lecturer notified the commissioner that the administration of a collective farm used the bells of a closed church to notify villagers of assemblies.[52] In another village, the church had been refitted as a grain store and chicken coop without changing its outward appearance, which "led to a steep rise in the religious feelings of the believers, who demanded that the church be returned to them."[53]

Such accounts of an unfinished or unsuccessful secularization of a sacred building are rare and usually kept separately from the registration file of a church or mosque, where procedures relating to its closure are documented. By contrast, popular accounts of confrontations between Soviet officials and sites of religious practice often focus on the long-term consequences for the willing or unwilling agents of the state. The injuries and calamities they suffered serve as evidence of the inherent danger of meddling with spiritual forces. Throughout the Soviet Union, Stalin-era anti-religious campaigns provoked rumors about people who destroyed churches, removed bells, and exhumed relics being struck by lightning, paralyzed, or otherwise meeting with sudden death or injury.[54] In the 1920s and '30s, some of these rumors made it into secret police records as evidence of popular discontent.[55] A post-war version of such rumors is the story of "Zoia's vigil," referring to a young girl from Kuibyshev on the Lower Volga who was said to have turned to stone in her family's apartment in 1956 when she danced with an icon of St. Nicholas in her hand. The story provoked official investigation as part of a number of religious rumors circulating during the uncertain time of transition after Stalin's death.[56] I found no mention of comparable stories in later reports from the Tatar and Mari republics, indicating that official attention to the genre diminished to the degree that religious narratives and institutions ceased to pose a threat to Soviet existence.

However, in Marii El in 2005, residents of the republic who had grown up during the 1960s and '70s told stories about workers who cut down Mari sacred groves and policemen who disturbed prayer ceremonies or pilgrimages, very similar to those found in pre-war archival records. For them, destructions of sacred sites were not so much one-time decisive events but rather slight shifts in an ongoing constellation of relationships: the coexistence of humans and non-human forces in a particular place. The same retired Mari teacher who relearned the proper way to visit cemeteries remembered that a member of her gardening association built a house from wood cut from a sacred grove close to Ioshkar-Ola. The house burned down soon after it was finished. Another teacher, born in 1963 in a Christian Mari family but a later convert to Islam, claimed that her father, a rural party secretary, died in a car accident because he had removed the icons her mother cherished from the family's new house. And an ethnic Russian who had worked for the forest service since the 1970s remembered what care she and her colleagues took to identify former sacred groves and old cemeteries in order to avoid cutting down any trees there. "I don't want to be cursed," she explained.

This pattern of explanation was shared even by former Communist Party members. A former district party secretary recalled that she received her post in the early 1980s because her predecessor was paralyzed after kicking the water spout of the sacred spring of Shabashi. He was trying to disperse a pilgrimage on the feast day of the Kazan icon of the Mother of God (July 20) at this site of popular veneration. His successor told me about this as an uncontroversial point of fact, while recalling in the same breath that her years as a party secretary were the best of her life.

Told as stories about unavoidable causality rather than moral evaluation, such rumors are not necessarily a discourse of resistance to Soviet power. But they do point to a deep disconnect between popular modes of explanation and those that were fit to write down in official paperwork. Local officials were often immersed in the same networks in which explanations of supernatural retaliation made sense, but as the decades of Soviet rule went on they increasingly understood that references to spiritual agents would not only be disbelieved in Moscow but also seen as irrelevant.[57] For an archival researcher, hearing oral stories that follow a different logic can make it easier to hear the silences of the archives and appreciate the skilled assembly of documentation that made it possible to construct acts of church or mosque closings as decisive events.

Workers pose before the demolished church of St. George, Nizhnii Novgorod/ Gorkii, 1932. Photos such as this one indicate a certain pride in the labor that went into dynamiting houses of worship, and perhaps a sense of demonstrative bravery. They stand in contrast to oral narratives, which almost invariably claim that the people who participated in acts of destruction or desecration later suffered divine retribution. *Photo by M. Dmitriev, courtesy of Russian Museum of Photography, Nizhnii Novgorod.*

The commonplace nature of such stories of divine retribution indicates that large numbers of Soviet citizens continued to subscribe to ideas of sacred places as animated by powerful and real forces. They also indicate that many of those who accepted atheism did so more as a performance of loyalty to the party and their position in the Soviet system than as a matter of rational assent to ideas of the non-existence of nonhuman powers. Rather than denying the powers of a place, blasphemers act in an official capacity that forces them to interact with sacred places and objects in ways that lack deference.[58] Where punishment results, it is somewhat detached from ideological arguments about the rights and wrongs of atheism but rather shows that placing oneself outside community norms has inevitable consequences.

It would thus be wrong to argue that divergences between oral stories and written documents are caused by ideological differences between "the believers" and "the atheists." Venerators and detractors of sacred objects could be as intimately connected as the wife who transferred the family icons to the new house and the husband who removed them. The difference lies, somewhat counter-intuitively, in the short attention span of paper and the longer patience of embodied memory. Bureaucratic documentation works in discrete steps designed to yield results so that focus can shift to other issues. Its plotlines are oriented toward one-time acts and decisive interventions. When people reflect back on their lives, by contrast, there is time for plots to take unexpected twists and turns: jealousy brings down an overly diligent milkmaid, divine retribution cuts short a career as a party secretary or saves a statue from destruction, and a self-defined atheist family retains an option to connect to religion through a pious grandmother. Oral history thus involves reflection on longer-term legacies and open-ended processes, always expressed in a particular interview situation. When my interlocutors talked about the irrepressible power of sacred sites, they were not only celebrating the triumph of religious faith over atheism but also affirming the superior strength and resilience of Russia's spiritual traditions to a foreign researcher.

Sources in Conversation

The examples in this chapter come largely from the Volga region under Soviet rule, but the problems of historical interpretation that they raise are relevant to the relationship between archival documents and oral history more broadly. What we can know about Soviet-era religious life is limited by the interested nature of official documents and by the way in which religious sensibilities both stood at odds with and were reshaped by a modernization process that was intended to exclude religion. There are also issues of retroactive judgment, selection, and standardized plotlines that are present in all oral history research, but that are especially pronounced for aspects of life that have undergone such dramatic reversals of public value as has religion in former Soviet spaces. From a social stigma that could only be discussed in circumscribed contexts, being religious has become a matter of some prestige and something whose absence rather than presence needs to be explained—all the more reason to use all available sources on this phenomenon with a mixture of caution and respect, and to be aware of the circumstances in which they were created.

By doing so, we discover a late Soviet society that, far from stagnant and monopolistic, contains surprising ideological diversity, and whose governing authorities are becoming less vigilant about combating it. Ideological vigilance flares up in archival documents on the occasion of a new political campaign or a local change in officeholders, in encounters with proselytizing groups that consciously set their own ideology against the convictions of Soviet officials, or in confrontation with mass events such as pilgrimages.[59] Otherwise, it seems clear from the memories of religious believers and officials that much everyday ritual activity remained under the radar of the producers of archival records. This did not happen because of the ignorance of bureaucrats unable to see life as it was; it occurred because locally established ritual observances neither fit into the expected plots of routine Soviet recordkeeping nor were threatening enough to trigger special surveillance efforts. As religion no longer posed an institutional threat to the socialist state, the task of monitoring religiosity became routinized to performing audits on registered religious groups and periodically dropping in on unregistered ones with warnings about registration. This turned religious traditions into tacitly tolerated sources of heteroglossia and depositories of ideas and ways of being that had their origin outside of Marxism-Leninism.

Although this means that there was much religious activity in the Soviet Union that was never described in an archival document, there is also the risk of seeing too much of it. Both archival documents from bureaucracies devoted to monitoring religious life and oral eyewitness accounts may overemphasize aspects of religious life. In his report, Commissioner Savel'ev makes "sectarianism" seem far more central to community life in the Zvenigovo district than it might appear if he had described social and economic life there in full, and spoken to a greater range of residents about changes in their lives. Inquiries about ritual practice and sacred sites are likely to elicit stories that confirm these sites' importance rather than tales of hard work and indifference to the supernatural. So one should be careful not to overemphasize religion as the only source of non-socialist sensibilities, nor to call every pursuit of such sensibilities "religious."[60] Recognizingthe challenge of defining the boundaries of their object of analysis, Brezhnev-era academic researchers came up with increasingly sophisticated methods to gauge the extent to which religion or its absence mattered in socialist life. Their work constitutes another set of rich and problematic sources on Soviet religiosity.

CHAPTER 3

From Documents to Books, and Back

Atheist Sociology through an Archival Lens

If it takes some imagination to use the documentary practices of Soviet bureaucracies to learn about the conditions of religious life, the publications of Soviet scholars may appear to be an even more compromised set of sources. To be published in the Soviet Union, studies of religious life had to go through processes of scholarly review as well as of political censorship, and at both stages there was likely to be skepticism regarding any findings that indicated too much vitality and ongoing appeal of religious traditions under socialism.

And yet, as long as Western researchers had limited access to Soviet archives and virtually none to communities of Soviet believers, the published works of Soviet sociologists and ethnographers constituted important sources of information on overall levels of religious and atheist commitment in the Soviet Union, as well as on substantive changes in religious practice. A number of Anglophone and Francophone scholars published books on aspects of religious life in the Soviet Union that were largely based on data from a school of empirical research on socialist society that took its beginning in the late 1950s and emerged full-fledged in the 1960s and '70s. Though aware of the need to assess flaws and biases in the data, scholars such as Christel Lane, Alexandre Bennigsen, Stephen and Ethel Dunn, and David Powell drew on Soviet published sources because gathering in-depth primary data in the Soviet Union was rarely an alternative.[1] "[A]pply directly to the [Soviet] Academy of Sciences bookstore," was anthropologist Ethel Dunn's advice to scholars interested in the Soviet experiment with directed culture change.[2]

Since the collapse of the Soviet Union, it is no longer clear what to do with the large body of published Soviet research on religion and secularization. Some Western scholars still rely on Cold War–era distillations of published Soviet research for drawing theoretical conclusions about the course of secularization under socialism.[3] Others largely ignore published Soviet work and turn to the newly accessible archives, expecting to get closer to the truth there.[4] Another group of researchers is beginning to piece together the history of Soviet religious studies from a mix of published sources, archives of state and academic institutions, and scholars' reminiscences.[5] This chapter looks at examples from the empirical sociology of religion of the 1960 and '70s to see how such a combination of archival and published sources, along with a touch of oral history, can help us appreciate both the sophistication and the limitations of these studies and use their findings more judiciously.

In some cases, archives can provide access to information that was omitted in published studies. In addition to the records of the Knowledge Society and regional Communist Party archives I examine here, relevant collections include the archives of scholarly institutions such as the Soviet Academy of Sciences, the Museum of the History of Religion and Atheism, and local research institutes. Field diaries, interview notes, and unpublished theses and dissertations are being accessed by post-Soviet scholars to ask new questions about popular responses to socialist development or folk customs with roots before the revolution.[6] But the problem of reading the Soviet-era scholarship cannot be reduced to the effects of print censorship. To the extent that published studies are flawed by limited understandings of religion and power imbalances between researchers and their subjects, these same problems are present in unpublished archival notes and reports.[7] What archives do provide is a glimpse of the struggles and intentions behind empirical research on religion in the Soviet Union, allowing more nuanced readings of the publications and a deeper understanding of the collaborative efforts of fact-assembly involved.

To use an analogy from archaeology, Soviet-era books sitting on North American library shelves are like inscribed tablets in a museum collection that have been stored without proper identification. Archival collections that document the preparation, carrying out, and reception of research projects place the artifact back into its context of excavation, giving it a place within a constellation of other objects and layers of information. As Michel Foucault pointed out, such an "archaeological" approach to knowledge does not look for the real truths that are hidden behind the surfaces of artifacts but pays attention to the surface itself—the relationship between (discursive) objects on an excavated quadrant.[8]

Rather than using archival records to debunk or correct Soviet-era scholarship, the archaeological vantage point places documents and publications on the same plane and allows them to recontextualize one another within a contested field of knowledge production. Approached from this angle, archival documents never answer all the questions raised by the published books, and they certainly provide no direct encounter with what religious believers really thought. But they show what was at stake in Soviet attempts to understand religion from an atheist point of view. They also sometimes reveal unexpected proximities between groups of people and ideas of different origin that jointly contributed to this endeavor. One proximity that has been explored in some depth is the role played by scholars of pre-revolutionary training in developing Soviet approaches to governing its multi-ethnic and multi-religious state. Ethnographers such as Lev Iakovlevich Shternberg and Vladimir Germanovich Bogoraz and Orientalists such as Sergei Fëdorovich Ol'denburg had been critical of the tsarist regime and were sympathetic to the revolutionary cause, but not necessarily Marxist in their approach to social analysis.[9] Under the Soviet regime, this group of scholars found new opportunities to shape policy but was also vulnerable to accusations of bourgeois idealism and misguided cosmopolitanism. In the post-war Soviet Union, a similarly complex and tense relationship developed between propagandists charged with eradicating religion and scholars interested in studying its changing forms. Overlapping in membership because of the involvement of scholars in the atheist work of the Knowledge Society, both groups shared the drive to refine knowledge about religious practice in the post-war Soviet Union and defended the value of this knowledge against critics who found it too trivial or threatening. Although the political mission may seem strange to twenty-first century readers, the intellectual dilemmas of demarcating religion and secularity in a changing social landscape will be quite familiar.

In Search of Concreteness

Some histories of Soviet empirical social science cast it as an oppositional enterprise that was suppressed under Stalin, resurfaced during the Khrushchev Thaw, and blossomed in the dissident circles of the Brezhnev era, representing an attempt to rescue the views and experiences of the individual from the generalizing demands of Soviet society.[10] It is true that empirical studies of popular practices and attitudes were discredited in the mid-1930s, despite their important earlier role in such areas as shaping policies for the education of ethno-linguistic minorities and monitoring the reactions of the peasantry to collectivization drives. In 1936, the discipline of pedology (the study of child development in different cultural and economic environments) was banned for bringing too much psychology into Marxism. The journal *Sovetskaia etnografiia* (Soviet Ethnography) went into a ten-year hiatus the following year. Research on religion during this time was largely philological and oriented toward the past.

A reason for the precarious situation of empirical social science during the pre- and immediate post-war years was that Stalin's government treated knowledge of the population as potentially explosive. The results of the 1937 census were held back from publication, in part because they revealed too much persistent adherence to religion after two decades of atheism.[11] When the Baltic states came under Soviet rule after the Second World War, archives of folkloric manuscripts compiled during previous decades were censored for anti-Soviet but also overtly sexual and otherwise "immoral" content.[12] Even in unpublished form accessible only to researchers, certain kinds of records were treated as too risky to exist.

The generation of scholars who survived the purges of the 1930s may have concluded that it was safer to conduct an exegesis of Marxist stages of world-historical development than to look at social transformations under actually existing socialism.[13] Despite this difficult history, a look at archival and published materials from the 1950s onward indicates that interest in empirical social research reemerged before Stalin's death and rapidly developed during the early Khrushchev years. The impulse was not always to criticize the state. Arguments for the value of knowing a more differentiated Soviet public were as much a part of Khrushchev's participatory populism as the newly unleashed campaigns against religion and social deviance. Why did women and rural dwellers cling to religious practice with greater tenacity, and how could they be persuaded to let go? How could male factory workers be stopped from drinking, and made to realize their personal responsibility for bringing about the communist future? What motivated people to engage in educational and healthy leisure pursuits, such as reading literary journals, visiting libraries, or participating in sports? These were practical questions for administrators and managers as well as party and trade union propagandists, and they were taken up by young scholars eager to experiment with the new set of approaches that came to be known as "concrete sociological research."[14]

In archived meeting minutes and reports from the late 1950s and '60s, efforts to bring concreteness back into research appear as struggles between empiricists and philosophers. On the empiricist side, managerial-propagandistic and scholarly interests came together in the records of the Knowledge Society. As the institution in charge of conducting atheist propaganda alongside lectures on other popular scientific topics, the Society was both a sponsor and disseminator of research on the state of religious life in the post-war Soviet Union. Because of its broad mandate to promote a scientific worldview and spread enthusiasm about the achievements and potential of Soviet science, its records provide insights into the connections between research on religion and more general attempts to understand the USSR's changing society.[15]

As a mass organization with local cells all across the Soviet Union, the Knowledge Society was an important agent in signaling the political acceptability of concrete sociological research and promoting emerging methodologies. Its records show that this was not an oppositional effort but was fostered by central scholarly and political organizations and intentionally spread to the periphery. At the same time, the Society responded to atheist practitioners on the ground who felt that they needed better training to perform their work. In 1963, a report on the state of atheist propaganda in the Mari regional division of the Knowledge Society laments that "no one is studying the state of religious belief in the republic, neither MarNII [Mari Scientific Research Institute, the local branch of the research network of the Soviet Academy of Sciences] nor other institutions and organizations, no one generalizes approaches to scientific-atheist propaganda."[16] The need for more knowledge about particular religious traditions and their contemporary forms was an ongoing refrain at unionwide and regional atheist meetings, coming especially from practitioners in multi-ethnic and multi-confessional regions. Comparable to the nineteenth-century Russian Geographical Society and its network of provincial teachers, clergy, and exiled intellectuals, the Knowledge Society's extensive provincial membership made it uniquely placed to elicit and collect such information.[17]

As empirical social science became more institutionalized, the Knowledge Society helped disseminate its research methods. In July 1966, the minutes of the atheist section of the Mari division reported that a member, N. S. Kapustin, had just returned from a seminar in Moscow "on the methodology of concrete sociological research."[18] Back in Ioshkar-Ola, he gave a presentation on what he had learned. These training efforts were put to practical use. In December 1967, the atheist section had begun preparations for "sociological research in the factory district of Ioshkar-Ola and in rural localities." Four questionnaires, 2,000 copies each, were to be printed. Kapustin and his colleague Nikolai Sofronov were to travel to the Gornomari district on the south bank of the Volga River, known for its Orthodox Christian traditions, to conduct training seminars for local lecturers in survey methodology.[19]

Sofronov, a philosophy lecturer at the Mari State Technical Institute, published the results in his book on "the atheist education of the collective farm peasantry."[20] According to this publication, the questionnaire asked ethnic Maris of Orthodox Christian background whether they attended church and what attracted them there, whether they had baptized their children, and who or what prompted them to do so. Some questions called for open-ended answers that were written down by the interviewer, generating verbatim quotes for use in the publication. The book presents statistics and quotes to show the internal inconsistencies of contemporary religious ideas, interpreted as a sign of a moribund tradition. But sometimes voices of rural dwellers are also deployed to defend their communities from the charge of being ignorant of modern life or anti-Soviet in orientation. For example, "Ol'ga Petrovna I. from Sernur district" is quoted as explaining the presence of icons in her house in terms of attachment to family memory rather than to religion:

> I stopped believing in god soon after the collectivization of agriculture. But I keep icons in the house in a prominent place. No, I don't use them for prayer (*ne molius' na nikh*). But I can't throw them out or put them away. I am keeping them in memory of my mother. No photograph remains of her. But the icon with which she blessed me and sent me off before my wedding is still there. So don't judge me harshly. This memory is very dear to me. And as long as I live, let the icon stand in the "red corner." And when I die, let the children do as seems best to them.[21]

This statement in the voice of a rural dweller is made non-threatening by her profession of non-belief and the reference to the collectivization of agriculture as a normative landmark in a Soviet biography. But what is striking is that the reported speech of an ordinary believer is allowed to justify persisting religious practice as an expression of filial piety. Rather than destabilizing the text with their ideologically alien point of view, villagers' voices seem to increase the authority of the scientific publication. This methodological and stylistic trend did not receive universal acceptance, as discussions recorded in archives show.

Personal Experience and Historical Laws

One insight that emerges from the archives of the Knowledge Society is the hybrid character of many early concrete-sociological studies, located somewhere between information gathering and consciousness raising. In this respect, the new Soviet sociology was not so different from approaches now known as participatory or collaborative research, where the research process is intended to bring community members together toward a common goal.[22] In the Soviet context, the goal was usually aligning local efforts with the direction of development set by party congresses and official decrees.

In the early 1960s, for instance, the Institute of Philosophy of the Soviet Academy of Sciences set out to publish a book series on the transition to communism in the wake of the 1961 party program, which announced that the construction of communism would be completed by 1980. The final volume was to be dedicated to "the spiritual world" of people living through this transition.[23] The records of the Knowledge Society preserve the stenographic transcript of a conference of experts where a draft of this volume was discussed in May 1963. The process of gathering material for the book, as described by the editor Tsolak Aleksandrovich Stepanian, involved a series of workers' conferences in twenty-five factories throughout the Soviet Union, co-organized by the Knowledge Society and the Institute of Philosophy. At these conferences, "progressive workers" spoke on the lives of their work collectives, generating reflections that were included as "concrete-sociological material" in the book. The workers also commented on draft chapters by the contributing scholars . In the mind of the editorial team, philosophers and workers had to work together to find adequate descriptions for the new social relations that were emerging as a secular, work-oriented culture took over the "spiritual world" of Soviet citizens.[24]

Not all of Stepanian's colleagues who were present at the conference saw the value of the empirical materials thus generated. Critics were less concerned with how workers were selected for participation or who might have coached them in preparing their statements describing harmonious relationships and inter-ethnic friendships in their work collectives. Rather, the question was what the personal views and experiences of workers could contribute to the theorization of stages

The display at the polling station in the Kalinin Culture Club, Gorkii, in 1960 is entitled "Toward a Communist Economy." This wall of posters greeted voters with an anticipatory vision of the near future, which included advances in aviation, greater agricultural productivity, new light and chemical industries, and new housing blocks in cities. *Photo by B. A. Alekseev, courtesy of State Archive of Audio Visual Documentation, Nizhnii Novgorod, Russia, sn. 29845.*

of development as they had been outlined by Marx, Engels, and Lenin. In his opening statement, the economist and philosopher Petr Nikolaevich Fedoseev said that "facts from particular conversations with workers" could at best "enliven" the account as illustrations. What really mattered was their correct interpretation within the right philosophical and temporal framework:

> What is needed is a philosophical sociological analysis from the angle of vision of what is happening, from the angle of vision of what is to come, what are the tendencies of development and how can we practically assist in the education and formation of

the new human being, in the development of the full spiritual life of socialist society.[25]

For Fedoseev, who was director of the Institute of Philosophy and a member of the Central Committee of the Communist Party of the USSR, communist spiritual life lay in the future and could only be anticipated by theory, not described through interviews or surveys. Countering such criticism, the psychologist Platonov argued that there could be a specifically Marxist use of statistics in the field of "scientific prognostics." In a move recalling the paradoxical requirement for socialist realist literature to realistically portray society not as it was, but as it was to become,[26] Platonov said that ordinary statistics only reflected static means and averages. A Marxist approach, however, would draw attention to "that which does not yet exist or only exists as seedlings, but which is indisputably anticipated." Data collected to include such seedlings of anticipation would represent the "dynamic typicality" of developmental trends.[27]

At stake in this debate was the capacity of empirical data to describe more than the meaningless pieces of a transitory present. Volume editor Tsolak Stepanian countered his critics by arguing that in "mature socialist society," consciousness no longer merely reflected being but could advance ahead of it. Through engagement in progressive work collectives, workers under socialism could already advance to a communist consciousness, so that their statements could teach researchers what that consciousness would look like once it spread to all citizens.[28] Another organizer of the workers' conferences explained that learning about the practices of "collaboration and mutual aid" in multi-ethnic work collectives added *positive* content to the idea of communist social relations rather than defining them in negative terms as "liquidating class differences between intellectual and physical labor and differences between town and country."[29] Religious persistence under socialism, he argued, was an example of phenomena that had to be studied empirically because

Marxist evolutionist philosophy with its teachings of survivals could not explain them. If 40 percent of the Soviet population identified as religious believers "can we count that simply as a question of inertia, a question of the vitality of these survivals or are there such phenomena even in the present that nourish this survival and reproduce it"?[30] For its defenders, empirical research was necessary because existing philosophical tenets did not account for the surprising outcomes of Soviet secularization.

Forty-six years after the Bolshevik revolution, evidence of religious persistence challenged not only the success of atheist campaigns but also the prevailing Marxist historiography, according to which religious dynamics were fed by the inequalities of feudalism and capitalism but should find no further nourishment under socialism. In the course of empirical research, the new sociologists encountered unintended effects of state-sponsored secularization that contradicted the assumption that everything harmful belonged to the past. Platonov cited the spread of alcohol use in formerly tea-drinking Central Asia as a social problem that was caused, rather than solved, by Soviet secularizing policies.[31] In the face of such troubling evidence of historical complexity, some of the resistance against a return to empirical approaches came from the conviction that trained Marxist academics (and, by extension, the Communist Party) knew best where Soviet society was headed and did not need to listen to "facts from particular conversations with workers."

But unease with the limitations of positivist research did not only come from blind commitment to Marxist dogma. The critique of surveys and quantifications as reflecting only an assortment of (more or less trivial) facts extracted from a more complex, dynamic social reality is part of long-standing debates about empirical social science outside the Soviet Union as well. An Anglo-American example not far removed in time from these Soviet debates is Clifford Geertz's playful use of a quote from a nineteenth-century predecessor: "It is not worth it, as Thoreau said, to go round the world to count the cats in

Zanzibar."[32] Instead of counting up isolated facts from a static present, Stepanian and his team argued that they were giving positive content to negative concepts such as "liquidation" and "atheism," thereby helping provide a glimpse of incipient social relations. Preserving this utopian, prefigurative element in their increasingly routinized approaches to concrete sociological research, studies of religious life under advanced socialism strove to discern an emerging set of atheist values even as they acknowledged complex reasons for religious persistence. They represent a search for a desired future as much as a description of the Soviet present, but their authors also thought creatively about the task of grounding predictions in empirical findings via the notion of dynamic types.

Confronting Vitality

As a part of this broader trend toward studying the lives of ordinary socialist collectives, empirical research on religion picked up speed from the 1950s onward, focusing initially on rural areas. Ethnographers working with peasants in Soviet collective farms came upon evidence of ongoing religious observance and of the effects of anti-religious campaigns. In addition to the general philosophical disagreements about the merits of empiricism, research on religious life in the Soviet Union faced additional obstacles. The debate about religious survivals shows that it was politically sensitive to proclaim that religion continued to develop decades after the Bolshevik revolution. At the same time, the renewed political attention given to questions of atheist propaganda after Stalin's death helped to raise the profile of village research that might otherwise be accused of dealing with trivial and marginal traditions.

Following a number of studies of collective farm villages in non-Russian regions, a seminal study of a Russian village's adaptation to changing political and economic conditions was *The Village of Viriatino in Past and Present*, published in 1958.[33] Based on repeated visits to the village in Tambov region during the years of 1952–1954 by a team of researchers from the Institute of Ethnography of the Academy of Sciences in Moscow, this study showed how central Russian peasants responded to changing times. Religion is not a central category in the book's structure, and some North American readers thought its presence was deliberately underemphasized.[34] But the chapters on family and cultural life mention religious traditions in passing, usually in association with the wishes and preferences of older villagers.

A strategy used in the book to make continued religious observance seem less explosive is to locate both firm religious commitments and passionate opposition to religion among past generations. For example, elderly residents who married in the 1920s recall the dynamics of negotiations around religious and non-religious marriage ceremonies. One woman describes her marriage to a member of the Komsomol (Communist Youth League), who was "a typical member of the progressive Komsomol youth of the 1920s, with its characteristic passionate intolerance of religion (*neprimirimost' s religiei*) as an ideology of class enemies, and with the urge to break with the routines of family life."[35] Since the bride's family refused to consent to a marriage without church blessing, the young couple circled the church three times; a compromise reported by another couple as well. While religion as the "ideology of class enemies" is treated as dead and non-existent in the ethnographic present of the book, religious practice appears quite alive in the context of family relationships and ritual. It is noted that religious holidays are marked by better food, a lull in domestic work, and family gatherings, but the "ritual specificity" of each holiday is no longer discernible.[36] As in the later study from the Mari republic, the continued presence of icons in homes is explained (by the researchers and their quoted interviewees) as deference to the expectations of neighbors and the feelings of older family members.[37]

In post-war Viriatino, religious sensibilities had a palpable but variable influence on family relationships. The authority of the head of the household remained strong, but many households were now headed by war widows. A daughter-in-law continued to enter her in-laws' household and had to respect the authority of her husband's mother in questions ranging from cooking to the treatment of sacred objects. But the researchers noted subtle ways in which the old were beginning to give precedence to the young. A mother-in-law gave the best wool for spinning to her daughter-in-law, who used the proceeds to buy factory-made dresses. The Soviet slogan of "everything to the children" (*vse detiam*) increasingly shaped how families allocated their cash budget, and villagers emphasized this change "when contrasting the new order with old family customs."[38] For reasons of affordability and propriety, elderly villagers tended to send their children and grandchildren to the village club for entertainment while staying at home themselves. The ethnographic description leaves the reader with a subtle sense of collusion and mutual accommodation between the generations as villagers navigated changing times and expectations, quite different from standard Soviet discourses that opposed seniors clinging to old ways to their younger, progressive descendants.[39]

Antagonistic Interest

The circumscribed way in which the presence of "religious survivals" is acknowledged in this early study shows the risks of raising the subject, and the investment of the researchers (and possibly their interviewees) in portraying the village as modern and Soviet. [40] The return to active atheist propaganda in the early Khrushchev years gave portrayals of religion practical relevance, as sources of information but also as models for politically safe expression. During the 1956 seminar of the Knowledge Society that signaled a new emphasis on atheist work, Section Chairman

Khudakov's address caricatured the prevailing style of lectures as far too general:

> In his lecture "Marxism-Leninism on religion," Comrade Shabinskii (Chistozernyi district, Novosibirsk region) talked about everything imaginable—about the income of a Buddhist monastery in Ulan-Bator [Mongolia], the number of churches and monasteries in Spain, the wines and delicacies that were consumed at the bishop's table in Mitrofan monastery in Voronezh in 1840, but not about the harm done by religious survivals in our time, in the life of the Chistozernyi district of Novosibirsk region, where he works.[41]

There are two sides to these calls for locally specific information. First, Knowledge Society leaders argued that familiar, local examples would make lectures about the harm of religion relevant and convincing. Second, they were uncertain about politically permissible ways of talking about religion and were looking for guidance. In January 1956, a month before the Secret Speech at the Twentieth Party Congress, where Khrushchev denounced Stalin's "cult of personality," the boundaries of what could be discussed in public were expanding, but the new norms were unclear and would remain so for years to come.[42] In such a political climate, lack of knowledge may not have been the only reason to avoid speaking about contemporary social problems in the region where one worked. In order to stop talking about monasteries in remote countries and the gluttony of pre-revolutionary clerics, atheist propagandists needed models for discussing the effects of religion on Soviet society in a way that would be interpreted as politically loyal and conducive to the building of communism.

Frequent requests at the 1956 conference for "methodological guidelines" and instructions on what is "possible to say" to various kinds of audiences reflect this atmosphere of uncertainty.[43] For lecturers and other applied intellectuals who popularized scientific knowledge that they did not themselves produce, finding reliable facts was not so much an epistemological problem but a political liability.

The emerging research on Soviet-era religious life interested atheist lecturers because it promised just such a combination of information about religious practices in the contemporary Soviet Union and models for talking about them. This is the context in which the organizers of the 1959 Knowledge Society conference on "questions of theology and Orthodox Christianity" invited the ethnographer L. A. Pushkareva, a member of the team that had conducted the study of Viriatino, to present findings from a more recent research project in a village in Kalinin (Tver') region. As preserved in the stenographic transcript of the conference from which I quote in the introduction, her presentation contained no more unexpected revelations than the published account of the research, which was in some ways more laden with clichés than the earlier book on Viriatino.[44]

Pushkareva spoke about religious persistence in the linen-producing village almost entirely in terms of conflict between generations: young people keep icons and baptize their children out of fear of "standing out" or being denied help from older relatives. Contradicting this strict generational argument somewhat, the ethnographer also notes that rates of church marriage and baptism were much higher in the village at the time of her study than they were in the 1920s.[45] She explains this not by deep religious commitments but by indifference to the meaning of rituals and the inability of peasants to understand the incompatibility of Soviet culture and religious traditions. Only a few families that participated in a voluntary commune movement in the 1920s have "no icons, none of the children goes to church, they don't hold church weddings, and all these people are bound together by deep friendship and a great sense of collectivism."[46] Again, the early years after the revolution appear as a time of genuine anti-religious passion and ideological consciousness-raising that left some traces but has not been preserved among the majority of the population.

Perhaps because she is addressing an audience of lecturers and festival planners, the only aspect of religious persistence on which Pushkareva speaks with greater frankness than is common in published work is the failure of new, secular Soviet holidays to replace and rechannel religious sentiments. When the district celebrates the Day of the Harvest, for example, "collective farm workers see this day not as a new holiday, but as a transfer of the village feast day (*prestol'nyi prazdnik*) to that date, and they assign a saint's name to it."[47] In the usual logic of Soviet reports, it was common to offer a list of new secular rituals as proof of the effectiveness of anti-religious work. Speaking to a gathering of people who were in charge of organizing such events, the ethnographer questions this logic and notes that a "new ritual" is not necessarily perceived as new by those who participate in it, but as an opportunity to follow traditional protocols with the apparent backing of state authority.

With the exception of this quite serious challenge to the Society's assumptions about effective atheist work, the talk demonstrates the possibility of acknowledging religious persistence while also making sense of it within established social frameworks. Familiar explanatory schemes of old versus young, traditional patriarchy versus socialist gender equality, public versus private help to neutralize the threat of religion. At the same time, the persistence of this threat casts Soviet values in a flattering light, making them appear empowering to those in weaker social positions. In showing the social pressures to uphold ritual traditions, Pushkareva represents those who abandon such traditions as freed from familial lines of authority rather than giving in to the authority of the state.

For an audience schooled in the "citationality" of late Soviet political discourse, where it was always safer to model one's utterances after those of authoritative sources,[48] presentations such as this one opened up ways of discussing religious persistence without making it seem as if socialism was succumbing to an alien ideology. A biologist and physical anthropologist attending the conference commended "the comrade from the Ethnographic institute" for showing the vitality of Orthodoxy in a "correctly-scientific" way: through data gathered in the field instead of an analysis of theological doctrine. Describing his own encounters with village religiosity during expeditions in Ukraine, this speaker concluded that what was needed were not studies that dug "in the history of religious beliefs" but those that "bring clarity about their social roots."[49]

Practitioners who faced evidence of religious persistence in their work were interested in sociological data because it acknowledged the everyday incongruities of Soviet life that were absent from more philosophical approaches to historical development. Seeing the names of authors of sociological publications on religion appear in the archival records of organizations dedicated to atheism, we gain a better understanding of the needs these books served in the Soviet Union. But empirical studies of belief and ritual were not only concerned with explaining religious persistence. In the spirit of prefigurative empiricism, they also looked for evidence of the emerging secular society of the future.

Positive Atheism

Population statistics are an oft-cited example of the way in which the drive to know aspects of social life and the desire to control or eliminate them come together in modern statecraft.[50] So it is perhaps no coincidence that Soviet sociology of religion evolved to increasingly emphasize statistical data as a method of creating, disseminating, and operationalizing knowledge. Compared to the relatively small scale and ad hoc approaches of Khrushchev-era inquiries into "spiritual culture," the methodological and institutional base of Soviet sociology solidified after Leonid Brezhnev took over as General Secretary of the Communist Party in 1964. This institutional base supported ever-more specialized studies of religion and atheism. Archival records from this period show the impressive amount of inter-agency coordination that went into organizing large-scale surveys, while published work testifies to the ways in which this research continued to push the boundaries of orthodox historical materialism. Parallel readings of publications, archival files, and oral reminiscences show that Soviet scholars were quite reflexive about the implications of their methodology, which presupposed encounters across ideological differences.

Khrushchev's ouster in 1964 and Brezhnev's accession to power brought many changes to Soviet governance, but a number of initiatives in the study of atheism and religion continued. Stepanian's volume on spiritual life during the transition to communism was published in 1966, and later studies of religious adherence among Soviet youth still echoed the themes of gender and generation that appeared in the village studies of the 1950s.[51] As was the case with other innovative developments of thaw-era academic and cultural life, their legacy persisted in more carefully circumscribed and monitored forms, even as the idea of an imminent transition to communism faded into the world of jokes. Brezhnev-era research on religion became more securely institutionalized and methodologically routinized, but its practitioners continued to work together with such institutions as the Knowledge Society and the Communist Party in the quest for politically useful knowledge.

One outcome of the Khrushchev-era interest in using (social) science to combat religion that survived into the Brezhnev era was the Institute of Scientific Atheism at the Moscow Academy of the Social Sciences, established in January 1964 by order of the Central Committee of the Communist Party.[52] Under the direction of the sociologist Viktor Grigor'evich Pivovarov, the institute's researchers soon began to conduct large-scale surveys based on standardized questionnaires with questions about "everyday life, culture, national traditions, and religious beliefs." The studies were conceived to allow for a comparative view of the development of atheist convictions across geographical regions and religious traditions, as shown by the locations of two pilot studies conducted by Pivovarov: the central Russian region of Penza (1968–70), where Russian Orthodox Christianity had been dominant before the revolution, and the Chechen-Ingush Autonomous Republic in the North Caucasus, a traditionally Muslim region (1970–71). Variations followed in five more regions of European Russia and western Siberia, as well as in parts of the Tadzhik, Ukrainian, and Moldovan Union Republics.[53] Additional studies were carried out by Pivovarov's students under the aegis of regional research institutes. Everywhere, emphasis was put on surveying inhabitants of rural regions, although residents of regional capitals were also interviewed. Part of the reason for this was continuing reluctance to see religiosity as a fully contemporary phenomenon. Studies that specifically investigated urban religiosity remained rare and sometimes went unpublished until the collapse of the Soviet Union.[54] Another reason is the specific interest of Brezhnev-era planners in modernizing and industrializing the countryside, often expressed under the slogan of "liquidating the difference between town and countryside."[55]

The survey research always proceeded with the assistance of the regional committee of the Communist Party, whose support was assured by the fact that the Academy of Social Sciences was a school for cadres directly subordinate to the Central Committee in Moscow. In the Mari ASSR, Pivovarov's doctoral student Viktor Stepanovich Solov'ev carried out a study in 1972–73. Born in 1934 in a Mari village in the northeast of the republic, Solov'ev was sent to Moscow for postgraduate study after several years of serving as instructor in the Communist Party office for propaganda and agitation (agitprop) and lecturer for the Knowledge Society.[56]

As the republic's first academically trained sociologist, Solov'ev relied on his links to both organizations to administer the survey. The Mari regional party committee passed a resolution in April 1972 calling for city and district committees to "choose from the ranks of party and council activists and representatives of the intelligentsia the necessary number of interviewers-instructors, take charge of their training and create the necessary conditions for their work."[57] Organizational and in-kind support for the project from the regional committee included the paper required to print over 10,000 questionnaires and the labor of more than 600 rural party members, teachers, and cultural workers who went door-to-door with the survey and interviewed respondents.[58] Newspaper articles and radio coverage announced the project to the population and asked for input from members of the local intelligentsia. Several hundred local "experts" were asked about their understanding of key terms during the design stage of the questionnaire, preserving some of the participatory forms of earlier sociological projects.[59] Solov'ev went on to become the second ethnic Mari to be elected to the Soviet Academy of Sciences, and follow-up surveys with slightly modified questionnaires were carried out in the Mari republic in 1985, 1994, and 2004, thus shaping the understanding of religious dynamics of post-Soviet governments as well.[60]

The questionnaires designed by Pivovarov and his students were lengthy—the one used in the Chechen-Ingush ASSR in 1970 contained more than 200 questions; the one used in the Mari ASSR in 1972 had 366. A conversation between the interviewer and an interviewee could last forty minutes to two hours.[61] Questions covered a wide range of topics from basic demographic information about gender, date and place of birth, and marital status, to educational level, occupation, housing conditions, layout and interior furnishings of the home, participation in social and volunteer activities, access to cultural services, and knowledge about and evaluation of ethnic traditions. Questions about religious convictions and observances and knowledge of atheist literature came at the very end.

Together with the questions about the ethnic traditions, the sections dealing with religion were the most variable across different surveys but always reflected the general Soviet understanding of ethnic and religious identities as catalogues of interchangeable traits. The questionnaire for the Chechen-Ingush republic asks about practices of bride price (*kalym*), hospitality, service for elders, familiarity with the Qur'an, and participation in Islamic rituals such as fasting during Ramadan, home gatherings with scripture recitation to mark family rites of passage (*mavlud*), and male circumcision. The survey for the Mari republic inquires after visits to Mari sacred groves and observance of Orthodox Christian and Islamic festivals.[62] All surveys devote several questions to attitudes toward friendship and marriage with members of other nationalities. This was a common late Soviet yardstick of the growth of the new Soviet super-ethnos that is still used in post-Soviet studies designed to monitor inter-ethnic coexistence.[63]

Rapport and Reliability

Combining the study of religion with that of other social characteristics reflected the broad political aim of "illuminating . . . the levels of influence of social and cultural changes on overcoming survivals of the past and forming an all-round developed personality," as the Mari regional committee resolution authorizing the survey puts it.[64] But there were also practical reasons for broaching the topic of religion within a more wide-ranging conversation. Pivovarov and his students were well aware that people might try to please the interviewers and present themselves as more atheist than they really were. Placing questions about religion at the end of a lengthy survey was meant to give the interviewer time to gain the respondent's trust and receive more candid answers.[65]

The sociologists thus shared some of the concerns of post-Soviet readers about the reliability of the published data. For Pivovarov and Solov'ev, ensuring reliability was a matter of establishing rapport between interviewer and respondent. When I interviewed him in 2005, Viktor Solov'ev claimed that employing locally known interviewers and introducing the survey through radio and print media helped to build trust and encouraged respondents to speak frankly. Commenting on the dramatic drop in the number of declared atheists between the last Soviet-era survey and the first post-Soviet study, he acknowledged that survey responses reflected the changing social and political prestige associated with atheism and religiosity. In 1985, 32.2 percent of respondents had declared themselves to be nonbelievers, and 37.8 percent said they were indifferent to matters of religion. In 1994, only 18.4 claimed unbelief, and indifference was no longer listed among the possible responses.[66]

As Solov'ev was quick to point out, it is impossible to say which pressure was greater—the one to declare oneself an atheist during the Soviet period or the one to remake oneself as a religious believer after the collapse of the Soviet system. In the case of these large-scale surveys, archival access to the raw data does little to address concerns about their reliability. The problem lay in the interview situation and its dynamics of interaction. By taking steps to avoid possible intimidation, the researchers indirectly acknowledged that religious believers may have had concerns about speaking their minds freely. Using local interviewers who knew respondents personally may have helped keep the conversations more realistic but also may have increased people's apprehensions about possible consequences of their answers. At the same time, by asking about a range of other issues besides religious practices and beliefs, the surveys document the wider changes occurring in rural life.

Other researchers working with more small-scale, qualitative methods agreed that trust could be difficult to achieve and a shared base of local knowledge was important, but they insisted that the scholar herself had to build this trust through long-term contact. Tamara Dragadze, a British anthropologist of Georgian origin who conducted research in the Soviet Union in the 1970s, recounts an anecdote from Georgia where villagers told her about a recent visit by Moscow academician Iurii Vartanovich

Arutiunian, whose family name betrayed his Armenian roots. In accordance with the ethnos theory that gained ground at the time, Arutiunian asked questions about attitudes toward inter-ethnic marriage, and the respondents understood only too well what answers were expected of them. A farmer told Dragadze how he had answered: "What? Would I mind if my daughter married a Russian, he asks? Tell the son of a bitch . . . whatever he wants to hear: say I'd love it!"[67]

The idea that a shared ethnic background and personal presence in the field mattered for establishing honest rapport was echoed by the Tatar ethnographer Raufa Karimovna Urazmanova, whom I visited in her office in the Institute of History of the Academy of Sciences of the Republic of Tatarstan in 2012. Urazmanova had conducted ethnographic research on recent Tatar migrants to the new oil-producing cities of Al'metevsk and Leninogorsk between 1962 and 1965. As a doctoral student at the Kazan branch of the Academy of Sciences of the USSR, she lived in each city for several months, staying with local families and conducting household surveys and interviews. The emergence of new industrial working classes was a topic of political importance at the time, so she shifted away from her original research interest in the field of traditional Tatar folklore. Successfully defended in 1968, Urazmanova's dissertation was only published in 2000, as part of a series on the history of the Tatar oil industry sponsored by the regional oil companies.[68]

Originally trained as a geographer, Urazmanova had been inspired by the work on Viriatino and other ethnographies of modern villages, and by university instructors in Kazan who enlisted their students as research assistants for village surveys. But when she began postgraduate research, "suddenly workers were important." Her work on rural migrants in new industrial cities underscores changes in family structure and gendered lines of authority, but also points out continuity when it came to life cycle rituals and maintaining connections to relatives who remained in the villages. When I asked her if she felt she received accurate information about religious observances, the ethnographer immediately drew a contrast between her work and the large-scale surveys that were conducted with the help of the district party committees in the Tatar ASSR, following Pivovarov's approach.[69] "Of course everyone answered those as required (*kak nado*)." In her own work she let herself be guided by field observations and did not even ask *if* people conducted religious life cycle rituals. Rather she asked "where did you do *nikah*, at home or in the mosque?" Being spared the decision of whether to reveal that their family solemnized marriages through the traditional contract mandated by sharia law, people discussed the details on how they organized these rituals. The young ethnographer met interviewees through introductions from her hosts and other existing contacts, different from the randomized sampling approach based on residential registers used by Pivovarov and his students. "I know that the data is correct within the sample population; how exact the sample selection was is hard to say."

The large-scale surveys thus represent only a part of Soviet research on changing religious life, but it is a part that received a great deal of state support. The enduring interest of the surveys lies not so much in their statistical breakdowns between believers and unbelievers but in the insights they provide into late Soviet efforts to conceptualize the shifting relationships of religion and secularity. In a country committed to bringing the achievements of modernity to the countryside, current and former religious believers presented a significant test case, whose grateful or admonishing voices contributed to socialism's internal "processes of validation."[70] The archival context of the Mari studies shows that interpreting the data as demonstrating the progress of atheism required advanced mathematics, while the less sophisticated readings of bureaucrats tended to treat them as evidence of failure and tools of self-critique.

Statistical Documentation and Its Uses

The wide thematic range of survey questions allowed sociologists to establish statistical correlations between expressions of atheist or religious convictions and other social characteristics. Through a form of regression analysis that was new in the Soviet Union at the time, calculated with the help of early forms of computer technology, atheists were shown to be more likely to participate in voluntary social service or trade union activities, and to put the interests of society before their own more often than believers. Even when analysis of the 1985 survey controlled for age and place of residence, atheists were still found to read more books, attend the cinema more often, and have a higher rate of approval of inter-ethnic marriages. These seemingly random correlations all showed a connection between the denial of religion and the embrace of various signs of Soviet cultural modernity, whether education, "cultured" forms of entertainment, or the fading away of differences between ethnic groups.[71] They were hopeful signs that decades of atheist work had indeed begun to produce a new type of citizen who was not only non-religious but also community-minded, diligent, and interested in film and literature.

In their quest to demonstrate this constructive side of atheism, sociologists and lecturers who analyzed the results of this and other surveys deliberately steered away from the claim that only ignorant or disloyal people would hold on to religious convictions. Instead, they identified such reasons as lack of cultural services for rural residents, dearth of child care options for young parents, and not offering ethnic minorities enough outlets for maintaining their own traditions within the framework of Soviet secular culture.[72] If religious believers were not backward, hostile, or deluded, the responsibility for convincing them of the value of atheism lay with the Soviet state as the sole authorized provider of social services. Archival files that refer to the large-scale surveys suggest that state and party officials took

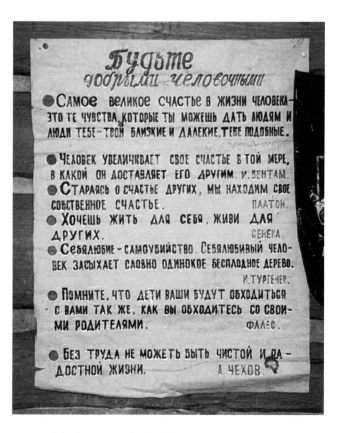

"Be good, be humane." This hand-written poster from the home of a rural school principal and long-time lecturer for the Knowledge Society probably dates from the 1980s but expresses some of the principles of secular morality that sociologists sought to elicit in the 1970s. Red bullets mark a series of quotes from Jeremy Bentham, Plato, Seneca, Aleksandr Turgenev, and Anton Chekhov, all talking about the positive effects of working for the good of others. The source of the uppermost quote is partly painted over, but it is from Feliks Dzerzhinskii (first head of the Soviet secret police), who said, "The greatest happiness in life are the feelings you can give people and that they give you." *Sovetskii district, Republic of Marii El, 2005. Photograph by Sonja Luehrmann.*

note of the findings but used them as familiar tools of internal critique rather than to initiate the complex social reforms suggested by the researchers.

The 1972–73 survey of the Mari ASSR was a central subject of discussion at the 1975 regional party plenum, at which the Moscow sociologist Pivovarov was a special guest. Viktor Solov'ev remembered this event as a great honor and sign of how seriously the party took his research. But comparing Pivovarov's statement to those of second regional party secretary I. S. Gusev and representatives of district and city committees, one gets the impression of a disconnect between scholars and officials in terms of their understanding of the purposes of sociological research. The officials read the surveys to document little-known practices that were slated for disappearance, serving as a reminder of "questions that used to fall by the wayside in ideological intervention."[73] The sociologist, by contrast, presented his work as an innovative way to measure the positive forces at work in Soviet society.

The stimulus prompting the regional party organization to take an interest in the results of the survey came from outside the republic. In his opening statement, Gusev uses the research project, carried out in 1972–73, as his prime example of how the republic had responded to the Central Committee's fall 1974 resolution "On the work of selection and formation of ideological cadres in the Belorussian party organization." This resolution called for the training of party cadres who were well versed in ideology and knew how to put their theoretical knowledge to practical use. In a temporal reversal characteristic of bureaucratic modes of action, the Mari party organization showcased the data gathered by the sociologists two years earlier as proof of their advance fulfillment of this order.[74] At a time when political elites became ever more enamored with the idea of rational planning and quantifiable results, speakers with varying levels of mathematical sophistication were happy to use statistics to bolster their authority.[75]

The officials speaking at the plenum mainly used survey data as didactic illustrations. Where the sociologists fully recognized the challenges of representing dynamic tendencies and causal connections in the language of mathematical correlations, the party officials contented themselves with citing figures for one year and claiming that they either represented a tendency for the better, or anachronisms in need of pedagogical intervention. If 4.7 percent of teachers and 15.6 percent of medical professionals called themselves religious believers or undecided "waverers," 15 percent of white-collar employees did not read a single book during the month when they were interviewed, and 26 percent of party members had icons in their home, these numbers illustrated the work that lay ahead on the way to a society free of outdated prejudice:

> A person who has linked his life to the party of Lenin, to please his mother-in-law or whomever else, lives year-in, year-out under the god-corner with the image of the mother of god or Nicholas the miracleworker, and we consider him an ideological fighter for the political aims of the party. . . . We need a serious reorganization of the work of forming a scientific world view, of atheist education, of the study of problems of atheism and religion by Komsomol members and communists, members of the intelligentsia, and all categories of workers.[76]

Against such illustrative use of isolated percentages that marginalized and exoticized religious practice, the sociologist Pivovarov warned that all survey findings "need a profound analysis":

> And if this analysis is carried out incorrectly, that is if the analysis focuses only on particular aspects, for example, on the negative aspects of particular phenomena as the outcome of the study, then the task of our work was first and foremost to illuminate the positive experiences, illuminate the good things that have been done by party committees in the field of education and formation of the person [*vospitaniia cheloveka*], and at the same time create or reconstruct an image of, for example, religion, or of the use of the mass media and propaganda.[77]

Pivovarov wanted his audience to see the results of the study as a complicated field of evidence in which media use, remaining religious practice, and aspirations for education and employment all came together to shape contemporary Soviet citizens. Pivovarov praised the involvement of volunteer data collectors in the Mari study and pointed out that the locally formed institute was unusual in its use of emergent forms of computer technology to analyze the data. The message he sought to convey was that sociological data could be used to understand the legacies of past social orders (religion) as well as the anticipated fruits of socialist modernization (mass media and education). Understanding complex interrelationships through statistics required the help of salaried experts as well as the enthusiastic support of volunteers. Taking the wider Soviet context into account, the results of the survey in the Mari republic were not as threatening as they seemed in isolation: the percentage of religious believers in the Mari republic was similar to "the level of religiosity in Voronezh and even in the Moscow region."[78]

Although the survey deliberately brought together spheres of labor, free time, and religious and cultural practice for what today might be called intersectional analysis, the party officials who discussed its results rarely made connections between different sets of numbers. Instead, they singled out particular percentages in order to call for isolated measures of correction: higher levels of religiosity among women demanded atheist lectures targeted to a female audience, whereas the reluctance of rural youth to seek higher work qualifications required more training courses in popular specialties. In bureaucratic readings of the surveys that focused on acknowledging problems and finding solutions, religion again appeared as an isolated survival in marginal communities rather than a dynamic factor in Soviet life.

In the end, the sociologists' hope to provide a numerical language for understanding social change did not reach far beyond their own group. But by providing numbers and the promise of scientifically founded "concrete recommendations for working with different demographic categories,"[79] empirical research on religion and atheism was able to normalize itself and gain acceptance. Once they were no longer expressed as quotes but in the relatively safe language of numbers, the views and opinions of simple Soviet citizens (including religious believers) became so valuable that considerable public resources were devoted to soliciting them.

Surrounding Books with Documents

Studies of secret police documents in various socialist states have shown the intimate imaginative entanglements that could develop between the agents and objects of surveillance.[80] The story of Soviet research on religion is part of these larger dynamics in which the drive to create and store knowledge about ideological deviance could come into conflict with fear of its destabilizing potential. But a joint reading of archival and published sources shows that Soviet empirical social science did not develop by political mandate alone. Like their counterparts in the natural sciences and mathematics, empirical social scientists were both constrained by the political demand to produce evidence of the laws of historical materialism and productively engaged with some of its concepts. Debates about positive and harmful traditions, intergenerational authority, and survivals showed that applying historical-materialist categories to Soviet society yielded fresh and controversial results.[81] Soviet sociologists never entirely abandoned the assumption that religion was a unified phenomenon whose manifestations in different denominational forms and personal practices all functioned to isolate believers from the modern world. At the same time, the doctrine of incompatibility between socialist modernity and religion, while shutting down inquiry in some areas such as religiosity among educated urban youth, also provided a powerful impetus to seek out believers and find out how their lives differed from those of an average Soviet citizen. Just as the shape of area studies in the North Atlantic world would not look the same without the Cold War drive to "know your enemy,"[82] the Soviet social science literature that so fascinated Western contemporaries would be less extensive without this sense of internal ideological competition.

If the Western readers who eagerly consumed the offerings of the bookstore of the Soviet Academy of Sciences in the 1960s and '70s had to wonder about the methods and assumptions behind Soviet statistics, archival access can help answer some of these questions. For anyone who is suspicious of the accuracy of Soviet statistics on religious observance, the archival records that show the politicized context of their production confirm that they need to be taken with a grain of salt. But the same records also show that those who carried out these studies approached them with seriousness and methodological reflexivity, and fought hard to defend the necessity of accurate and up-to-date information about the forms and motivations of religious belief.

In hindsight, perhaps the most interesting findings of the empirical research projects lie in the description of a Soviet countryside in flux, where cinema, television, and libraries were changing the way people demarcated their time, and factory-made clothing and furniture were assigning new meanings to traditional handicrafts. Not unlike their twenty-first century successors in the study of secularism, Soviet sociologists who sought to identify substantive characteristics of a society without gods looked to changing ideas about kinship, gender, and inherited identities. They also probed the ethical implications of the commitment to finite biological life as the only possible framework of existence. When it comes to analyzing the social forces that drove secularization, the relative weight of outright anti-religious measures compared to general processes of modernization and Sovietization remains an open question.[83]As international debates turn away from measuring secularization to describing how secularity is lived and experienced, there might still be something to learn from the breadth of topics covered by the Soviet surveys.

CHAPTER 4

Counter-Archives

Sympathy on Record

At first glance, Waco, Texas, is an unlikely destination for archival research on Soviet religious history. The city of roughly 120,000 people is most readily associated with the schismogenic and violent tendencies of U.S. religious culture: when I mentioned to colleagues that I was traveling to Waco for research, most assumed I was interested in the 1993 standoff between FBI agents and the Branch Davidians led by David Koresh.[1] A less spectacular feature of Waco's religious landscape is Baylor University, a Baptist institution founded in 1845. In 2007, Baylor entered the world of Soviet records by acquiring the Keston archive and library, a collection of documents and books relating to religious life in the USSR and other socialist countries, compiled in Great Britain by a group led by an Anglican priest, Canon Michael Bourdeaux. Originally founded in 1969, the Keston Institute acted as an important switchboard through which knowledge about Soviet religion traveled westward during the Cold War. Through a targeted distribution system and open press releases, information gathered by Keston staff fueled an emerging field of activism whose proponents framed religious freedom as a core indicator of human rights. Reflecting the internal operating categories of this advocacy group, the institute's collection of records is an example of a counter-archive that tries to correct the blind spots left by state logics of documentation. The Keston archive uses its own unique filing system and presents an intriguing example of the degree to which the perspectives of the creators of archival depositories can shape our readings of the documents they collect.

Arriving at the Waco airport on a Sunday afternoon in February 2014, I learned about some parallels between this area of Texas and parts of the Soviet Union from a cab driver with a penchant for local history. The town had grown up in the late nineteenth century around the cultivation of cotton—"cotton is good to sell, but bad for the soil"; a statement that residents of the cotton-growing regions of Central Asia would confirm.[2] Long before the Branch Davidian standoff, the town had its own episode of struggle between proponents and critics of organized religion. Pointing out the old cemetery next to the freeway that separates the Baylor campus from the town of Waco, the cab driver explained that this was where William Cowper Brann was buried. Brann was the owner of a newspaper tellingly named *Iconoclast*, which published critical stories about Baylor administrators and local religious elites. He died in 1898, following a shootout in which he also killed his opponent, the father of a female Baylor student offended by the *Iconoclast*'s allegations of widespread sexual misconduct at the university.[3]

This incident can serve as a reminder that violent controversy about the place of religion in society is not limited to state socialism. Historical parallels notwithstanding, the experience of doing research in the Keston archive was very different from archives in Russia. From the time I entered the arched front door of the neoclassical building of Carroll Library and settled in a reading room where part of the collection was directly accessible in drawers (other parts were still stored in boxes waiting to be unpacked), the familiar archival world of order forms and restrictions on numbers of files to be checked out seemed far away. Finding records in this depository is also a different process from that in most state archives, because institutional provenance is not the organizing principle. If the term counter-archive implies that a depository not only represents a different perspective from that of state archives but is organized according to a different logic, Keston is a good case in point. But there are also moments when its perspective quotes and mirrors a state archive in interesting ways, and others when its primary angle of critique does not seem to be aimed at the state at all but at the church hierarchy. Although the Keston archive's logic of classification assumes the same binary opposition between religion and non-religion as Soviet state archives, the narratives constructed by its files sometimes point to more complicated lines of division.

Documenting Dissent

A brochure produced for the twentieth anniversary of the Keston Institute tells the origin story of that institution. Participating in an exchange program, British student of theology and Russian language and literature Michael Bourdeaux spent a year in Moscow in 1959–60. During a return visit in 1964, now an ordained Anglican priest, he found that many churches that had been open for worship four years earlier were reduced to rubble or had been expropriated for other purposes. Near one of these destroyed churches, he met two women who gave him "a written appeal recounting the persecution of Christians in the Soviet Union and begging people to intervene with the Soviet government on their behalf."[4] The women, who had traveled all the way from Ukraine to find a foreigner who might transmit their letter, made a request that provided the motto for the new organization: "Be our voice where we cannot be heard."[5]

Bourdeaux responded to this call by founding an organization devoted to collecting and disseminating information on the situation of religious believers in the Soviet Union and other socialist countries. As he and his colleagues set up office first in the village of Keston in South London and then in Oxford, the archive grew from accumulated letters, originals and copies of samizdat (literally "self-publish") publications, and newspaper clippings. It also preserved evidence of how those documents were processed into newsletters and press releases. The point of all this collecting, translating, and excerpting was to prompt Western governments and international bodies such as the World Council of Churches to attend to the problems faced by religious believers in socialist states and advocate for them during encounters with Soviet politicians. As late as 1988, the aim remained to "speak for those who cannot be heard and help those who demand their 'right to believe.' "[6] Compiled to support this task of Cold War advocacy, the Keston archive is a counter-archive in relation to Soviet depositories, engaged in a kind of documentary arms race. While Soviet recordkeeping was designed to demonstrate procedural correctness in dealing with believers, the Keston archive is organized around a notion of inherent rights of religious communities, whose violation by the Soviet state it documents meticulously.

Similar to "identity archives" that collect historical evidence from the point of view of a group that is marginalized in official historical records, counter-archives challenge the state-centered perspective that pervades archival collections.[7] Since the nineteenth century, most public archives adhere to the organizing principle of provenance, meaning that records are grouped together according to the agency or individual who created or accumulated them.[8] This means that researchers can look beyond the contents of an individual file and find information about the context in which it was created and circulated. But it also means that accessing information in a modern archive often requires "thinking like a state," and conceptualizing one's topic in terms of the bureaucratic division of labor.

In Soviet archives, topics relating to religion will most obviously be covered in the documents of the Council for Religious Affairs. If translated into "ideology," religion might also be dealt with by the ideological wing of the Communist Party (agit-prop); if translated into "deviance" it can find its way into court or police records. If religion is framed as the opposite of science, questions of how to understand and deal with it will be covered in the records of organizations devoted to promoting scientific knowledge, such as educational institutions, libraries, and the Knowledge Society. In a dynamic that is familiar to scholars working on women's or indigenous histories, such efforts to think like the archive almost force the researcher to decenter the primary subject of inquiry and adopt the perspective of record-producing bureaucracies. This can shape the questions that historical studies pursue, favoring work that focuses on women as objects of protection rather than figures of authority in their communities, or on native-newcomer interactions rather than relations among indigenous groups. Since most bureaucratic agencies operate within the boundaries of nation-states and their subdivisions, provenance as an organizing principle also makes it difficult to study groups whose activities extend across several jurisdictions.[9]

To avoid these problems, a counter-archive would need to not only collect information that state archives neglect or overlook but also organize it in different ways.[10] Indeed, the Keston archive eschews the principle of provenance and instead organizes its information thematically. In any given folder, letters, newspaper clippings, and photocopies from Soviet and Western publications on a particular topic are put together. Rather than privileging the offices that created and assembled documents, this system of classification adopts the perspective of users who look for information by subject, as they would in a library catalogue.

Such a user-centered perspective makes it hard to trace where a document originated and how it made it to the West. At the same time, it creates new contexts within which the document will be read. When archives digitize their materials, some offer options for users to compile and annotate their own digital collections, creating "'parallel but linked' access systems" that allow users to record their own interests and priorities.[11] Some depositories use this approach as a deliberate counterpoint to the state's prerogative to sort, collect, and preserve historical evidence. For example, the Open Society Archives in Budapest digitized parts of their collection of Eastern European samizdat and other documents of human rights cases around the world, and also offer a platform called "Parallel Archive," created in 2008. Here, users can upload, store, and annotate their own documents and make them accessible to others, within the limits of restrictions imposed by the original depository. At the University of Toronto, historian Ann Komaromi maintains an online database of samizdat periodicals stored in thirty-one archives and libraries around the world, which offers more limited possibilities to annotate and ask questions via a discussion forum.[12]

These are post–Cold War attempts to deal with the lack of a central archive documenting dissent in socialist states and help users make connections between dispersed materials. They explore user-centered ways to categorize and annotate materials as part of a general ethos of making the past accessible for varied and flexible use.[13] When browsing the Keston archive's older and more low-tech version of a user-centered system of classification, we are reminded that archival users themselves have history. The imagined user for whom Keston's cataloging and storage system was designed had a set of questions and priorities different from those of users today. For the institute staff of the 1970s and '80s, socialist states loomed large as powerful adversaries, but so did concern over the future of Christianity at home. The experiences of believers under socialism served as testimony to the universality of religious commitment and its resilience under social and political pressure. Comparable to the comments and tags made by users of the digital age, the users and compilers of the Keston archive have left traces of their readings and interpretations in the form of notes and cross-references.

Ironically, the eventual success of Keston's opposition to socialist atheism turned the archive itself into an endangered historical artifact. In the 1990s, the Keston Institute began to look for a permanent home for its archive because of problems with space and funding after the end of the Cold War. One of the conditions was that the new host should be willing to take the collection in its entirety, implicitly turning the institute into the new provenance of the documents.[14] The new center at Baylor University does indeed preserve the original cataloging and filing system and treats the notes and cross-references of the original users as part of the archival record. This allows for greater visibility of the cumulative work of using, classifying,

The reading room, Keston College, Kent, England. This photo from the 1980s shows the Keston archive and library in its original location, before it was moved to Baylor University in the United States in 2007. *Courtesy of the Keston Center for Religion, Politics, and Society, Baylor University, Waco, Texas, kc-misc-pho-93-06-01.*

and circulating documents than is often the case in public archives. Assembled to suit the needs of users outside the Soviet Union with a particular political interest in Soviet affairs, this counter-archive of Soviet life preserves the history of such use, although the most immediate purpose of the cataloging system is to provide access to information on religious communities.

The Catalogue: Heroic Religion

The classification system used in the Keston archive catalogue was devised by Alexandra Kolarz, wife of the Sovietologist Walter Kolarz.[15] Documents are organized by countries, and then by topics for each country. Instead of taking its structure from state organizations, the catalogue reads like a list of grievances against the state. Under SU 12 (Soviet Union—religion), for example, the subcategory "oppressive practices" (SU 12/6) includes folders on the following topics: harassment, physical assault, fines, inter-rogations, trials, state interference in church affairs, interference in parish life, discrimination in employment, discrimination in education, misuse of psychiatry, and loss of parental rights. Another subcategory, "activities disapproved by state" (SU 12/11) lists many activities that would be considered quite legitimate for religious congregations in Western parliamentary democracies, thereby casting the Soviet state itself as abnormal: demonstra-tions/protests, refusal to do military service, charitable activity, and underground religious education. In a reversal of the sub-ject catalogues of Soviet libraries, where books about religious history and particular religious traditions fell under the general heading of "scientific atheism," in this catalogue the section on atheism (SU 13) comes after religion. It consists mainly of news-paper clippings and journal articles, with much less unpublished content than the richer files on religious life.

This classification scheme still places the relationship between believers and the state at center stage, even though it denormalizes the state by refusing to take its bureaucracy as the guiding structure. As Adalaine Holton notes, a counter-archive necessarily stands in a "supplementary relationship to dominant historiographic knowledge," as if asking follow-up questions to those that are asked in standard historiography.[16] This gives it the advantage of the reacting critic, but it also means that state-centered narratives continue to set the agenda to some extent. For an archive built on the premise that religious believers could not be heard inside or outside the Soviet bloc, it is striking how many copies of Soviet publications are in the files. Newspaper reports on atheist work and journal articles that denounced abusive conditions in religious families constituted precious sources for Keston researchers. In most instances, it was up to the staff to read between the lines and interpret what such reports meant for religious believers. For subsequent users, the filing system solidifies and reinforces their interpretations.

For example, an article from the daily newspaper *Izvestiia* about a group of six Leningrad children who moved out of their religious parents' home and were cared for by their oldest brother is filed under "oppressive practices—loss of parental rights." The article itself does not mention whether the parents were formally deprived of their parental rights, but instead celebrates the brother, Robert, who takes on responsibility for caring for his siblings "family-style" (*po semeinomu*) in addition to putting in long work hours at a factory.[17] It could be read as a story of how atheism strengthens wholesome kinship bonds while empowering young people to sever relationships that have become abusive or oppressive. The English summary attached to the article by a Keston staff member, however, preempts this reading by referring to "Robert and his 'family'" in ironic quotation marks. Functioning as a framing device that imposes its own tone on quotations from the article, the summary suggests injustice by noting that the parents are "depicted as self-willed, social outcasts" simply because they are Christians.[18] Different from Council of Religious

Affairs documents in Soviet archives, where the commissioner's authorial voice organizes quotations of religious believers and imprints its own evaluative framework on them, here atheist discourse turns into "foreign speech" that is managed through external notes and commentaries.[19] In contrast to public archives in Russia, where the classification system and the documents collude to maintain an overall appearance of even-handed legality, in the Keston archive frequent clashes in tone and content between catalogue, commentary, and individual documents encourage users to adopt ironic, skeptical attitudes toward the official Soviet accounts.

Some of these clashes come from the fact that files contain documents of different origins that present conflicting information and represent contradictory stances toward a set of events. In these cases, custodial practices such as assigning categories, adding notes and cross-references, and determining the physical order of items in a file take on a crucial role in guiding the user's interpretation. For researchers most comfortable with reading English, Western newspaper clippings, press releases, and summary notes will likely be consulted first and color the reading of Russian-language items. This unequal dialogue is at work in the file on Boris Vladimirovich Talantov (1903–1971), an Orthodox layman and grandson of a priest from Kirov, a regional center northeast of Moscow. It starts with clippings from Western newspapers that document the interest Talantov aroused after sending an open letter to Patriarch Aleksii I in 1966, together with eleven other named believers from his city. The letter expressed support of an earlier letter written by the Moscow priests Nikolai Eshliman and Gleb Iakunin.[20] Talantov concurred with the Moscow priests' criticism of the compliant church hierarchy and added his own examples to their description of the devastating effects of recent Soviet policies on church life. Following additional critical writings, he was arrested in 1969 and sentenced to two years in prison, where he died of heart failure shortly before the end of his term.[21]

Western interest in Talantov's activities seems to have peaked around the time of the fourth assembly of the World Council of Churches in Sweden in July 1968, where the Russian Orthodox Church was represented by hierarchs who affirmed the fair treatment of Christians in the Soviet Union.[22] Clippings from the *New York Times*, the *Los Angeles Times*, and the *Washington Post* speculate about the emergence of a new protest movement among Russian Orthodox laypeople. An earlier press release from the BBC argued that the Orthodox Church might be facing a similar split as the Soviet Baptists, who had divided over the issue of whether to follow state restrictions preventing the baptism and instruction of young people.[23] A particular Cold War "prose of pro-insurgency" is obvious from the coverage, which infers the existence of a protest movement from the writings of a very small number of people.

Because documents in the file quote and comment on one another, they enter into a conversation in which critical readings of official Soviet sources in Western and émigré media set the tone. A report on Talantov's arrest by the Possev News Service in West Germany, founded and operated by first-wave émigrés from the Soviet Union, notes that a woman who had been entrusted with mailing materials to the West was found dead on the way to a remote village. While no direct allegation of murder is made, the account strongly suggests foul play while also condemning the practices of mail censorship that made it necessary for critics to mail packages from remote locations in order to escape official attention. Later in the file, the typescript copy of an article from a regional Soviet newspaper corroborates the same incident but offers a different interpretation. The article reports that the elderly woman died in the cold due to "acute cardio-vascular failure," carrying with her audited financial statements from the cathedral in Vladimir, a city much closer to Moscow than to Kirov. The elderly woman, the article hints, was being exploited as a courier by the "slanderer and mudslinger" Talantov, and died as a result of transporting illic-itly obtained documents.[24]

In this technique of collating divergent accounts from differ-ent sources, the files in the Keston archive resemble police files assembled on a single suspect, only with the evaluation reversed. Whereas the ultimate sense of the Soviet police file is deter-mined by the sentence (or record of a decision to close the file),[25] in Keston's files the interpretive framing is provided by the com-mentary on Soviet accounts offered by Western press releases and summary translations of documents by institute staff. Not every researcher who peruses Talantov's file will read the seventeen-page letter by Talantov and his co-signatories, which is preserved in Russian and French versions. In an archive in Kirov it would be included in a file of believers' complaints and petitions, surrounded by scores of other complaint letters that were routinely sent back from Moscow to be dealt with locally.[26] Its inclusion with other unsuccessful complaints would diminish its importance and credibility. By contrast, the media reports filed together with this Western copy underline its significance as an intervention that provoked violent responses at home and was carefully read and taken seriously as evidence abroad. As late as 1984, a research brief by Radio Free Europe speculates that a recent article in the newspaper *Sovetskaia Rossiia* that singles out Kirov as a city with "shortcomings" in atheist propaganda may be a reaction to the "traditionally strong" religious belief of the residents as expressed in Talantov's letters.[27]

Alongside these media speculations about an ongoing resis-tance movement in the Russian Orthodox Church, the let-ter itself comes across as a relatively standard example of the Soviet genre of complaint to higher-standing authorities against the lower ones. In this case, the patriarch is being petitioned to intervene against abuses committed by the local bishop. In addition to figures about church closures that would have been precious evidence for Western readers at the time (forty out of seventy-five churches in Kirov diocese were closed between 1960 and 1964), the text provides vivid descriptions of parish life under great pressure. "Pastors have been turned into hired soothsayers (*naemnykh zhretsov*)" while lay Christians "are parishless visitors of divine services" as a result of stricter applications of the law on religious organizations.[28] Blaming the current bishop who strictly follows the orders of the commissioner of religious affairs, Talantov recounts that children have been barred from receiving communion even when brought by their parents, and beggars are chased from church grounds. The story he tells paints a picture of collusion between the commissioner of religious affairs, the bishop, and local police, undermining the attempts at resistance by lay members of the church. It makes it clear why Talantov, though canonized by the émigré Russian Orthodox Church Abroad, remains an ambivalent figure for the Orthodox Church in post-Soviet Russia.

For example, the letter recounts how police and voluntary militia (*druzhinniki*) surrounded St. Seraphim's Church in Kirov in August 1963 to prevent women and children from attending mass and communion there. "But this act of violence brought about the opposite result. The women bravely entered into hand-to-hand combat with the militiamen and easily broke the chain. The police and militia understood that it's shameful to openly fight women and children!"[29] The bishop then forbade his priests from admitting children under eighteen to confession and communion, under penalty of being barred from office. "At first the reigning atheists tried to banish children from the churches by means of violence. They did not succeed. Then they easily and peacefully achieved the same immoral goal with the help of the clergy."[30]

A common thread between Soviet police files and files on individual dissidents at Keston is that seemingly innocuous and inconsequential details, by association and framing, are magnified into evidence of activity that threatens the Soviet state. The custodial history of both types of files begins with initial collectors who, for their own interested uses, brought together writings of individuals and things written about them. The resulting composite portrait served the purposes of the original collectors or users but may not reflect the value that the documents have for later readers. For a twenty-first-century historian interested in the conditions of religious life in the Soviet Union, the question of whether Talantov's letter indicated the existence of an Orthodox Christian protest movement has lost its immediate political import. But the letter is still interesting for what it suggests about the stress of parish life under tightening controls. It hints at changes in the relationship between clergy and laypeople because of the priest's triple dependency on the parish council who employed him and the bishop and commissioner who had to affirm his appointment. The reader is made to wonder about new social dynamics in congregations increasingly bereft of young people. Finally, Talantov's account suggests complicated formal and informal relationships between the commissioner of religious affairs and the local bishop, who allegedly told his priests: "I will bar [from the priesthood] anyone who dares not to listen to the commissioner!"[31]

In public archives, whose documents show the commissioner's own struggle for recognition in the administrative hierarchy, such collusion would look more like a tactical alliance in which each side tried to survive while keeping sight of their divergent purposes. But since the authorial voice of the Keston files adopts the perspective of laypeople and practitioners at some remove from positions of power in religious institutions, the relationship between religious dignitaries and state agents appears as a complete fusion, to the detriment of ordinary committed believers. The fullest sympathy of the archive is not with "Soviet believers" in general but with the figure of the ordinary lay believer thought to face pressure and betrayal from clerical hierarchies as well as from state organs. The genre of samizdat, with its aura of independent and unassisted authorship, is perhaps the clearest embodiment of this individualistic conception of religiosity.

Samizdat: Amplifying Readings

One of the points of pride of the Keston archive is its collection of more than four thousand samizdat publications from the Soviet Union and other socialist countries.[32] Samizdat is the Russian term for uncensored typescripts that circulated through unofficial channels throughout the post-war decades—some of a political nature, others works of literature or scientific treatises.[33] Organized by country and religious denomination or political cause and marked by an (S) at the end of the call number, Keston's samizdat documents are accessible to users in labeled drawers in the reading room, with little need to consult a catalogue or finding aid. Some are original typescripts that reached the Keston staff directly from the countries of authorship. Others are preserved as photocopies from the Samizdat Archive in Munich, which served as a distribution center that assigned unique numbers to each publication that became known in the West.[34] By its sheer bulk and through evidence of intensive use by Keston staff, the samizdat collection dominates the overall narrative told by the archive. Taken together, the drawers full of documented dissent present an image of a population in uproar against the suppression of its rights, and for whom the freedom to worship and believe was a leading concern.

Originals and copies of samizdat documents constituted a highly prized source of information for the Keston staff, as shown by the fact that every document in the collection has an attached "samizdat processing form." The form allowed staff members to record where copies of the document were forwarded, if a translation was made and where it was sent, and whether it was published or excerpted in the "information sheets" that were periodically circulated by the Keston News Service. There are also rows for cross-references to other Keston files and indexes. In essence, the processing forms are tools to track the further circulation of information that reached Keston via samizdat. They reflect the institute's self-understanding as a switch point from which knowledge that had made the difficult passage across the

Iron Curtain could be amplified and reformatted to influence media coverage and policy toward the Soviet Union.

In addition to the processing form, many of the documents have attached handwritten or typed sheets with notes and summary translations that provide a record of readings by Keston staff. These notes often assign a value to the document, telling subsequent users if it is worth reading or excerpting. For example, a Russian-language note on one treatise reads: "Disjointed stream of consciousness, quotations from books are mixed with quotations from the Bible. The whole text is similar to the [long and confusing] title."[35] By contrast, an anonymous text entitled "Russia and the Church today," written by a Moscow convert to Orthodoxy in the early 1970s, is validated by a set of notes in Father Michael Bourdeaux's handwriting. Written in English in red ink and attached to the document with a paper clip, the notes provide a page-by-page synopsis as well as evaluation. Referring to one page in particular, Bourdeaux notes: "Return to faith. Marvellous spiritual passage—<u>exactly</u> what I've been saying."[36]

The passage that elicited such an enthusiastic response claims that there is "an obvious stream of new believers to the church" and describes the surprising circumstances that lead citizens of a highly secularized society to Orthodox Christianity:

> Every idea and even the mere memory of God and religion, it would seem, have been banished from the life of the average well-adjusted Soviet citizen. The church has been brought to manifest silence, and a hypocritical silence at that, since when it comes to reassuring the world of the comfortable position of the church in Russia the mouths of its official representatives are open, one could say, without cease . . . . Alas, no enlightening apostolic word can be heard in the Moscow Patriarchate. But still, by the unfathomable pathways of the Lord, Russian people are led to God's House by themselves: where else should they go in search of truth? There it is—an astonishing testimony that indeed, the Spirit breathes where it will![37]

The passage resonated with Bourdeaux's experience as a student in Moscow, where he was surprised to find that the church was in demand among Soviet citizens despite the political passivity of its leaders in the face of state restrictions. It must also have resonated with the experience of an Anglican priest in 1970s Great Britain, which was going through a strong decline in church membership and attendance. In a book sent to print not long before this document was written, Bourdeax himself had argued that "the present-day life and thought of the Russian Orthodox Church" revealed the "work of the Holy Spirit, which so often triumphs where the human odds are stacked impossibly against it."[38] As historian Ian Jones observes, tales about the survival of religion under communism published in Cold War Britain "called church members to re-examine the depth of their *own* commitment, in light of the resilience of their Christian brothers and sisters in the East."[39] If resilience in the East seemed to be strongest among laypeople, this reaffirmed the Protestant teaching of the priesthood of all believers. It also constituted a call to Western lay Christians to take responsibility for the survival of their own churches instead of leaving the clergy to deal with this task alone.

With its copious notes and traces of systematic forwarding, the samizdat collection can be read as a document of the collaborative creation of knowledge about religion under socialism by Soviet dissidents and their Western allies. The enthusiasm with which Keston staff greeted and amplified signs of religious resilience behind the Iron Curtain suggests a possible genealogy for current claims that a religious revival was under way in the Soviet Union under Brezhnev, as well as for the broader idea that religion is a universal human tendency whose free expression is an important part of democratic governance. Although popular tendencies in Soviet society were difficult to verify then and remain elusive now, several scholars claim that religious life was becoming reinvigorated long before perestroika, often with evidence from residents of urban centers who were engaged in circles around particular clergy.[40] Documentary assemblages in the Keston archive neither prove nor disprove these claims, but they do suggest that the Western circulation of Soviet samizdat helped to popularize the notion of a country in hidden spiritual turmoil. The sympathetic attention of Western co-believers and human rights activists, and their skilled publishing work, may have made Soviet believers look more numerous and socially influential than they were.

Not all samizdat authors represented in the Keston collection identify themselves as religious believers, and the presence of writings where religion is only a minor theme bolsters the over-all impression that all dissidence had a religious aspect. Keston staff received and archived the well-known and long-lived "Chronicle of Current Events" as well as the information bulletin of the "working group for the investigation of the use of psychiatry for political purposes."[41] Both present a digest of events and reports, some of which touch on the experiences of religious believers. Outside of these samizdat periodicals, the majority of documents are filed under the actual or assumed religious denomination of their authors, sometimes independently of the actual subject matter. For example, a letter by Semën Gluzman (an obviously Jewish name) describing an encounter with a Lutheran Christian in a prison camp was cross-referenced under "Jews", although the author never discusses any personal religious beliefs.[42] Religious affiliation is a default category required by the grammar of this archive, making it difficult to see the diversity of motivations that drove Soviet citizens to dissent.

Although denominational categories are important to the internal logic of the filing system, their use as mutually equivalent labels ultimately suggests that the experiences of lay believers in each community were interchangeable. A large part of the samizdat collection comes from the non-registered Baptists (*initsiativniki*) and Seventh-day Adventists, who had split off from their officially recognized bodies in the early 1960s and published regular bulletins such as *Bratskii Listok* (Fraternal

Leaflet, since 1965). Press releases and staff notes interpret complaints from Orthodox believers about the passive and compliant church hierarchy as evidence of the potential for a similar split in the Orthodox Church.[43] In the Jewish section of the samizdat collection, there is an open letter to the chief rabbi of Moscow that expresses a comparable protest against corrupt and immoral clergy whose presence during a conference allegedly desecrated the Moscow Choral Synagogue.[44] Since internal records of religious institutions were leaked to the West far more rarely than individual complaints, the collection itself supports no alternative readings that would show what these compromises and concessions looked like to members of the religious hierachies. Not all Western readers of samizdat privileged religious content, and some of the most original post-Soviet analyses of the phenomenon pay relatively little attention to religious writings.[45] But faith-based Cold War activists contributed to framing religion as an essential human characteristic and Soviet dissidents as embodiments of eternal spiritual dilemmas, two themes that outlasted the fall of the Iron Curtain and continue on in contemporary human rights debates.[46] As Bourdeaux explains in the preface to his book on Russian Orthodoxy in the USSR, he understood the "creative tension" between established clergy and "explosive calls to repentance from the prophet" as two poles that shaped religious consciousness from the times of ancient Israel to the twentieth century.[47] With a cataloging system based on denominations and state-imposed restrictions, the Keston archive represents Soviet citizens as "naturally faith-based"[48] and places their state and their churches together in a long line of compromised institutions that persecuted creative individuals. How Western advocacy for Soviet religious believers helped shape ideas about religious freedom as a core democratic value would need to be pieced together from the records of more than one archive. Clues to Keston's place in this larger network of advocacy lie in the most unusual aspect of this archive: its visible preservation of the custodial history of its collections.

The Content of the Filing System

As a depository that is tailored to the interests of an original group of users, the Keston archive exemplifies the problems and advantages of moving beyond the traditional archival emphasis on provenance. The argument for provenance as an organizing principle is that it reflects an organically emerging order rather than one that was willfully created by an archivist: "Archives are not artificial collections acquired, arranged, and described in the first instance by theme, subject, place or time; rather, they are acquired, arranged, and described, in a contextual, organic, natural relationship to their creator and acts of creation."[49] By keeping together records that originated from the same bureaucratic processes, each document is embedded in a context of creation that can accommodate a maximum number of different questions to be pursued by unknown future users. The respect for provenance that emerged as a principle of archival administration in the nineteenth century thus helped to separate the functions of the archivists who manage records from the historians who draw conclusions from them. This separation was central to justifying claims to objectivity and professionalism on the part of both groups.[50]

By these standards, Keston is not really an archive; it is a private collection of records accumulated by a group of users in the way that best served their immediate needs. And true enough, a researcher is left with many questions to which traditional archival catalogues provide at least partial answers. For example, it is often unclear how a particular document made it into the collection. Press releases usually refer simply to documents being "smuggled out of the Soviet Union," and the policy of the Samizdat Archive was to retype all documents that reached it rather than circulating originals.[51] Obscuring pathways of provenance and accession was a matter of safety. As a result, documents not only lack information about the pathways by which they became part of the archive but also about the uses for which they were originally created.

For example, the collection of Orthodox samizdat includes two hand-made books authored by a monk from the Pskov-Pechery Monastery who identifies himself as D.O.S., translated as "abbot Savva" in a penciled annotation. One is a prayer book, the other a history of the monastery and autobiographical account of the author's experience of becoming a monk. Both are obviously laborious creations, with typewritten pages folded and bound by hand. The prayer book is even illustrated with images of Jesus, Mary, and the saints, reproduced as photographs and glued to the pages. Judging by the texts, these one-of-a-kind books were made for a spiritual follower or group of followers who knew the monk personally and looked to him for guidance in prayers and daily life.[52] Within the Keston collection, these volumes represent another genre of samizdat, where there is no direct political commentary but subversion of state restrictions on the production of literature that was not deemed useful for socialist readers. Such literature speaks most directly of the religious needs and interests of citizens who did not see themselves as engaged in oppositional activity. But since the filing system does not document how and through whom a document reached the archive, it is not clear for whose use the volumes were made and how these presumably valuable possessions of Soviet believers ended up in a Western archival collection. In a conventional archive these books would be part of the papers of the person who received them from Abbot Savva, allowing more conjectures about the nature of such unofficial spiritual ties.

While these open questions show that respect for provenance can be a good thing, Keston's user-centered filing system preserves two aspects of the life of an archival document that are often neglected in archival description: custodial history and history of use. Custodial history refers to what happens to a document after it becomes an archival file: this includes movements from one depository to another, in and out of storage, and acts of reclassification or restoration.[53] In addition to preserving the classification system as created in Great Britain, the new owners of the collection at Baylor decided to keep together originals and photocopies as accumulated by the Keston staff, and also to keep the library intact in the archival reading room rather than integrating it with the larger university library. This preservation of custodial history allows researchers to turn their eye toward the relationship between Soviet religious dissidents and their Western publics, an area of research where much is still unknown.[54]

The history of use is, as discussed earlier, the main force that shaped the classification system in the Keston archive. While erasing some valuable information and reinforcing the view of heroic individuals united in the battle against religious discrimination, it also allows later researchers to benefit from the work of their predecessors. While not allowing users to make modifications to the records is an important principle of archival objectivity, it works to preserve logics of documentation that may be biased against particular topics from the start. In a state archive in Russia, users are left to their own devices in identifying where religion comes up in the records of a state that limited its official dealing with it to a deceptively narrow range of issues. Only a user's personal file preserves the list of documents he or she has requested, and such files are not accessible to other users. At Keston, the work of identifying information on religion in secular media and unpublished papers has already been done. The files reflect decades of work by staff members who collected informal writings and monitored newspapers, journals, and other publications. The categories used in the catalogue preserve their conclusions about major issues facing religious communities, from publishing and education to involvement in charity and family relationships. Having looked at the collection of newspaper clippings collected under the heading of "loss of parental rights," a researcher who before looked only at the records of the commissioner for religious affairs in public archives may start requesting the records of child protection agencies or court proceedings for divorce and custody cases.

Since the real life implications of religious adherence were too broad for any one bureaucracy to encompass, a counter-archive built around the use of records for religious advocacy can give new generations of users fresh ideas for locating evidence of religious practices in state archives. Neither conventional nor counter-archives have any claim to presenting information in a neutral, objective manner, and going back and forth between them will help sharpen a researcher's sensitivity for *how* files are presented as well as what they say.

Quoting the State

In compiling evidence of religious life in socialist states, Western sympathizers sought to go beyond state records, but also prized them as hard-to-obtain sources of information. Scholars have pointed out the particular aesthetics of samizdat typescripts that was often "fetishized" by readers who saw the thin, dog-eared pages, jumping or missing typewriter keys, and unevenly set lines as indicative of non-conformist content that would never be printed in the official press.[55] Others, however, have noted the resemblances between samizdat and *spetsizdat* ("special publications"), classified or restricted circulars and publications put out by state offices and marked "top secret" (*sovershenno sekretno*) or "for official use" (*dlia sluzhebnogo polzovaniia*). These were typed on typewriters with similar fonts and often reproduced with the help of the same kind of carbon paper, or as brochures with small print runs. The content of spetsizdat also differed from what might be printed in the newspapers, and, when diverted from its intended readership, could have the same appeal of forbidden and non-standardized information. In a playful book on "new sectarianism" in twentieth-century Russia as reflected in imaginary files of the Moscow Institute of Atheism, literary critic Mikhail Epshtein plays on the similarity between samizdat and spetsizdat in style as well as content. Both reported on phenomena that officially did not exist in the Soviet Union, such as new religious growth.[56] While neither type of literature always contained surprising, verifiable, or novel information, both had an aura of increased truthfulness because their circulation was restricted and had not gone through censorship. The "wretched material manifestation" thus stood for honesty and unadorned truth in both cases.[57]

At Keston, this reading of uncensored and restricted as truthful and rare erases distinctions between samizdat and official documents. For example, a folder in the samizdat collection contains a four-page typed list of Moscow churches as of 1972, including their addresses.[58] From research in the files of the Council of Religious Affairs, I am accustomed to such lists as a common genre of sources that provides the historian with useful information on the shrinking numbers of houses of worship in a given region. But in the 1970s, precise information on the numbers and locations of churches, mosques, or synagogues was unavailable to ordinary Soviet citizens and Western researchers alike, so that something as seemingly absurd as a samizdat reproduction of an official document constituted a subversive act. Circulating classified documents challenged the myth of unrestricted freedom of worship that the Soviet Union sought to convey to foreign partners and visitors. It also punctured the air of secrecy and exclusive control over information that was central to the power that socialist states could wield over their citizens.[59]

Documents and restricted publications obtained from the Soviet Union show the international dimension of this economy of secrecy and scarcity. The Samizdat Archive (AS) in Munich circulated a typed copy of a blank survey on attitudes toward religion, atheism, and forms of atheist propaganda conducted at a technical college in Moscow "no later than summer 1982."[60]

The answers collected remained unknown, but even the questions that were being asked about religion in the Soviet Union were valuable knowledge to Western observers, and smuggling them out of the country was worthy of the name "samizdat." The labor that went into copying and recirculating relatively uninformative documents among institutions across western Europe shows the high symbolic significance of Soviet believers as well as the difficulty of obtaining information.

In the post-Soviet era, as information scarcity no longer posed a problem but reliability and authenticity of documents became more pressing concerns, staff members added photocopies of more than 400 documents from Russian archives to the collection. The institute's British website accurately describes these documents as coming "from the Archives of the KGB, the State Archives of Russia and regional archives of the Council for Religious Affairs."[61] At Baylor, however, the drawers containing these photocopies are simply labeled "KGB," probably reflecting the widespread assumption that the real truth of what happened in Eastern Europe is contained in the secret police files.[62] Actually, most of the files are photocopies from the records of religious affairs commissioners from various regional archives in Central Russia, focusing mainly on reports to Moscow. Different from the KGB archives in Moscow, the originals of these records are now easily accessible to researchers. Their genre and subject matter was immediately familiar to me from research with analogous records in the Volga region. A user who consults the photocopies at Keston is spared costly trips to several Russian cities and is able to compare the approaches of different commissioners. She also loses the opportunity to consult the files of other agencies or from later or earlier years than those chosen for copying. In a dilemma similar to what occurs when selected records are digitized and made available online, accessibility comes at the cost of contextual information.[63]

My initial reaction to seeing these photocopies was to think of them as products of the moment just after the collapse of the Soviet Union, when the quest to own previously inaccessible information often became an end in itself. At the same time, the official records are recontextualized in a way that changes how users interact with them. They are not only juxtaposed to samizdat accounts that challenge their picture of correct and orderly treatment of believers. They have become just as deterritorialized as samizdat, calling attention to the geographic dimension of archival authority. In most of my experiences with conducting archival research, having seen a document in the administrative jurisdiction where it was created or sent added to my sense that it was authentic and that I was considering it in its proper context. The archival photocopies at Keston are one step removed from such jurisdictional verification, creating a sense of uncertainty that is similar to the "epistemological instability"[64] that adheres to samizdat itself, where links to individual authors and pathways of circulation were often deliberately obscured.

On the part of Keston staff, the move to integrate declassified materials from other archives could be seen as another attempt to "quote" the state in a larger authorial narrative that contradicts Soviet claims about religious freedom and legality. Their collecting practice had never privileged originals, but had been based on accumulating whatever information available no matter what form it took. For a researcher used to associating archives with unique documents stored in the context of territorial jurisdiction, the disconcerting effect of encountering regrouped and misattributed photocopies shows how expectations of provenance influence our reading of documents. If, like samizdat, archival documents were not thought of as unique pieces of paper tied to a particular geographic location, but could be part of different collections spread across continents, how would that change the effects we think they can have?

Sympathy and Hostility in the Archives

As many commentators on Soviet historiography have noted, the changes that made the Soviet past accessible also took away part of the institutional support for studying it in the West.[65] Keston was among those affected by these changes, losing some of its funding base at the same time the information it collected became more abundantly available. In the post-Soviet decades, the institute continued to publish an influential journal on religion in Eastern Europe and the former Soviet Union, renamed from *Religion in Communist Lands* to *Religion, State and Society*. Seeking collaboration with Russian scholars who document religious diversity and church-state relations, it has shifted focus to issues of religious freedom and monitoring of religious conflicts.[66] From being an integral part of the institute's activities, the archive became a relic of a past era, allowing it to be more easily relocated to another continent.

Now that Keston no longer serves as a living depository, it is perhaps easier to see what this religious counter-archive tells us about the value of sympathetic documentation. It certainly contains many narratives one would be unlikely to find in a Russian state archive—detailed chronicles of the conversations between dissidents hospitalized as mentally ill and their doctors, for example, and texts of prayers circulated by a spiritual father in defiance of tight restrictions on printing religious literature. Other narratives that are preserved in state archives as well, such as believers' complaints about corruption within their religious institution, take on a more dignified, less futile tone. If uptake by other documents is one indication of how effective a document was in its time, then the documentary acts of dissatisfied citizens seem far more powerful at Keston than in post-Soviet state archives.

In other ways, however, the archive shows that sympathetic perspectives can be just as limited as critical ones: the search for evidence of a "movement" behind an individual author might as easily be adopted by the secret police trying to neutralize dissidents as by a Western admirer. In the polarizing context of the Cold War, the atheist state's prose of counter-insurgency is too easily mirrored in the "hope of insurgency" nurtured in the Western press. Just as Soviet sociology lovingly anticipated the emerging atheist society, Western Christian observers amplified all signs of persistent religiosity. The deepest affinity between atheist and faith-based practices of recordkeeping lies perhaps in the tendency to create an environment that confirms the significance of their object of study: religious belief. Hannah Arendt's observation of how circles of sympathizers and specialized information create closed feedback loops that give political activists an exaggerated sense of their movement's importance applies to activist archives as well.[67]

Where users work in an archive whose categories have been created to suit their particular interests, there is a high likelihood that the archive will yield evidence to confirm these interests. As the end of the Cold War and of state atheism makes older preoccupations with religious resistance redundant, new generations of users will need to treat Keston's filing system and documentation of custodial history as historical artifacts in their own right. Keeping in mind that the bulletins, letters, philosophical treatises, prayers, and complaints can never represent the whole spectrum of religious experience in the Soviet Union, these new users will have to speculate about the place of self-conscious religious practice among the broader life concerns of Soviet citizens. They will also be able to ask questions about the relationship of mutual affirmation and misunderstanding between Soviet and Western publics of religious samizdat. The Keston archive contains fascinating materials to answer these questions precisely when it flaunts archival conventions of territorial provenance and singular originals.

Epilogue

Reversible History and Fragile Archives

Throughout this book, I have argued that hostile documents can stimulate productive and thought-provoking readings, especially if we see them not just as true or false descriptions of an outside reality but as tools that acted on that reality. If we look at state records in this way and combine them with other available sources, a picture of the place of religion in late Soviet society emerges that is in many ways in flux. Believers contend with similar bureaucratic forces as all Soviet citizens, although the dice are more heavily loaded against them; the boundaries of religion and non-religion are debated by scholars and called to question by lived ritual practice. In the Soviet Union governed by Khrushchev and especially Brezhnev, religion continued to be seen as ideologically alien but it no longer posed an institutional threat. While remaining an adversary, it slowly turned into a possible object of nostalgia, and this contributed to multi-faceted reconsiderations of the topic by scholars and bureaucrats as well as by citizens making practical decisions about ways to bury deceased relatives or the advisability of cutting down prayer groves for use as building materials.

If the 1960s and '70s appear as a time of increasing indeterminacy and opening up of interpretive possibilities, doing research in Russia two decades after the fall of the Soviet Union often feels like living through a moment when particular interpretations of the past and the future are consolidated at the expense of others. In this struggle over reinterpretation, archives retain their explanatory power but come to be read in new ways, and religious institutions cease to be among the voiceless in need of protection. Rather, they actively shape how history is conceptualized. To close my reflections on the contexts of production and use of Soviet archival collections, I would like to offer a story about the reversibility of archival fortunes in the context of shifts in the balance of power between secularism and religion in Russia.

One of the archives in which I spent a lot of time is the State Archive of the Republic of Marii El (GARME) in Ioshkar-Ola, a regional capital of about 300,000 inhabitants an overnight train ride away from Moscow. Founded as a military outpost named Tsarevokokshaisk (the tsar's city on the Kokshaga) in the sixteenth century, the city's history is closely tied to Moscow's subjugation of Finno-Ugric populations on the middle Volga. Until it became capital of the Mari Autonomous region (later to be upgraded to Autonomous Republic) in the 1920s, the city was part of the province (*guberniia*) of Kazan and had no archival building of its own. As in many Sovietizing cities, space was made available on the grounds of a destroyed religious institution: the archive was established in an L-shaped, single-story wooden building at the spot where the convent of Our Lady and St. Sergius had stood until it was destroyed in the 1930s. It was in this wooden building, aged by several decades, that I spent many days in 2005, looking at the records of the commissioner for religious affairs. The floorboards creaked, the reading room was damp and not very well heated, and space constraints forced the archivists to use an even colder outlying storage facility for less frequently used records—for example, those of the Knowledge Society.

For all its inconveniences, the main archival building was located on one of the central streets of the city, just steps from two newly opened churches and the historical museum, and a few blocks away from the government building whose basement still housed the Communist Party archive. It formed an integral part of the infrastructure of a city whose Soviet past still very much determined its present look.

When I returned to Ioshkar-Ola in 2008, after an absence of a little more than two years, the city had begun to change profoundly, and so had the place of the archive in it. The wooden building was empty and slated to be torn down, and the archive had moved across the river into a three-story brick building constructed amid the concrete apartment blocks of the 1970s. The new facility offered more space and climate-controlled storage, and the reading room staff I talked to said they were happy to work in warmer and brighter rooms. But a recently retired archivist whom I visited at her home complained that the move had been done in haste, before leaving proper time for the mortar in the new brick building to settle and dry. As a result, the nineteenth-century documents that she and her colleagues had carefully aired and dried in their old environment were now infected with mold.

Ironically, the move that relocated the archive away from the cultural and political center of the city and damaged some of its documents was carried out under the slogan of a "reconstruction of historical heritage." A wave of construction in red brick had filled the city center with buildings that did not exactly look "historical" but certainly had nothing in common with Soviet concrete architecture. A new art gallery and shopping center in the style of a Venetian plaza had appeared across from the republic's government building. United Russia (the party of Russia's president Vladimir Putin and Marii El's president

Leonid Markelov) had headquarters built in neogothic style, and government offices were moving into gabled brick houses along the river bank that were dubbed "little Holland". A concrete footbridge across the Little Kokshaga river now started at the foot of a tower modeled on the Spassky Gate of Moscow's Kremlin. As part of this construction boom, a number of previously destroyed churches were also being reconstructed at their historical locations. The archive had had to move to make room for a rebuilt convent church, to be surrounded not by an actual nunnery but by an upscale apartment building.

It was clear that none of this construction activity was aimed at restoring the city to its pre-revolutionary state. The last remaining wooden houses from the early twentieth century were falling victim to the new construction, and archaeologists complained that there was no time for excavation in the construction schedule. Rumor had it that the republic's president had toy construction bricks on his desk and used them to demonstrate to the city architect what he wanted to build; many of the buildings were cheap brick copies of church and military architecture from St. Petersburg and Moscow. Gradually, the Soviet planning that had defined the city center was losing its importance, both visually and in terms of the structural grid of streets and parks. Buildings from the 1960s and '70s such as a concrete puppet theater and a house of culture were torn down, and the ample green spaces that had surrounded large Soviet buildings were being repurposed for commercial uses. Like the planetarium of the Knowledge Society and several cultural institutions, the archive had simply taken up too much space on valuable real estate.[1]

If the archive was forced to leave the city center, the Russian Orthodox Church has become more entrenched in it. Between 1960 and 1995, there was no functioning church within the city limits of Ioshkar-Ola. By 2005, there were two active churches in the city center, and two more were under construction. At the time of my last visit in 2012, there were six functioning

Orthodox churches and two new ones were under construction, all within easy walking distance from one another. Several of them held services only on festival days, since there were neither enough churchgoers nor priests to fill them every Sunday. In the residential areas outside the historical center, where most of the city population lived, only one new church had been built. As a result, Russian Orthodox Christianity has become a more prominent part of the face of the city, without becoming any more easily accessible to lay worshippers.

Among friends in Ioshkar-Ola who are neither archival researchers nor churchgoers, the changes in the cityscape have aroused some pride—"finally, we have something to show guests when they visit the city"—and suspicious speculations as to who is making money selling all those bricks to the government. Muslims and Mari pagans felt alienated from the city, which they suddenly perceived as "Christian" in a way that it had not been before. Considered from the perspective of how cityscapes change along with changing horizons of historical expectation, I am tempted to agree with Michel-Rolph Trouillot's observation that when it comes to engaging the past, "the production of traces is always also the creation of silences," achieved in part through turning the built environment into monuments: "Too solid to be unmarked, too conspicuous to be candid, [the remains of historical buildings] embody the ambiguities of history. They give us the power to touch it, but not to hold it firmly in our hand—hence the mystery of their battered walls."[2] In the absence of tangible walls from before the revolution, elites in Marii El were able to construct a narrative of unity, prosperity, and loyalty to Moscow, borrowing the authority of monumental architecture without having to deal with the messiness of an evolved historical city.

Throughout Russia, part of the way in which a changing view of the past imposes itself on people in the present is through the increased visibility of regionally dominant religions in cityscapes, where worship buildings and religious symbols come to represent a historically established order. The few steadfast atheists I met in post-Soviet Russia felt that they now had to defend themselves against charges of immorality rather than representing human solidarity and responsibility against the otherworldly promises of religion. Once part of the rush of a revolutionary state to secularize its past, archives as buildings and institutions are also caught up in this latest reversal of history. As the embattled fates of libraries and archives in post-conflict societies in Europe, Latin America, and the Middle East have shown, the institutional power of an archive to authorize narratives of the authentic past finds limits in its physical reality as a building filled with paper.[3] Once the state that underwrote them is gone, the documents of powerful bureaucracies have the same wretched paper existence as samizdat. Both must be recognized as traces of a valuable and usable past in order to last.

In the late Soviet period, scholars and officials saw signs of a secular society emerging, but they also had to acknowledge that religion remained a part of the present. What the mutual relationship and relative weight of secular and religious forms would be remained a matter of philosophical and practical debate. If from the hindsight of post-Soviet developments records of this period seem to reveal the first stirrings of religious revival, an alternative future in which atheism had become more entrenched might well find signs of the slow progress of secularization in the same records. Knowing that the project of transformation that these records once served was abandoned inevitably colors our readings of them, but they also serve as reminders of alternative historical trajectories.

Reading Soviet records at a time when the balance of power between secular and religious self-representations is being renegotiated in many parts of the world, one of the most striking features of these documents is the attempt to speak with critical curiosity about others whose perspective the authors do not wish to share. Today, many historians and social scientists are concerned with whether disciplines committed to methodological suspension of belief can do justice to religious worlds. Seeing the reconstruction of Russian cities, but also watching US television or browsing through book stalls in airports in many parts of the world, one finds it hard to deny the power of religious institutions and inclinations, but it is also clear that this power does not emanate from an unchanging essence of what religion is or does. Soviet atheists never stopped trying to identify such an essence and to provide an exhaustive explanation of the harm done by religion. At the same time, they insisted that it was possible to learn something about Soviet society from talking to believers as well as unbelievers, and developed a program of inquiry into religion's meanings and social effects that sometimes led them to challenge and revise orthodox Marxist assumptions. Examining the writings of these scholar-administrators, we can easily note the blindness and self-fulfilling prophecies imposed by their contradictory position. But we may also wonder if our own attempts to understand others across ideological and experiential boundaries will stand the test of time any better than theirs.

Notes

Introduction

1. Deborah Field, *Private Life and Communist Morality in Khrushchev's Russia* (New York: Peter Lang, 2007); Brian LaPierre, *Hooligans in Khrushchev's Russia: Defining, Policing, and Producing Deviance during the Thaw* (Madison: University of Wisconsin Press, 2012); William Taubman, *Khrushchev: The Man and His Era* (New York: Norton, 2003), 236–69; Mikhail Shkarovskii, *Russkaia pravoslavnaia tserkov' i sovetskoe gosudarstvo v 1943-1964 gg.: Ot peremiriia k novoi voine* (St. Petersburg: DEAN-ADIA-M, 1995); Andrew Stone, "Overcoming Peasant Backwardness: The Khrushchev Anti-Religious Campaign and the Rural Soviet Union," *Russian Review* 67:2 (2008): 296–320.

2. GARF, f. A-561, op. 1, d. 65, l. 54, Transcript of an all-Russian seminar of chairmen of atheist and natural-scientific sections of regional organizations of the Knowledge Society, Moscow, January 10-11, 1956.

3. Natalie Zemon Davis, *Fiction in the Archives: Pardon Tales and Their Tellers in Sixteenth-Century France* (Stanford, CA: Stanford University Press, 1987); Ann Laura Stoler, *Along the Archival Grain: Epistemic Anxieties and Colonial Common Sense* (Princeton, NJ: Princeton University Press, 2009); Kathryn Burns, *Into the Archive: Writing and Power in Colonial Peru* (Durham, NC: Duke University Press, 2010); Matthew Hull, *Government of Paper: The Materiality of Bureaucracy in Urban Pakistan* (Berkeley: University of California Press, 2012); Katherine Verdery, *Secrets and Truth: Ethnography in the Archive of Romania's Secret Police* (Budapest: Central European University Press, 2014).

4. Craig Campbell, *Agitating Images: Photography Against History in Indigenous Siberia* (Minneapolis: University of Minnesota Press, 2014), x.

5. Michel-Rolph Trouillot, *Silencing the Past: Power and the Production of History* (Boston: Beacon, 1995), 26. For a slightly different application of this passage to the context of post-socialist archives, see Verdery, *Secrets and Truth*, 34–35.

6. GARF, f. A-561, op. 1, d. 65, l. 7.

7. Emily Baran, *Dissent on the Margins: How Soviet Jehovah's Witnesses Defied Communism and Lived to Preach about It* (New York: Oxford University Press, 2014); Miriam Dobson, "Child Sacrifice in the Soviet Press: Sensationalism and the 'Sectarian' in the Post-Stalin Era," *Russian Review* 73:2 (2014): 237–59.

8. Daniel Peris, *Storming the Heavens: The Soviet League of the Militant Godless* (Ithaca, NY: Cornell University Press, 1998); David Powell, *Antireligious Propaganda in the Soviet Union: A Study of Mass Persuasion* (Cambridge, MA: MIT Press, 1975).

9. Ulrike Huhn, *Glaube und Eigensinn: Volksfrömmigkeit zwischen orthodoxer Kirche und sowjetischem Staat 1941 bis 1960* (Wiesbaden: Harrassowitz, 2014), 25–26; Baran, *Dissent on the Margins*, 155–157.

10. Michael Froggatt, "Renouncing Dogma, Teaching Utopia: Science in Schools under Khrushchev," in *The Dilemmas of De-Stalinization: Negotiating Cultural and Social Change in the Khrushchev Era*, ed. Polly Jones (London: Routledge, 2006), 250–66; Thomas Schmidt-Lux, "Das helle Licht der Wissenschaft: Die Urania, der organisierte Szientismus und der ostdeutsche Säkularisierungsprozess," *Geschichte und Gesellschaft* 34:1 (2008): 41–72. On Western debates about creationism, see Simon Coleman and Leslie Carlin, eds., *The Cultures of Creationism: Anti-Evolutionism in English-Speaking Cultures* (Aldershot: Ashgate, 2004). For some of the intellectual genealogy of the contrast between faith and knowledge, see Christopher Lane, *The Age of Doubt: Tracing the Roots of Our Religious Uncertainty* (New Haven, CT: Yale University Press, 2011).

11. Victoria Smolkin-Rothrock, "Cosmic Enlightenment: Scientific Atheism and the Soviet Conquest of Space," in *Into the Cosmos: Space Exploration and Soviet Culture in Post-Stalinist Russia*, ed. James T. Andrews and Asif A. Siddiqi (Pittsburgh, PA: University of Pittsburgh Press, 2011), 159–94; Slava Gerovitch, *From Newspeak to Cyberspeak: A History of Soviet Cybernetics* (Boston: MIT Press, 2002).

12. Kate Brown, *Plutopia: Nuclear Families, Atomic Cities, and the Great Soviet and American Plutonium Disasters* (New York: Oxford University Press, 2013); Joseph Masco, *The Nuclear Borderlands: The Manhattan*

Project in Post–Cold War New Mexico (Princeton, NJ: Princeton University Press, 2006).

13. Karl Marx, "Contribution to the Critique of Hegel's Philosophy of Law: Introduction," in *The Collected Works of Karl Marx and Frederick Engels*, vol. 3 (New York: International Publishers, 1975), 175–87, quote from p. 175; William Husband, *"Godless Communists": Atheism and Society in Soviet Russia, 1917–1932* (DeKalb: Northern Illinois University Press, 2000).

14. Tatiana Chumachenko, *Church and State in Soviet Russia: Russian Orthodoxy from World War II to the Khrushchev Years* (Armonk, NY: Sharpe, 2002), 17–27; Christel Lane, *Christian Religion in the Soviet Union: A Sociological Study* (London: George Allen and Unwin, 1978); Yaacov Ro'i, *Islam in the Soviet Union: From the Second World War to Gorbachev* (New York: Columbia University Press, 2000), 217–25.

15. Quoted in Taubman, *Khrushchev*, 262. On contradictions created by de-Stalinization and appeals to popular conscience, see Polly Jones, ed., *The Dilemmas of De-Stalinization: Negotiating Cultural and Social Change in the Khrushchev Era* (London: Routledge, 2006); Miriam Dobson, *Khrushchev's Cold Summer: Gulag Returnees, Crime, and the Fate of Reform after Stalin* (Ithaca, NY: Cornell University Press, 2009).

16. Sheila Fitzpatrick, "Social Parasites: How Tramps, Idle Youth and Busy Entrepreneurs Impeded the Soviet March to Communism," *Cahiers du monde russe* 47:1–2 (2006): 377–408.

17. Vladlen Izmozik and Nataliia Lebina, *Peterburg sovetskii: "Novyi chelovek" v starom prostranstve, 1920–1930e gody* (St. Petersburg: Kriga, 2010); Paul Stronski, *Tashkent: Forging a Soviet City, 1930–1966* (Pittsburgh: University of Pittsburgh Press, 2010).

18. Leon Trotsky, "Culture and Socialism" (1926) in his *Problems of Everyday Life: Creating the Foundations for a New Society in Revolutionary Russia* (New York: Pathfinder Press, 1973), 281–308, esp. 297–98. See also Richard E. Lonsdale and John H. Thompson, "A Map of the USSR's Manufacturing," *Economic Geography* 30:1 (1960): 36–52.

19. GARF, f. A-561, op. 1, d. 65, l. 103.

20. GARF, f. A-561, op. 1, d. 65, ll. 103–104.

21. GARF, f. A-561, op. 1, d. 65, l. 107.

22. GARF, f. A-561, op. 1, d. 65, l. 106; Victoria Smolkin-Rothrock, "Problema 'obyknovennoi' sovetskoi smerti: Material'noe i dukhovnoe v ateisticheskoi kosmologii," *Gosudarstvo, Religiia, Tserkov'* 30:3–4 (2012): 429–62.

23. The latter was a theme of much of the debate about religiosity among women and old people that developed from the mid-1960s onward. See, for example, GARF, f. R-6991, op. 6, d. 80, ll. 219–22, Report

on religiosity among women, Commissioner of Religious Affairs Viktor Savel'ev to the Regional Party Committee of the Mari ASSR, June 16, 1967.

24. Luehrmann, *Secularism Soviet Style: Teaching Atheism and Religion in a Volga Republic* (Bloomington: Indiana University Press, 2011).

25. Sonja Luehrmann, "On the Importance of Having a Method, or What Does Archival Work on Soviet Atheism Have to Do with Ethnography of Post-Soviet Religion?" in *Anthrohistory: Unsettling Knowledge, Questioning Discipline*, ed. Edward Murphy et al. (Ann Arbor: University of Michigan Press, 2011), 273–85.

26. Reinhart Koselleck, *Vergangene Zukunft: Zur Semantik geschichtlicher Zeiten* (Frankfurt: Suhrkamp, 1979), 98.

27. See the critiques in Hugh McLeod, *European Religion in the Age of the Great Cities, 1830–1930* (London: Routledge, 1995); Brian Porter-Szűcs, "Introduction: Christianity, Christians, and the Story of Modernity in Eastern Europe," in *Christianity and Modernity in Eastern Europe*, ed. Bruce Berglund and Brian Porter-Szűcs (Budapest: Central European University Press, 2010), 1–34.

28. E. P. Thompson, *The Making of the English Working Class* (New York: Vintage, 1966), 365, 368.

29. On the pitfalls of uncritically accepting clerical narratives of religious decline, see Callum Brown, *The Death of Christian Britain: Understanding Secularization, 1800–2000* (London: Routledge, 2001).

30. Bernard Lewis, *The Emergence of Modern Turkey* (London: Oxford University Press, 1961); Alexandre Bennigsen and Chantal Lemercier-Quelquejay, *L'Islam en Union soviétique* (Paris: Payot, 1968).

31. Gregory Freeze, *The Russian Levites: Parish Clergy in the Eighteenth Century* (Cambridge, MA: Harvard University Press, 1977); Hugh McLeod, *Class and Religion in the Late Victorian City* (Hamden, CT: Archon Books, 1974).

32. For discussions of the political contexts of the—partly overlapping—shifts toward "culture" and "religion," see Geoff Eley, *A Crooked Line: From Cultural History to the History of Society* (Ann Arbor: University of Michigan Press, 2005); Bruce Lincoln, *Holy Terrors: Thinking about Religion after September 11* (Chicago: University of Chicago Press, 2006); Porter-Szűcs, "Introduction."

33. Talal Asad, *Formations of the Secular: Christianity, Islam, Modernity* (Stanford, CA: Stanford University Press, 2003); José Casanova, *Public Religions in the Modern World* (Chicago: University of Chicago Press, 1994); Rodney Stark, "Secularization: RIP," *Sociology of Religion* 60:3 (1999): 249–73.

34. Brown, *The Death of Christian Britain*; Steve Bruce, *God Is Dead: Secularization in the West* (Oxford: Blackwell, 2002); Detlef Pollack, *Säkularisierung—ein moderner Mythos? Studien zum religiösen Wandel in Deutschland* (Tübingen: Mohr-Siebeck, 2003).

35. On "forced secularity," see Monika Wohlrab-Sahr, Uta Karstein, and Thomas Schmidt-Lux, *Forcierte Säkularität: Religiöser Wandel und Generationendynamik im Osten Deutschlands* (Frankfurt: Campus, 2009); for comparative data from different post-socialist countries, see Gert Pickel, "Areligiosität, Antireligiosität, Religiosität: Ostdeutschland als Sonderfall niedriger Religiosität im osteuropäischen Rahmen?" in *Atheismus und religiöse Indifferenz*, ed. Christel Gärtner et al. (Opladen: Leske & Budrich, 2003), 247–69; Detlef Pollack, Irena Borowik, and Wolfgang Jagodzinski, eds., *Religiöser Wandel in den postkommunistischen Ländern Ost- und Mitteleuropas* (Würzburg: Ergon, 1998).

36. Bruce, *God Is Dead*, 31–36; Thomas Luckmann, *Die unsichtbare Religion* (Frankfurt: Suhrkamp, 1991); Matthew Engelke, *God's Agents: Biblical Publicity in Contemporary England* (Berkeley: University of California Press, 2013).

37. Dmitrii Furman and Kimmo Kaariainen, *Religioznost' v Rossii v 90e gody XX—nachale XXI veka* (Moscow: OGNI TD, 2006), 48; *Obshchestvennoe mnenie—2014: Ezhegodnik* (Moscow: Levada Center, 2015), 129.

38. Nikolai Mitrokhin, *Russkaia Pravoslavnaia Tserkov': Sovremennoe sostoianie i aktual'nye problemy* (Moscow: Novoe Literaturnoe Obozrenie, 2004), 38; see also Sergei Filatov and Roman Lunkin, "Statistics on Religion in Russia: The Reality behind the Figures," *Religion, State and Society* 34:1 (2006): 33–49.

39. Chaeyoon Lim, Carol Ann MacGregor, and Robert Putnam, "Secular and Liminal: Discovering Heterogeneity among Religious Nones," *Journal for the Scientific Study of Religion* 49:4 (2010): 596–618; Phil Zuckerman, *Faith No More: Why People Reject Religion* (New York: Oxford, 2012).

40. Charles Taylor, *A Secular Age* (Cambridge, MA: Belknap, 2007).

41. Talal Asad, "Trying to Understand French Secularism," in *Political Theologies: Public Religions in a Post-Secular World,* ed. Hent de Vries and Lawrence Sullivan (New York: Fordham University Press, 2006), 494–526; Jean Baubérot, *Laïcité 1905–2005, entre passion et raison* (Paris: Seuil, 2004); Callum Brown, "The Secularisation Decade: What the 1960s Have Done to the Study of Religious History," in *The Decline of Christendom in Western*

Europe, 1750–2000, ed. Hugh McLeod and Werner Ustorf (Cambridge: Cambridge University Press, 2003), 29–46; Christian Smith, "Introduction: Rethinking the Secularization of American Public Life," in *The Secular Revolution: Power, Interests, and Conflict in the Secularization of American Public Life,* ed. Christian Smith (Berkeley: University of California Press, 2003), 1–96.

42. Making a space for religiously inspired action in conceptualizations of anti-colonial resistance has been a concern of members of the subaltern studies group; see Dipesh Chakrabarty, *Provincializing Europe: Postcolonial Thought and Historical Difference* (Princeton, NJ: Princeton University Press, 2000); Ranajit Guha, "The Prose of Counter-Insurgency," in *Selected Subaltern Studies,* ed. Ranajit Guha and Gayatri Spivak (New York: Oxford University Press, 1988), 45–86. Scholars looking for sympathetic approaches to so-called religious fundamentalists have made similar arguments about the secularist bias of the social sciences. See Susan Harding, "Representing Fundamentalism: The Problem of the Repugnant Cultural Other," *Social Research* 58:2 (1991): 373–93; Saba Mahmood, *Politics of Piety: The Islamic Revival and the Feminist Subject* (Princeton, NJ: Princeton University Press, 2005).

43. Katherine Ewing, "Dreams from a Saint: Anthropological Atheism and the Temptation to Believe," *American Anthropologist* 96:3 (1994): 571–83; Diane Goldstein, "The Secularization of Religious Ethnography and Narrative Competence in a Discourse of Faith," *Western Folklore* 54 (1995): 23–36.

44. Marianna Shakhnovich, *Ocherki po istorii religiovedeniia* (St. Petersburg: Izdatel'stvo Sankt-Peterburgskogo universiteta, 2006); Viktor Shnirel'man, personal communication, May 2011.

45. GARF, f. A-561, op. 1, d. 282, l. 9, Transcript of a theoretical conference on questions of theology and Russian Orthodoxy, Moscow, May 29–30, 1959. The research in which Pushkareva participated was published as Liudmila Anokhina and Margarita Shemeleva, *Kul'tura i byt kolkhoznikov Kalininskoi oblasti* (Moscow: Nauka, 1964).

46. GARF, f. A-561, op. 1, d. 282, l. 10. "The Great Patriotic War" is the common Soviet designation for the fight against Nazi Germany during the Second World War.

47. GARF, f. A-561, op. 1, d. 282, l. 11.

48. GARF, f. A-561, op. 1, d. 282, ll. 11–12.

49. Tamara Dragadze, "The Domestication of Religion under Soviet Communism," in *Socialism: Ideals, Ideologies, and Local Practice,* ed. Chris Hann (London: Routledge, 1993), 148–56; Douglas Northrop, *Veiled Empire: Gender and Power in Stalinist Central Asia* (Ithaca,

NY: Cornell University Press, 2004), 176; Irina Paert, "Demystifying the Heavens: Women, Religion, and Khrushchev's Anti-Religious Campaign, 1954–64," in *Women in the Khrushchev Era*, ed. Melanie Ilič, Susan Reid, and Lynne Attwood (Basingstoke: Palgrave Macmillan, 2004), 203–21.

50. Viktor Solov'ev, "Nekotorye osobennosti formirovaniia ateisticheskoi ubezhdennosti cheloveka," in *Ateizm i sotsialisticheskaia kul'tura: Materialy nauchnoi konferentsii*, ed. Viktor Solov'ev (Ioshkar-Ola: Mariiskoe knizhnoe izdatel'stvo, 1982), 56–67. On attempts to regulate baptism through required paperwork, see GARF, f. R-6991, op. 6, d. 470, l. 219, Commissioner of Religious Affairs Savel'ev's report on the state of religiosity and control over the observance of the law on religious cult in the Gornomari district, Mari ASSR, March 1972.

51. Stoler, *Along the Archival Grain*, 45.

52. Guha, "The Prose of Counter-Insurgency"; Carlo Ginzburg, *The Cheese and the Worms: The Cosmos of a Sixteenth-Century Miller*, transl. Anne and John Tedeschi (Baltimore: Johns Hopkins University Press, 1980).

53. Davis, *Fiction in the Archives*.

54. Gayatri Chakravorty Spivak, "Can the Subaltern Speak?" in *Marxism and the Interpretation of Culture*, ed. Cary Nelson and Lawrence Grossberg (Urbana: University of Illinois Press, 1988), 271–313; Irene Silverblatt, "New Christians and New World Fears in Seventeenth-Century Peru," in *From the Margins: Historical Anthropology and its Futures,* ed. Brian Keith Axel (Durham, NC: Duke University Press, 2002), 95–121; Ann Laura Stoler, *Race and the Education of Desire: Foucault's History of Sexuality and the Colonial Order of Things* (Durham, NC: Duke University Press, 1995).

55. Boris V. Ananich, "The Historian and the Source: Problems of Reliability and Ethics," in *Archives, Documentation, and Institutions of Social Memory*, ed. William Rosenberg and Francis Blouin (Ann Arbor: University of Michigan Press, 2006), 490–96; Jörg Barberowski, "Arbeit an der Geschichte: Vom Umgang mit den Archiven," *Jahrbücher für Geschichte Osteuropas* 51:1(2003): 36–56; Stephen Kotkin, "The State—Is It Us? Memoirs, Archives, and Kremlinologists," *Russian Review* 61:1 (2002): 35–51; Donald J. Raleigh, "Doing Soviet History: The Impact of the Archival Revolution," *Russian Review,* 61:1 (2002): 16–24.

56. The degree to which the Soviet Union can and should be compared to colonial or dynastic empires is a matter of ongoing debate. For different takes on the issue that all emphasize the way in which Soviet policies aimed to eradicate key social and educational differences between

groups, see Terry Martin, *The Affirmative Action Empire: Nations and Nationalism in the Soviet Union, 1923–1939* (Ithaca: Cornell University Press, 2001); Northrop, *Veiled Empire*; Adeeb Khalid, "Backwardness and the Quest for Civilization: Early Soviet Central Asia in Comparative Perspective," *Slavic Review* 65:2 (2006): 231–51.

57. Sheila Fitzpatrick, "Signals from Below: Soviet Letters of Denunciation of the 1930s," *Journal of Modern History* 68:4 (1996): 831–66; Igal Halfin, "Poetics in the Archives: The Quest for 'True' Bolshevik Documents," *Jahrbücher für Geschichte Osteuropas* 51:1(2003): 84–89, *Red Autobiographies: Initiating the Bolshevik Self* (Seattle: University of Washington Press, 2011); Jochen Hellbeck, *Revolution on My Mind: Writing a Diary under Stalin* (Cambridge, MA: Harvard University Press, 2006); Miriam Dobson, "Letters," in *Reading Primary Sources: The Interpretation of Texts from Nineteenth- and Twentieth-Century History*, ed. Miriam Dobson and Benjamin Ziemann (London: Routledge, 2009), 57–73.

58. Verdery, *Secrets and Truth*, 40.

59. Sonja Luehrmann, "Antagonistic Insights: Evolving Soviet Atheist Critiques of Religion and Why They Matter for Anthropology," *Social Analysis*, forthcoming; Marianne Kamp, *The New Woman in Uzbekistan: Islam, Modernity, and Unveiling under Communism* (Seattle: University of Washington Press, 2006).

60. Stoler, *Along the Archival Grain*; Burns, *Into the Archive*; Francis Blouin Jr. and William Rosenberg, *Processing the Past: Contesting Authority in History and the Archives* (New York: Oxford University Press, 2011).

61. John Austin, *How to Do Things with Words* (New York: Oxford University Press, 1965); Blouin and Rosenberg, *Processing the Past*, chapter 8. On the role of the circulation of files for the agency of administrative bureaucracies, see Matthew Hull, "The File: Agency, Authority, and Autography in an Islamabad Bureaucracy," *Language and Communication* 23:3–4 (2003): 287–314; Terry Martin, "Interpreting the New Archival Signals: Nationalities Policy and the Nature of the Soviet Bureaucracy," *Cahiers du monde russe* 40:1–2 (1999): 113–24.

62. Benjamin Ziemann and Miriam Dobson, "Introduction," in *Reading Primary Sources: The Interpretation of Texts from Nineteenth- and Twentieth-Century History*, ed. Miriam Dobson and Benjamin Ziemann (London: Routledge, 2009), 1–18, quote p. 11.

63. Bruce Grant, "Shrines and Sovereigns: Life, Death, and Religion in Rural Azerbaidjan," *Comparative Studies in Society and History* 53:3 (2011): 654–81.

64. Sonja Luehrmann, "The Spirit of Late Socialism and the Value of Transformation: Brezhnevism through the Lens of Post-Soviet Religious Revival," *Cahiers du monde russe* 55:3–4 (2013): 543–64.

65. Ananich, "The Historian and the Source"; Cristina Vatulescu, *Police Aesthetics: Literature, Film, and the Secret Police in Soviet Times* (Stanford, CA: Stanford University Press, 2010), 14; Verdery, *Secrets and Truth*, 51–52; Stoler, *Along the Archival Grain*, 186.

66. Laura Engelstein, "The Archives Talk Back: Unofficial Collections in Imperial, Soviet and Post-Soviet Russia," *Jahrbücher für Geschichte Osteuropas* 51:1 (2003): 70–76; Douglas Rogers, *The Old Faith and the Russian Land. A Historical Ethnography of Ethics in the Urals* (Ithaca, NY: Cornell University Press, 2009), 165–73.

67. Laura Engelstein, *Castration and the Heavenly Kingdom: A Russian Folktale* (Ithaca, NY: Cornell University Press, 2003).

68. For studies that use secret police files from Ukraine, see Baran, *Dissent on the Margins*; Sergei Zhuk, *Rock and Roll in the Rocket City: The West, Identity, and Ideology in Soviet Dniepropetrovsk, 1960–1985* (Baltimore, MD: Johns Hopkins University Press, 2010). On an unsuccessful attempt to get access to Russian KGB files relating to post-war religious life, see Huhn, *Glaube und Eigensinn*, 24–25.

69. Peter Holquist, " 'Information is the Alpha and Omega of Our Work': Bolshevik Surveillance in Its Pan-European Perspective," *Journal of Modern History* 69:3 (1997): 415–50.

70. Andreas Kappeler, *Russlands erste Nationalitäten: Das Zarenreich und die Völker der mittleren Volga vom 16. bis 19. Jahrhundert* (Cologne: Böhlau, 1982); Robert Geraci, *Window on the East: National and Imperial Identities in Late Tsarist Russia* (Ithaca, NY: Cornell University Press, 2001); Paul Werth, *At the Margins of Orthodoxy: Mission, Governance, and Confessional Politics in Russia's Volga-Kama Region, 1827–1905* (Ithaca, NY: Cornell University Press, 2002).

71. Sonja Luehrmann, "A Multireligious Region in an Atheist State: Unionwide Policies Meet Communal Distinctions in the Postwar Mari Republic," in *State Secularism and Lived Religion in Soviet Russia and Ukraine*, ed. Catherine Wanner (New York: Oxford University Press, 2012), 272–301; Boris Kolymagin, *Krymskaia ekumena: Religioznaia zhizn' poslevoennogo Kryma* (St. Petersburg: Aleteiia, 2004).

72. A study that uses Communist Party archives extensively to look at the evolution of Soviet atheist ideology over time is Victoria Smolkin-Rothrock, "A Sacred Space Is Never Empty: Soviet Atheism, 1954–1971." Ph.D. dissertation, University of California, Berkeley, 2010.

73. Luehrmann, *Secularism Soviet Style*.

74. Arjun Appadurai, "The Past as a Scarce Resource," *Man*, n.s., 16:2 (1981): 201–19.

75. Tat'iana Khorkhordina and Tamara Volkova, *Rossiiskie arkhivy: Istoriia i sovremennost'* (Moscow: Izdatel'stvo RGGU, 2012), 214.

76. Il'ia Viktorovich Semenenko-Basin, *Sviatost' v russkoi pravoslavnoi kul'ture XX veka: istoriia personifikatsii* (Moscow: RGGU, 2010).

77. See Gail Kligman and Katherine Verdery, *Peasants under Siege: The Collectivization of Romanian Agriculture, 1949–1962* (Princeton, NJ: Princeton University Press, 2011); Marianne Kamp, *The New Woman in Uzbekistan*; Catherine Wanner, *Communities of the Converted: Ukrainians and Global Evangelism* (Ithaca, NJ: Cornell University Press, 2007). For an approach that adds visual sources into the mix, see Campbell, *Agitating Images*.

78. Guha, "The Prose of Counter-Insurgency," 70.

79. Paul Eiss, "Notes on the Difficulty of Studying *El Pueblo*," in *Anthrohistory: Unsettling Knowledge, Questioning Discipline*, ed. Edward Murphy et al. (Ann Arbor: University of Michigan Press, 2011), 37–47. On the controversial values of change and tradition in the Soviet Union, see Yuri Slezkine, *The Jewish Century* (Princeton, NJ: Princeton University Press, 2004); Bruce Grant, *In the Soviet House of Culture: A Century of Perestroikas* (Princeton, NJ: Princeton University Press, 1995); Sheila Fitzpatrick, *Education and Social Mobility in the Soviet Union, 1921–1934* (Cambridge: Cambridge University Press, 1979).

80. Winnifred Sullivan, *The Impossibility of Religious Freedom* (Princeton, NJ: Princeton University Press, 2007); Wendy Brown, *Regulating Aversion: Tolerance in the Age of Identity and Empire* (Princeton, NJ: Princeton University Press, 2008).

81. For the former Soviet Union, see Adeeb Khalid, *Islam after Communism: Religion and Politics in Central Asia* (Berkeley: University of California Press, 2007); Irina Papkova, *The Orthodox Church and Russian Politics* (New York: Oxford University Press, 2011); Anya Bernstein, "An Inadvertent Sacrifice: Body Politics and Sovereign Power in the Pussy Riot Affair," *Critical Inquiry* 40:1 (2013): 220–41.

Chapter 1: Documentary Acts

1. National Archive of the Republic of Tatarstan (NART), f. R-873, op. 1, d. 11, l. 159, Letter dated July 7, 1964.

2. Jack Goody, *The Logic of Writing and the Organization of Society* (Cambridge: Cambridge University Press, 1986); Ian Hacking, *The Taming of Chance* (Cambridge: Cambridge University Press, 1990); Jacques Derrida, *Archive Fever: A Freudian Impression* (Chicago: University of Chicago Press, 1996), 2.

3. NART, f. R-873, op. 1, d. 11, l. 55, Letter from the head of the archival section of the Council of Ministers of the Tatar ASSR to Mangutkin, May 31, 1962. On the intellectual cultures of twentieth-century Muslims in the Volga region, see Taufik Ibragim, Farit Sultanov, and Aidar Iuzeev, *Tatarskaia religiozno-filosofskaia mysl' v obshchemusul'manskom kontekste* (Kazan: Tatarskoe knizhnoe izdatel'stvo, 2002); Il'nur Minnullin, *Musul'manskoe dukhovenstvo i vlast' v Tatarstane (1920–1930e gg.)* (Kazan: Akademiia nauk Respubliki Tatarstan, 2006).

4. Museum collections created in the context of colonial expansion and under the paradigm of "salvage ethnography" can have a similarly ambiguous role even for the descendants of those who made the objects. See Ann Fienup-Riordan, *Yup'ik Elders in the Ethnologisches Museum Berlin: Fieldwork Turned on Its Head* (Seattle: University of Washington Press, 2005).

5. A number of relics and cult buildings were returned to religious groups across the former Soviet Union based on archival documents of the expropriations of the 1920s and '30s. See John and Carol Garrard, *Russian Orthodoxy Resurgent: Faith and Power in the New Russia* (Princeton, NJ: Princeton University Press, 2008); Vlad Naumescu, *Modes of Religiosity in Eastern Christianity: Religious Processes and Social Change in Ukraine* (Berlin: Lit, 2007).

6. On the archivist as historical actor or even activist, see Francis Blouin Jr. and William Rosenberg, *Processing the Past: Contesting Authority in History and the Archives* (New York: Oxford University Press, 2011), 141–43.

7. Matthew Hull, *Government of Paper: The Materiality of Bureaucracy in Urban Pakistan* (Berkeley: University of California Press, 2012), 23.

8. Laura Engelstein, "The Archives Talk Back: Unofficial Collections in Imperial, Soviet and Post-Soviet Russia," *Jahrbücher für Geschichte Osteuropas* 51:1 (2003): 70–76.

9. William Husband, *"Godless Communists": Atheism and Society in Soviet Russia, 1917–1932* (DeKalb: Northern Illinois University Press, 2000), 54–55.

10. Boris Kolymagin, *Krymskaia ekumena: Religioznaia zhizn' poslevoennogo Kryma* (St. Petersburg: Aleteiia, 2004), 15; Tatiana Chumachenko, *Church and State in Soviet Russia: Russian Orthodoxy from World War II to the Khrushchev Years* (Armonk, NY: Sharpe, 2002), 24–25.

11. Kolymagin, *Krymskaia ekumena,* 9.

12. Chumachenko, *Church and State*; Mikhail V. Shkarovskii, *Russkaia pravoslavnaia tserkov' i sovetskoe gosudarstvo v 1943-1964 gg.: ot peremiriia k novoi voine* (St. Petersburg: DEAN-ADIA-M, 1995).

13. Yaacov Ro'i, *Islam in the Soviet Union: From the Second World War to Gorbachev* (New York: Columbia University Press, 2000), 5; Nataliia Shlikhta, "Ot traditsii k sovremennosti: Pravoslavnaia obriadnost' i prazdniki v usloviiakh antireligioznoi bor'by (na materialakh USSR, 1950e-1960e gody)," *Gosudarstvo, Religiia, Tserkov'* 30:3–4 (2012): 379–406.

14. Sonja Luehrmann, "The Spirit of Late Socialism and the Value of Transformation: Brezhnevism through the Lens of Post-Soviet Religious Revival," *Cahiers du monde russe* 54:3-4 (2013): 543–64; Sergei Shtyrkov, "Prakticheskoe religiovedenie vremen Nikity Khrushcheva: respublikanskaia gazeta v bor'be s 'religioznymi perezhitkami' (na primere Severo-Osetinskoi ASSR)," in *Traditsii narodov Kavkaza v meniaiushchemsia mire: Preemstvennost' i razryvy v sotsiokul'turnykh praktikakh*, ed. Iurii Karpov (St. Petersburg: Peterburgskoe Vostokovedenie, 2010), 306–43.

15. Aleksei Beglov, *V poiskakh bezgreshnykh katakomb: Tserkovnoe podpol'e v SSSR* (Moscow: Arefa, 2008); Robert H. Greene, *Bodies like Bright Stars: Saints and Relics in Orthodox Russia* (DeKalb: Northern Illinois University Press, 2010); Catherine Wanner, ed., *State Secularism and Lived Religion in Russia and Ukraine* (New York: Oxford University Press, 2012); Emily Baran, *Dissent on the Margins: How Soviet Jehovah's Witnesses Defied Communism and Lived to Preach about It* (New York: Oxford University Press, 2014); Ulrike Huhn, *Glaube und Eigensinn: Volksfrömmigkeit zwischen orthodoxer Kirche und sowjetischem Staat 1941 bis 1960* (Wiesbaden: Harrassowitz, 2014). On the tendency to read vignettes in colonial archives as more immediately truthful accounts than aggregate judgments and statistics, see Ann Laura Stoler, *Along the Archival Grain: Epistemic Anxieties and Colonial Common Sense* (Princeton, NJ: Princeton University Press, 2009), 142.

16. Natalie Zemon Davis, *Fiction in the Archives: Pardon Tales and Their Tellers in Sixteenth-Century France* (Stanford, CA: Stanford University Press, 1987); Kathryn Burns, *Into the Archive: Writing and Power in Colonial Peru* (Durham, NC: Duke University Press, 2010); Stoler, *Along the Archival Grain*; Hull, *Government of Paper*; Katherine Verdery, *Secrets and Truth: Ethnography in the Archive of Romania's Secret Police* (Budapest: Central European University Press, 2014).

17. Cristina Vatulescu, *Police Aesthetics: Literature, Film and the Secret Police in Soviet Times* (Stanford, CA: Stanford University Press, 2010); Sheila Fitzpatrick, "Supplicants and Citizens: Public Letter-Writing in Soviet Russia in the 1930s," *Slavic Review* 55:1 (1996): 78–105.

18. Annelise Riles, ed., *Documents: Artifacts of Modern Knowledge* (Ann Arbor: University of Michigan Press, 2006).

19. John Austin, *How to Do Things with Words* (New York: Oxford University Press, 1965), 14–15.

20. Austin, *How to Do Things with Words*, 60.

21. Austin calls the things that can go wrong and invalidate a speech act "infelicities." Creating a more positive term, the sociologist Erving Goffman speaks of "felicity conditions" to describe the conditions under which a speech act is valid. Erving Goffman, "Felicity's Condition," *American Journal of Sociology* 89:1 (1983): 1–53.

22. Elena Zhidkova, "Sovetskaia grazhdanskaia obriadnost' kak al'ternativa obriadnosti religioznoi," *Gosudarstvo, Religiia, Tserkov'* 30:3-4 (2012): 407–28, esp. 422–23; "Sotsialisticheskoe pereustroistvo byta i bor'ba za novye traditsii," lecture typescript circulated by the All-Union Knowledge Society, on file at the Russian State Library, Moscow. On the symbolic load of the party membership card in the 1930s, see Vatulescu, *Police Aesthetics*, 103–8. On acts of signing and writing in bureaucratic form as moments where citizenship is performed and recognized, see Francis Cody, *The Light of Knowledge: Literacy Activism and the Politics of Writing in South India* (Ithaca, NY: Cornell University Press, 2013).

23. Verdery, *Secrets and Truth*, 66.

24. Paul Werth, "In the State's Embrace? Civil Acts in an Imperial Order," *Kritika* 7:3 (2006): 433–58; Jan Plamper, "Archival Revolution or Illusion? Historicizing Russian Archives and Our Work in Them," *Jahrbücher für Geschichte Osteuropas* 51:1 (2003): 57–69.

25. Tat'iana Khorkhordina and Tamara Volkova, *Rossiiskie arkhivy: istoriia i sovremennost'* (Moscow: Rossiiskii Gosudarstvennyi Gumanitarnyi Universitet, 2012), 59–60.

26. E. V. Isakova and Mikhail V. Shkarovskii, *Voskresenskii Novodevichii Monastyr'*, ed. Igumenia Sofiia [Silina] (St. Petersburg: Art Deko, 2007), 121–31; Scott Kenworthy, *The Heart of Russia: Trinity-Sergius, Monasticism, and Society after 1825* (New York: Oxford University Press, 2010), 307; Georgii Mitrofanov, *Istoriia Russkoi Pravoslavnoi Tserkvi, 1900–1927* (Moscow: Novoe literaturnoe obozrenie, 2002), 208–211.

27. Greene, *Bodies like Bright Stars*; Husband, *"Godless Communists,"* 55–57; Huhn, *Glaube und Eigensinn*, 130.

28. NART, f. 873, op. 1, d. 11, l. 59.

29. The actual Tatar form would be Mikael kyzy Khanifa. On the politics of Russianizing Tatar names in the Soviet Union, see Helen

Faller, *Nation, Language, Islam: Tatarstan's Sovereignty Movement* (Budapest: Central European University Press, 2011).

30. Sheila Fitzpatrick, *Tear off the Masks! Identity and Imposture in Twentieth-Century Russia* (Princeton, NJ: Princeton University Press, 2005); Jochen Hellbeck, *Revolution on My Mind: Writing a Diary under Stalin* (Cambridge, MA: Harvard University Press, 2006).

31. NART, f. 873, op. 1, d. 11, l. 59. Caps in the original.

32. NART, f. R-873, op. 1, d. 7, l. 46, Act No 4, July 13, 1951.

33. On secrecy as an end in itself in secret police records, see Verdery, *Secrets and Truths*, 83–88.

34. On learning to read files of socialist bureaucracies through attention to genre, see Vatulescu, *Police Aesthetics*, 35–36; Caroline Humphrey, *Marx Went Away but Karl Stayed Behind* (Ann Arbor: University of Michigan Press, 1998), 113–14.

35. Mikhail Bakhtin, "Problema rechevykh zhanrov," in *Sobranie sochinenii*, vol. 5 (Moscow: Russkie slovari, 1996), 159–206.

36. For example, the files of the commissioner in Kazan contain a letter addressed to the council in Moscow from Tatar villagers in Tetiushi district asking for the opening of a mosque. The letter-writers complain that two previous petitions were forwarded to Kazan and to the local rural council, where they had been told from the start that their cause was hopeless (NART, f-873, op. 1, d. 10, l. 40, Letter from representatives of the religious community of Tatar-Muslims in Bol'shie Tarkhany to the Council for Religious Cult Affairs, August 2, 1961). For a similar forwarding pattern in another regional archive see State Archive of the Republic of Marii El (GARME), f. R-836, op. 1, d. 3, l. 264–65, Letter from believing citizens of the city of Ioshkar-Ola to Nikita Khrushchev protesting the closing of the Church of the Resurrection, December 23, 1960; GARME, f. R-836, op. 2, d. 18, l. 5–11, Letter from residents of Ioshkar-Ola to the chairman of the Council of Ministers of the USSR asking for the reopening of the Church of the Ascension, December 21, 1972.

37. On different ways of interpreting provenance in archival practice, see Terry Cook, "The Concept of the Archival Fonds in the Post-Custodial Era: Theory, Problems and Solutions," *Archivaria* 35 (1993): 24–37.

38. NART, f. R-873, op. 1, d. 4, l. 1–1v.

39. NART, f. R-873, op. 1, d. l. 31–32v, Act of October 18, 1949.

40. NART, f. R-873, op. 1, d. 8, l. 22, Head of the archival sector of the the Council of Ministers of the Tatar ASSR to the Commissioner of Religious Cult Affairs, March 24, 1962.

41. Aleksei Zhamkov, "Sovet po delam religii: stranitsy proshlogo." Interview with Vladimir Pudov, *Bogoslov.ru* (November 16, 2009), http://www.bogoslov.ru/text/498829.html (accessed June 17, 2013); Aleksandr Balyberdin, *Bezumie: Khrushchevskie goneniia na Viatskoi zemle* (Viatka: Bukvitsa, 2006), 22–23.

42. Ro'i, *Islam in the Soviet Union*, 2.

43. NART, f. R-873, op. 1, d. 7, l. 93, Letter from Mangutkin to Council Chairman Puzin, n.d. [spring 1963].

44. DUMS (*Dukhovnoe upravlenie musul'man Sibiri*—Spiritual directorate of the Muslims of Siberia) was the official governing organ of Soviet Muslims outside of Central Asia and the Causasus, created by government decree in 1944. The mufti of Ufa headed this board. Ro'i, *Islam in the Soviet Union,* 100–102.

45. Hull, *Government of Paper,* 138–40; Yoram Gorlizki and Oleg Khlevniuk, *Cold Peace: Stalin and the Soviet Ruling Circle, 1945–1953* (New York: Oxford University Press, 2004), 50.

46. NART, f. 873, op. 1, d. 9, January 1952 to April 1966, 15 sheets of paper.

47. NART, f. 873, op. 1, d. 9, l. 4–5, Letter from Commissioner Endakov (Rostov) to Mangutkin, January 14, 1963.

48. Raufa Urazmanova, "'Musul'manskie' obriady v bytu tatar," *Etnograficheskoe obozrenie* 1 (2009): 13–26.

49. NART, f. 873, op. 1, d. 9, l. 10, Undated letter from Mangutkin to the Commissioner for the Bashkir ASSR Arduanov.

50. NART, f. 873, op. 1, d. 10, October 1960 to December 1964, 151 sheets of paper.

51. NART, f. 873, op. 1, d. 10, l. 110–119, Two identical letters from Muslim believers of Kazan to the Council of Religious Cult Affairs and the Council of Ministers of the Tatar ASSR, April 10, 1963.

52. NART, f. 873, op. 1, d. 10, l. 110.

53. NART, f. 873, op. 1, d. 10, l. 141, Letter from Kazan Muslims to Leonid Il'ich Brezhnev, April 28, 1964.

54. NART, f. 873, op. 1, d. 10, l. 142, "Zhuliki v chalmakh," *Molodezh' Tatarii* 33, March 17, 1964.

55. NART, f. 873, op. 1, d. 10, l. 130, Letter from the Council of Religious Cult Affairs to Mangutkin, April 29, 1964, with handwritten note dated July 2, 1964.

56. Gorlizki and Khlevniuk, *Cold Peace*, 63; Oleg Khlevniuk, *Master of the House: Stalin and His Inner Circle* (New Haven, CT: Yale University Press, 2009), xxvi; Yoram Gorlizki, "Political Reform and Local Party Interventions under Khrushchev," in *Reforming Justice in Russia,*

1864–1996: Power, Culture, and the Limits of the Legal Order, ed. Peter H. Solomon (Armonk, NY: M. E. Sharpe, 1997), 256–81.

57. NART, f. 873, op. 1, d. 10, l. 66–67, Letter from Mufti Khialetdinov to Mangutkin, April 5, 1963.

58. On the police file as a composite biographical narrative, see Vatulescu, *Police Aesthetics,* 34–36.

59. NART, f. R-873, op. 1, d. 11, Materials of the Commissioner for Religious Cult Affairs relating to correspondence with local organs, February 1961 to April 1966, 215 sheets of paper.

60. NART, f. R-873, op. 1, d. 11, l. 74, Letter from Mangutkin to the head of the Organizational Department, March 26, 1963.

61. NART, f. R-873, op. 1, d. 11, l. 76, copy of a letter from Mangutkin to the Department of International Relations of the Muslim organizations of the USSR, n.d. [April 1963].

62. NART, f. R-873, op. 1, d. 11, l. 101, Letter from the chief of the Privolzhskii district police to Mangutkin, April 22, 1963.

63. NART, f. R-873, op. 1, d. 11, l. 135–36, Letter from Mangutkin to the chair of the Privolzhskii district executive committee, July 6, 1963.

64. NART, f. R-873, op. 1, d. 11, l. 139, Letter from Mangutkin to the cChair of the Sovietskii district executive committee, October 16, 1963.

65. Ann Laura Stoler, "Rethinking Colonial Categories: European Communities and the Boundaries of Rule," *Comparative Studies in Society and History* 31:1 (1989): 134–61; Patricia Galloway, "Introduction: How Deep Is (Ethno-)History? Archives, Written History, Oral Tradition," in her *Practicing Ethnohistory: Mining Archives, Hearing Testimony, Constructing Narrative* (Lincoln: University of Nebraska Press, 2006), 1–30.

66. Ro'i, *Islam in the Soviet Union,* 2.

67. A. P. Barinskaia and V.I. Savel'ev, *Sovetskoe zakonodatel'stvo o religioznykh kul'takh* (Ioshkar-Ola: Mariiskoe knizhnoe izdatel'stvo, 1973); Lucian Leustean, ed, *Eastern Christianity and the Cold War* (London: Routledge, 2010).

68. NART, f. R-873, op. 1, d. 10, l. 21, Decision of the Kazan city council of August 17, 1960.

69. Humphrey, *Marx Went Away,* 215; Katherine Verdery, *What Was Socialism and What Comes Next?* (Princeton, NJ: Princeton University Press, 1996).

70. NART, f. R-873, op. 1, d. 13, l. 102, Letter by commissioner for Russian Orthodox Church affairs Mikhalev to the head of the instructional division of the Council of Ministers of the Tatar ASSR, March 13, 1965.

71. NART, f. R-873, op. 1, d. 13, l. 26–27, Decision of the Bauman district executive committee, Kazan, April 7, 1964.

72. NART, f. R-873, op. 1, d. 13, l. 42, *Akt* signed by the candle seller and members of the executive organ of St Nicholas Cathedral, Kazan, November 19, 1964.

73. Gregory Grossman, "The 'Second Economy' of the USSR," *Problems of Communism,* 26:5 (1977): 25–40.

74. NART, f. R-873, op. 1, d. 15, l. 19, Chair of the Council of Ministers to the head of the Oktiabrskii district committee, November 21, 1964. On the ritual and economic significance of in-kind donations to Orthodox churches, see Douglas Rogers, *The Old Faith and the Russian Land: A Historical Ethnography of Ethics in the Urals* (Ithaca, NY: Cornell University Press, 2009); Detelina Tolcheva, "An Ethos of Relatedness: Foreign Aid and Grassroots Charities in Two Orthodox Parishes in North-Western Russia," in *Multiple Moralities and Religions in Post-Soviet Russia,* ed. Jarrett Zigon (New York: Berghahn, 2011), 67–91.

75. NART, f. R-873, op. 1, d. 62, l. 50a, Summary of a conversation with G. G. Zinatullin, May 27, 1974.

76. Ro'i, *Islam in the Soviet Union,* 161–63.

77. NART, f. R-873, op. 1, d. 17, Commissioner Mikhalev to the commissioner for the Latvian SSR Sakharov, January 31, 1966.

78. Adeeb Khalid, *Islam after Communism: Religion and Politics in Central Asia* (Berkeley: University of California Press, 2007); Catriona Kelly, "From 'counter-revolutionary monuments' to 'national heritage': The preservation of Leningrad churches, 1964-1982," *Cahiers du monde russe* 54:1-2 (2013): 131–64.

79. On such processes of inversion and compartmentalization of religious practice within secularizing societies, see Hans-Joachim Höhn, *Postsäkular: Gesellschaft im Umbruch, Religion im Wandel* (Paderborn: Schöningh, 2007).

Chapter 2: Mirrored Fragments

1. On the creative bookkeeping practices of Soviet collective farms, see Caroline Humphrey, *Marx Went Away, but Karl Stayed Behind* (Ann Arbor: University of Michigan Press, 1998), 215. On the ideas of witchcraft referenced in this anecdote, see Sonja Luehrmann, "The Magic of Others: Mari Witchcraft Reputations and Inter-ethnic Relations in the Volga Region," *Russian History* 40:3–4 (2013): 469–87.

2. David Ransel, *Village Mothers: Three Generations of Change in Russia and Tataria* (Bloomington: Indiana University Press, 2000); Donald Raleigh, *Russia's Sputnik Generation: Soviet Baby Boomers Talk about Their Lives* (Bloomington: Indiana University Press, 2006), Raleigh, *Soviet Baby Boomers: An Oral History of Russia's Cold War Generation* (New York: Oxford University Press, 2012); Anke Stephan and Julia Obertreis, eds., *Oral History und (post)sozialistische Gesellschaften* (Essen: Klartext, 2009). For work that combines oral and archival history and crosses the temporal divide between periods for which archives are accessible and those for which they are not, see Douglas Rogers, *The Old Faith and the Russian Land: An Historical Ethnography of Ethics in the Urals* (Ithaca, NY: Cornell University Press, 2009); Catherine Wanner, *Communities of the Converted: Ukrainians and Global Evangelism* (Ithaca, NY: Cornell University Press, 2007); and the project "From the Kolkhoz to the Djamaat: The Politicization of Islam in Rural Communities of the Former USSR, 1950s–2000s," directed by Christian Noack and Stéphane Dudoignon, www. uni-bielefeld.de/geschichte/abteilung/FlyerBerlin-1.pdf.

3. This division formed part of the original impulse of the oral history movement in Western Europe and North America, which set out to gather the voices of those excluded from official histories, such as workers and women. See Lutz Niethammer and Wilhelm Trapp, *Lebenserfahrung und kollektives Gedächtnis: Die Praxis der Oral History* (Frankfurt: Syndikat, 1980); Jacques LeGoff, *Histoire et mémoire* (Paris: Gallimard, 1988).

4. Ann Stoler and Karen Strassler, "Castings for the Colonial: Memory Work in 'New Order' Java," *Comparative Studies in Society and History* 42:1 (2000): 4–48; Rudolf Mrázek, *A Certain Age: Colonial Jakarta through the Memories of Its Intellectuals* (Durham, NC: Duke University Press, 2010).

5. Karen E. Rosenblum, "The In-Depth Interview: Between Science and Sociability," *Sociological Forum* 2:2 (1987): 388–400; Julie Cruikshank, *The Social Life of Stories: Narrative and Knowledge in the Yukon* (Lincoln: University of Nebraska Press, 1998); Marianne Kamp, "Three Lives of Saodat: Communist, Uzbek, Survivor," *Oral History Review* 28:2 (Summer/Fall) (2001): 28–51.

6. Leslie Robertson and the Kwagu'ł Gixsam Clan, *Standing Up with Ga'axsta'las: Jane Constance Cook and the Politics of Memory, Church, and Custom* (Vancouver: University of British Columbia Press, 2012).

7. Sonja Luehrmann, "Recycling Cultural Construction: Desecularisation in Post-Soviet Mari El," *Religion, State and Society* 33:1 (2005): 35–56; Mathijs Pelkmans, ed., *Conversion after Socialism: Disruptions, Modernism,*

and Technologies of Faith in the Former Soviet Union (New York: Berghahn, 2009); Justine Quijada, "What if We Don't Know Our Clan? The City Tailgan as New Ritual Form in Buriatiia," *Sibirica* 7:1 (2008): 1–22; Wanner, *Communities of the Converted*.

8. Sonja Luehrmann, *Secularism Soviet Style: Teaching Atheism and Religion in a Volga Republic* (Bloomington: Indiana University Press, 2011), 39. On similar processes of the interpenetration of official accounts and personal narratives, see Daniela Koleva, "Memories of the War and the War of Memories in Post-Communist Bulgaria," *Oral History* 34:2 (2006): 44–55; Andrea Zemskov-Züge, "Narrating the Siege of Leningrad. Official and Unofficial Practices in the Memorialization of the 'Great Patriotic War,'" in *Unsettling History: Archiving and Narrating in Historiography*, ed. Alf Lüdtke and Sebastian Jobs (Frankfurt: Campus, 2010), 199–217.

9. Rubie Watson, "Memory, History, and Opposition under State Socialism: An Introduction," in *Memory, History, and Opposition under State Socialism*, ed. Rubie Watson (Santa Fe: School of American Research Press, 1994), 1–20.

10. The term "emplotment" comes to historiography through Hayden White, *Metahistory: The Historical Imagination in Nineteenth-Century Europe* (Baltimore: Johns Hopkins University Press, 1975). On applying it to the reading of archival documents, see Ziemann and Dobson, "Introduction," 10–11.

11. On the narrative structures imposed by printed forms and charts, see Adam Reed, "Documents Unfolding," in *Documents: Artifacts of Modern Knowledge*, ed. Annelise Riles (Ann Arbor: University of Michigan Press, 2006), 158–77. On witchcraft accusations as commentaries on competitive social relations, see Harry West, "Who Rules Us Now? Identity Tokens, Sorcery, and Other Metaphors in the 1994 Mozambican Elections," in *Transparency and Conspiracy: Ethnographies of Suspicion in the New World Order*, ed. Harry West and Todd Sanders (Durham, NC: Duke University Press, 2003), 92–124.

12. The term "hidden transcripts" comes from James Scott, *Domination and the Arts of Resistance: Hidden Transcripts* (New Haven, CT: Yale University Press, 1992). For a critique that advocates against assuming clear distinctions between dominant and subaltern discourses, see Susan Gal, "Language and the 'Arts of Resistance'," *Cultural Anthropology* 10(3), 1995: 407–424.

13. David William Cohen and E. S. Atieno Odhiambo, *The Risks of Knowledge: Investigations into the Death of the Hon. Minister John Robert Ouko in Kenia, 1990* (Athens: Ohio University Press, 2004); Douglas Northrop, *Veiled Empire: Gender and Power in Stalinist Central Asia* (Ithaca, NY: Cornell University Press, 2004), 139–63.

14. GARF, f. R-6991, op. 6, d. 80, ll. 224–28. Report on a visit to Zvenigovo district, August 28, 1967.
15. GARF, f. R-6991, op. 6, d. 80, l. 224.
16. Tatiana Chumachenko, *Church and State in Soviet Russia: Russian Orthodoxy from World War II to the Khrushchev Years* (Armonk, NY: Sharpe, 2002), 161; Sonja Luehrmann, "A Multi-Religious Region in an Atheist State: Unionwide Policies Meet Communal Distinctions in the Post-War Mari Republic," in *State Secularism and Lived Religion in Soviet Russia and Ukraine*, ed. C. Wanner (New York: Oxford University Press, 2012), 272–301.
17. GARF, f. R-6991, op. 6, d. 80, l. 224.
18. GARF, f. R-6991, op. 6, d. 80, l. 225.
19. Wanner, *Communities of the Converted*, 63–66.
20. See, for example, a memorandum from Council Chairman Puzin sent to all commissioners in June 1965, which was entitled "On Some Facts of Violation of Socialist Legality in Relation to Believers," but ask for reports on violations committed *by* religious believers, most notably by "schismatic Baptists." GARF, f. R-6991, op. 4, d. 170, l. 14a.
21. GARF, f. R-6991, op. 6, d. 80, l. 225–26.
22. Valentin Voloshinov, *Marxism and the Philosophy of Language*, trans. Ladislav Matejka and I.R. Titunik (New York: Seminar Press, 1973); Mikhail Bakhtin, "Epic and Novel: Toward a Methodology for the Study of the Novel," in *The Dialogic Imagination: Four Essays*, by M. M. Bakhtin, ed. Michael Holquist (Austin: University of Texas Press, 1981), 4–40.
23. Sergei Shtyrkov, "Prakticheskoe religiovedenie vremen Nikity Khrushcheva: respublikanskaia gazeta v bor'be s 'religioznymi perezhitkami' (na primere Severo-Osetinskoi ASSR)," in *Traditsii narodov Kavkaza v meniaiushchemsia mire: Preemstvennost' i razryvy v sotsiokul'turnykh praktikakh*, ed. Iurii Karpov (St. Petersburg: Peterburgskoe Vostokovedenie, 2010), 306–43.
24. Heather Coleman, *Russian Baptists and Spiritual Revolution, 1905–1929* (Bloomington: Indiana University Press, 2005); Miriam Dobson, "Child Sacrifice in the Soviet Press: Sensationalism and the 'Sectarian' in the Post-Stalin Era," *Russian Review* 73:2 (2014): 237–59.
25. Voloshinov, *Marxism and the Philosophy of Language*, 116.
26. Alexei Yurchak, *Everything Was Forever until It Was No More: The Last Soviet Generation* (Princeton, NJ: Princeton University Press, 2006); Dominic Boyer and Alexei Yurchak, "American Stiob: Or, What Late-Socialist Aesthetics of Parody Reveal about Contemporary

Political Culture in the West," *Cultural Anthropology* 25:2 (2010): 179–221.

27. Voloshinov, *Marxism and the Philosophy of Language*, 116.

28. Marianne Kamp, *The New Woman in Uzbekistan: Islam, Modernity, and Unveiling under Communism* (Seattle: University of Washington Press, 2006), 6.

29. Raleigh, *Soviet Baby Boomers*, 42–44.

30. Raleigh, *Russia's Sputnik Generation*, 74.

31. Raleigh, *Soviet Baby Boomers*, 42.

32. Nikandr Popov, "Na mariiskom iazycheskom molenii," *Etnograficheskoe obozrenie*, 3 (1996): 130–45; Paul Werth, *At the Margins of Orthodoxy: Mission, Governance, and Confessional Politics in Russia's Volga-Kama Region, 1827–1905* (Ithaca, NY: Cornell University Press, 2002), 30; Luehrmann, *Secularism Soviet Style*, 27–29.

33. Nikolai Iarigin, *Evangel'skoe dvizhenie v Volgo-viatskom regione* (Moscow: Akademicheskii proekt, 2004).

34. Protestants in the Mari republic were not unique in that regard. See Olena Panych, "A Time and Space of Suffering: Reflections of the Soviet Past in the Memoirs and Narratives of the Evangelical Christians-Baptists," in *State Secularism and Lived Religion in Soviet Russia and Ukraine*, ed. Catherine Wanner (New York: Oxford University Press, 2012), 218–43.

35. The shift in the frequency of reporting seems to have been connected to a standardization of the content of commissioners' reports in other parts of the Soviet Union as well. See Ulrike Huhn, *Glaube und Eigensinn: Volksfrömmigkeit zwischen orthodoxer Kirche und sowjetischem Staate 1941 bis 1960* (Wiesbaden: Harrassowitz, 2014), 23, 274–5.

36. Caroline Humphrey, *Marx Went Away, but Karl Stayed Behind* (Ann Arbor: University of Michigan Press, 1998), 408–09; see also Rogers, *The Old Faith and the Russian Land*.

37. Interview, July 2005.

38. GARME, f. P-14, op. 1, d. 487, l. 58, Minutes of November 15, 1960.

39. GARME, f. P-14, op. 26, d. 7, l. 115, Minutes of August 24, 1973.

40. Victoria Smolkin-Rothrock, "The Confession of an Atheist Who Became a Scholar of Religion: Nikolai Semenovich Gordienko's Last Interview," *Kritika* 15:3 (2014): 597–620; Andreas Glaeser, *Political Epistemics: The Secret Police, the Opposition, and the End of East German Socialism* (Chicago: University of Chicago Press, 2011).

41. Luehrmann, *Secularism Soviet Style*, 52–53.

42. NART, f. R-873, op. 1, d. 10, l. 35, Letter from believers of Bondiuga district to Comrade Aristov, member of the Central Committee, June 12, 1961.

43. GARF f. R-6991, op. 6, d. 470, ll. 236–38, Letter from Commissioner Mikhalev to Council Chairman Kuroedov, October 10, 1972. The law in question was the law on religious organizations of 1929, which remained in force until 1990. See Felix Corley, *Religion in the Soviet Union: An Archival Reader* (Basingstoke: Palgrave, 1996).

44. NART, f. R-873, op. 1, d. 11, l. 21, Letter from Commissioner Mangutkin to the chairman of the Bondiuga district executive committee, June 26, 1961.

45. NART, f. R-873, op. 1, d. 11, l. 50; NART, f. R-873, op. 1, d. 11, l. 37, Letters of April 4, 1962 and November 5, 1961.

46. Bruce Grant, "Shrines and Sovereigns: Life, Death, and Religion in Rural Azerbaidjan," *Comparative Studies in Society and History*, 53:3 (2011): 654–81; Gail Kligman, *The Wedding of the Dead: Ritual, Poetics, and Popular Culture in Transylvania* (Berkeley: University of California Press, 1988); Marjorie Mandelstam Balzer, *The Tenacity of Ethnicity: A Siberian Saga in Global Perspective* (Princeton, NJ: Princeton University Press, 1999), 179–81. The relative persistence of death rituals in a situation of rapid secularization has parallels in Western Europe and North America, where concerns about caring for the dead in a ritual manner also continue after most other life transitions lose their religious framing. See Winifred Sullivan, *The Impossibility of Religious Freedom* (Princeton, NJ: Princeton University Press, 2005).

47. E. V. Isakova and Mikhail V. Shkarovskii, *Voskresenskii Novodevichii Monastyr'*, ed. Igumenia Sofiia [Silina] (St. Petersburg: Art Deko, 2007), 168–69.

48. The feminization of religious leadership and transmission is another oft-noted innovation from the Soviet era. More recently, Nadieszda Kizenko has analyzed changing practices of Orthodox Christian confession as forms of liturgical creativity rather than attrition. Tamara Dragadze, "The Domestication of Religion under Soviet Communism," in *Socialism: Ideals, Ideologies, and Local Practice*, ed. Chris Hann (London: Routledge, 1993), 148–56; Nadieszda Kizenko, "Sacramental Confession in Modern Russia and Ukraine," in *State Secularism and Lived Religion in Soviet Russia and Ukraine*, ed. Catherine Wanner (New York: Oxford University Press, 2012), 190–217.

49. Fernand Braudel, "Histoire et sciences sociales: La longue durée," *Annales* 13:4 (1958): 725–53; Veena Das, *Critical Events: An Anthropological Perspective on Contemporary India* (Delhi: Oxford University Press, 1995).

50. The closing of the last functioning church in Ioshkar-Ola and of a rural parish church in the Tatar ASSR in 1960 were each preceded by a series of such meetings whose participants voted for the closing. GARME, f. R-836, op. 1, d. 11a, Documents on the closing of the Church of the Resurrection, Ioshkar-Ola, August 1960; NART, f. R-873, op. 2, d. 24, l. 102–40, Minutes and correspondence related to the closing of the church in Taveli, January–February 1960; Luehrmann, *Secularism Soviet Style*, 95–107.

51. NART, f. R-873, op. 1, d. 13, l. 23, chairman of the Zelenodol'sk district committee to the Council of Ministers of the Tatar ASSR, March 6, 1964.

52. NART, f. R-873, op. 1, d. 13, l. 8, Letter from Commissioner Mikhalev to the chairman of the Zelenodol'sk district committee, January 27, 1964.

53. NART, f. R-873, op. 1, d. 11, l. 202–03, Letter from Commissioner Mikhalev to the vice chairwoman of the Council of Ministers of the Tatar ASSR, March 9, 1966.

54. Elena Levkievskaia, "The Silent People? Soviet Militant Atheism through the Eyes of the Russian Peasant," *Russian Studies in History* 38: 4 (2000): 33–52; Jeanne Kormina, "Pilgrims, Priest and Local Religion in Contemporary Russia: Contested Religious Discourses," *Folklore* 28 (2004): 26–40.

55. Robert Greene, *Bodies like Bright Stars: Saints and Relics in Orthodox Russia* (DeKalb: Northern Illinois University Press, 2009), 183–85; Glennys Young, *Power and the Sacred in Revolutionary Russia: Religious Activists in the Village* (University Park: Pennsylvania State University Press, 1997).

56. Huhn, *Glaube und Eigensinn*, 309–15.

57. Caroline Humphrey, "Janus-Faced Signs: The Political Language of a Soviet Minority before *Glasnost'*," in *Social Anthropology and the Politics of Language*, ed. Ralph Grillo (London: Routledge, 1989), 145–75.

58. Leskievskaia, "The Silent People."

59. Stella Rock, "'They Burned the Pine, but the Place Remains All the Same': Pilgrimage in the Changing Landscape of Soviet Russia," in *State Secularism and Lived Religion in Soviet Russia and Ukraine*, ed. Catherine Wanner (New York: Oxford University Press, 2012), 159–89.

60. Serguei Oushakine suggests the term "socialist romanticism" to describe a range of pursuits and sensibilities that took parts of the late Soviet population outside the realm of official ideology, such as poetic filmmaking, hiking clubs, neopastoral architecture, and

archaeological interests in pre-Soviet pasts. See Alexey Golubev, "Romanticheskii podryv sovetskogo prosveshcheniia: Otzyv o konferentsii," *The Bridge—Most* 3:12 (2014). http://thebridge-moct. org/, accessed October 20, 2014.

Chapter 3: From Documents to Books, and Back

1. Christel Lane, *Christian Religion in the Soviet Union: A Sociological Study* (London: George Allen and Unwin, 1978); Christel Lane, *The Rites of Rulers: Ritual in Industrial Society—The Soviet Case* (Cambridge: Cambridge University Press, 1981); Alexandre Bennigsen and Chantal Lemercier-Quelquejay, *L'Islam en Union soviétique* (Paris: Payot, 1968); Alexandre Bennigsen and Marie Broxup, *The Islamic Threat to the Soviet State* (London: Croom Helm, 1983); Stephen and Ethel Dunn, *The Peasants of Central Russia* (New York: Holt, Rinehart and Winston, 1967); Stephen and Ethel Dunn, *The Study of the Soviet Family in the USSR and in the West* (Columbus, OH: American Association for the Advancement of Slavic Studies, 1977); David Powell, *Antireligious Propaganda in the Soviet Union: A Study of Mass Persuasion* (Cambridge, MA: MIT Press, 1975); Edward Allworth, ed., *The Nationality Question in Soviet Central Asia* (New York: Praeger, 1973); Bohdan Bociurkiw and John W. Strong, *Religion and Atheism in the USSR and Eastern Europe* (Toronto: University of Toronto Press, 1975); Allen Frank, "Traditional Religion in the Volga-Ural Region: 1960–1987," *Ural-Altaische Jahrbücher* 63 (1991): 167–84.

2. Ethel Dunn, "Review of *Kul'tura i byt kolkhoznikov Kalininskoi oblasti* by L. A. Anokhina and M. N. Shmeleva," *American Anthropologist* 67: 4 (1965): 1031–33.

3. Paul Froese, *The Plot to Kill God: Findings from the Soviet Experiment in Secularization* (Berkeley: University of California Press, 2008).

4. Yaacov Ro'i, *Islam in the Soviet Union: From the Second World War to Gorbachev* (New York: Columbia University Press, 2000).

5. Marianna Shakhnovich, *Ocherki po istorii religiovedeniia* (St. Petersburg: Izdatel'stvo Sankt-Peterburgskogo universiteta, 2006); Sanami Takahashi, "Religion as an Object of Science in Atheistic Society: The Function of the Historical Museum of Religion and Atheism in Late Socialist Russia," in *India, Russia, China: Comparative Studies on Eurasian Culture and Society*, ed. Tetsuo Mochizuki and Shiho Maeda (Sapporo: Slavic Research Center, 2012), 11–19; Victoria Smolkin-Rothrock, "A Sacred Space Is Never Empty: Soviet

Atheism, 1954–1971," Ph.D. dissertation, University of California, Berkeley, 2010.

6. Galina V. Liubimova, *Ocherki istorii vzaimodeistviia sel'skogo naseleniia Sibiri s prirodnoi sredoi* (Novosibirsk: Izdatel'stvo Instituta arkheologii i etnografii Sibirskogo otdeleniia RAN, 2012), 178–96; Ol'ga Kalinina, ed., *Kalendarnye prazdniki i obriady mariitsev* (Ioshkar-Ola: Mariiskii nauchno-issledovatel'skii institut, 2003).

7. Devin DeWeese, "Islam and the Legacy of Sovietology: A Review Essay on Yaacov Ro'i's *Islam in the Soviet Union*," *Journal of Islamic Studies* 13:3 (2002): 298–330.

8. Michel Foucault, *L'archéologie du savoir* (Paris: Gallimard, 1969).

9. Sergei Kan, *Lev Shternberg: Anthropologist, Russian Socialist, Jewish Activist* (Lincoln: University of Nebraska Press, 2009); Francine Hirsch, *Empire of Nations: Ethnographic Knowledge and the Making of the Soviet Union* (Ithaca, NY: Cornell University Press, 2005); Yuri Slezkine, *Arctic Mirrors: Russia and the Small Peoples of the North* (Ithaca, NY: Cornell University Press, 1994).

10. Vladimir Shlapentokh, *The Politics of Sociology in the Soviet Union* (Boulder: University of Colorado Press, 1987).

11. Yuri Slezkine, "The Fall of Soviet Ethnography, 1928–1938," *Current Anthropology* 32:4 (1991): 476–84; Hirsch, *Empire of Nations*.

12. Kaisa Kulasalu, "Immoral Obscenity: Censorship of Folklore Manuscript Collections in Late Stalinist Estonia," *Journal of Ethnology and Folkloristics* 7:1 (2013): 65–81.

13. Roger Markwick, *Rewriting History in Soviet Russia: The Politics of Revisionist Historiography, 1956–1974* (New York: Palgrave Macmillan, 2001); Shakhnovich, *Ocherki po istorii religiovedeniia*.

14. Irina Paert, "Demystifying the Heavens: Women, Religion, and Khrushchev's Anti-Religious Campaign, 1954–64," in *Women in the Khrushchev Era*, ed. Melanie Ilič, Susan Reid, and Lynne Attwood (Basingstoke: Palgrave Macmillan), 203–21; Brian LaPierre, *Hooliganism in Khrushchev's Russia: Defining, Policing, and Producing Deviance during the Thaw* (Madison: University of Wisconsin Press, 2012); Dina Spechler, *Permitted Dissent in the USSR: Novy mir and the Soviet Regime* (New York: Praeger, 1982).

15. Powell, *Antireligious Propaganda*; Victoria Smolkin-Rothrock, "The Ticket to the Soviet Soul: Science, Religion, and the Spiritual Crisis of Late Soviet Atheism," *Russian Review* 73:2 (2014): 171–97.

16. GARME, f. R-737, op. 2, d. 161, l. 8, Report on the state of scientific-atheist propaganda carried out by the Mari division of the Knowledge Society between 1960 and 1963, prepared by G. Chistiakov, November 20, 1963.

17. GARF, f. A-561, op. 1, d. 65, Transcript of an all-Russian seminar of chairmen of atheist and natural-scientific sections of regional organizations of the Knowledge Society, Moscow, January 10-11, 1956; Z. S. Akhmerov, "Problemy nauchno-ateisticheskogo vospitaniia v natsional'noi shkole," in *Tezisy dokladov na nauchno-pedagogicheskoi konferentsii po voprosam kommunisticheskogo vospitaniia v natsional'noi shkole*, ed. Nauchno-issledovatel'skii institut natsional'nykh shkol (Maikop: Adygeiskii oblastnoi otdel narodnogo obrazovaniia, 1965), 22–24. On the Russian Geographical Society, see Claudia Weiss, *Wie Sibirien 'unser' wurde: Die Russische Geographische Gesellschaft und ihr Einfluss auf die Bilder und Vorstellungen von Sibirien im 19. Jahrhundert* (Göttingen: V & R Unipress, 2007).

18. GARME, f. R-737, op. 2, d. 161, l. 59, Minutes of the Atheist Section of the Mari division of the Knowledge Society, July 5, 1966.

19. GARME, f. R-737, op. 2, d. 161, l. 92, Minutes of December 15, 1967.

20. Nikolai Sofronov, *Ateisticheskoe vospitanie kolkhoznogo krest'ianstva* (Ioshkar-Ola: Mariiskoe knizhnoe izdatel'stvo, 1973).

21. Sofronov, *Ateisticheskoe vospitanie*, 24. The red/beautiful corner (*krasnyi ugol*) is the corner where icons and other sacred objects are kept.

22. Luke Eric Lassiter, *The Chicago Guide to Collaborative Ethnography* (Chicago: University of Chicago Press, 2005); Thomas Lindenberger et al., "Radical Plurality: History Workshops as a Practical Critique of Knowledge," *History Workshop* 33 (1992): 73–99; Louise White, Stephan Miescher, and David William Cohen, eds., *African Worlds, African Voices: Critical Practices in Oral History* (Bloomington: Indiana University Press, 2001); Leslie Robertson and the Kwagu Gixsam Clan, *Standing up with Ga'axsta'las: Jane Constance Cook and the Politics of Memory, Church, and Custom* (Vancouver: University of British Columbia Press, 2012).

23. Tsolak A. Stepanian, ed., *Stroitel'stvo kommunizma i dukhovnyi mir cheloveka* (Moscow: Nauka, 1966).

24. GARF, f. R-9547, op. 1, d. 1314, l. 41–44, Stenographic transcript of the conference "The Laws of Formation and Development of the Spiritual Life of Communist Society," May 9–11, 1963, presentation by Ts. A. Stepanian.

25. GARF, f. R-9547, op. 1, d. 1314, l. 17. For more on Fedoseev and debates between theoretically and empirically oriented social scientists, see Alexander Vucinich, "Marx and Parsons in Soviet Sociology," *Russian Review* 33:1 (1974): 1–19.

26. Katerina Clark, *The Soviet Novel: History as Ritual* (Chicago: University of Chicago Press, 1981). On the ubiquitous motif of anticipation in Soviet state discourse and ritual, see also Nikolai Ssorin-Chaikov, *The Social Life of the State in Subarctic Siberia* (Stanford, CA: Stanford University Press, 2003).

27. GARF, f. R-9547, op. 1, d. 1314, l. 284–85.

28. GARF, f. R-9547, op. 1, d. 1314, l. 34.

29. GARF, f. R-9547, op. 1, d. 1314, l. 462, statement by F. V. Konstantinov.

30. GARF, f. R-9547, op. 1, d. 1314, l. 457. See also Devin DeWeese, "Survival Strategies: Reflections on the Notion of Religious 'Survivals' in Soviet Ethnographic Studies of Muslim Religious Life in Central Asia," in *Exploring the Edge of Empire: Soviet Era Anthropology in the Caucasus and Central Asia*, ed. Florian Mühlfried and Sergey Sokolovskiy (Münster: LIT, 2011), 35–58.

31. GARF, f. R-9547, op. 1, d. 1314, l. 286.

32. Clifford Geertz, *The Interpretation of Cultures* (New York: Basic Books, 1973), 16.

33. I. P. Kushner, ed., *Selo Viriatino v proshlom i nastoiashchem: Opyt etnograficheskogo izucheniia russkoi kolkhoznoi derevni* (Moscow: Izdatel'stvo Akademii nauk SSSR, 1958). An English translation of this book was published in 1970 as *The Village of Viriatino: An Ethnographic Study of a Russian Village from before the Revolution to the Present*, trans. and ed. Sula Benet (Garden City, NY: Anchor Books). For earlier studies in other Soviet republics, see S. M. Abramzon, "Opyt etnograficheskogo izucheniia kirgizskogo kolhoza," *Sovetskaia etnografiia* 3 (1953): 38–60; N. N. Ershov et al., *Kul'tura i byt tadzhikskogo kolkhoznogo krest'ianstva* (Moscow: Izdatel'stvo Akademii nauk SSSR, 1954).

34. Stephen and Ethel Dunn, "Talks with Soviet Ethnographers and Some Reflections," *American Anthropologist* 67:4 (1965): 985–97.

35. Kushner, *Selo Viriatino*, 206. On the Komsomol as a force of anti-religious action in the 1920s whose enthusiasm was sometimes encouraged by the authorities, sometimes regarded as excessive, see William Husband, *"Godless Communists": Atheism and Society in Soviet Russia, 1917–1932* (DeKalb: Northern Illinois University Press, 2000); Anne Gorsuch, *Youth in Revolutionary Russia: Enthusiasts, Bohemians, Delinquents* (Bloomington: Indiana University Press, 2000).

36. Kushner, *Selo Viriatino*, 231.

37. Kushner, *Selo Viriatino*, 230.

38. Kushner, *Selo Viriatino*, 213.

39. Kushner, *Selo Viriatino*, 221. On changing practices of child rearing and the special meaning of children in Soviet social imaginaries, see Lisa Kirschenbaum, *Small Comrades: Revolutionizing Childhood in Soviet Russia, 1917–1932* (New York: Routledge Falmer, 2000); David Ransel, *Village Mothers: Three Generations of Change in Russia and Tataria* (Bloomington: Indiana University Press, 2000); Alla Sal'nikova, *Rossiiskoe detstvo v XX veke: Istoriia, teoriia i praktika issledovaniia* (Kazan': Kazanskii gosudarstvennyi universitet, 2007).

40. When the American anthropologists Stephen and Ethel Dunn met members of the study team during the International Congress of Anthropological and Ethnographic Sciences in Moscow in 1965, they were told that some of the descriptions were already out of date and that an updated edition was being prepared to show the latest changes. Dunn, "Talks with Soviet Ethnographers," 992–93.

41. GARF, f. A-561, op. 1, d. 65, l. 20, Stenographic transcript of an all-Russian seminar of chairs of atheist sections, January 10, 1956.

42. Polly Jones, ed., *The Dilemmas of De-Stalinization: Negotiating Cultural and Social Change in the Khrushchev Era* (London: Routledge, 2006); Denis Kozlov, *The Readers of Novyi Mir: Coming to Terms with the Stalinist Past* (Cambridge, MA: Harvard University Press, 2013).

43. GARF, f. A-561, op. 1, d. 65, l. 116.

44. Liudmila Anokhina and Margarita Shmeleva, *Kul'tura i byt kolkhoznikov kalininskoi oblasti* (Moscow: Nauka, 1964). For a contemporary North American commentary, see Dunn, "Review of *Kul'tura i byt.*"

45. GARF, f. A-561, op. 1, d. 282, l. 13, Stenographic transcript of a theoretical conference on "Questions of Theology and Orthodox Christianity," May 29–30, 1959.

46. GARF, f. A-561, op. 1, d. 282, l. 16. Voluntary agricultural communes had a brief existence in the late 1920s and early 1930s but were then replaced by the collective farm model, where individual households remained as units but shared the land and resources for large-scale agricultural production. See Louis Siegelbaum, "Production Collectives and Communes and the 'Imperatives' of Soviet Industrialization, 1929–1931," *Slavic Review* 45:1 (1986): 65–84.

47. GARF, f. A-561, op. 1, d. 282, l. 15. On the secularizing hopes connected with new Soviet festivals in the post-war decades, see Lane, *The Rites of Rulers*; Sonja Luehrmann, "Recycling Cultural Construction: Desecularisation in Post-Soviet Mari El," *Religion, State and Society*, 33:1 (2005): 35–56; Elena Zhidkova, "Sovetskaia grazhdanskaia obriadnost' kak al'ternativa obriadnosti religioznoi," *Gosudarstvo, Religiia, Tserkov'* 30: 3–4 (2012): 407–28.

48. Alexei Yurchak, *Everything Was Forever until It Was No More: The Last Soviet Generation* (Princeton, NJ: Princeton University Press, 2006), 61.

49. GARF, f. A-561, op. 1, d. 282, ll. 55, 57, statement by Preobrazhenskii.

50. Ian Hacking, *The Taming of Chance* (Cambridge: Cambridge University Press, 1990); James Scott, *Seeing like a State: How Certain Schemes to Improve the Human Condition Have Failed* (New Haven, CT: Yale University Press, 1998); Arjun Appadurai, "Number in the Colonial Imagination," in *Orientalism and the Postcolonial Predicament: Perspectives from South Asia*, ed. Carol Breckenridge and Peter van der Veer (Philadelphia: University of Pennsylvania Press, 1993), 314–39; Peter Holquist, "To Count, to Extract, to Exterminate: Population Statistics and Population Politics in Late Imperial and Soviet Russia," in *A State of Nations: Empire and Nation-Making in the Age of Lenin and Stalin*, ed. Terry Martin and Ron Suny (New York: Oxford University Press, 2001), 111–44.

51. Elena Blinova, *Religiia i zhenshchina* (Moscow: Znanie, 1976); Mikhail Nekhoroshkov, *Sem'ia i religiia* (Ioshkar-Ola: Mariiskoe knizhnoe izdatel'stvo, 1967).

52. Viktoria Smolkin, "Sviato mesto pusto ne byvaet: Ateisticheskoe vospitanie v Sovetskom Soiuze, 1964–1968," *Neprikosnovennyi zapas* 65(3), 2009: 36–52.

53. Viktor Pivovarov, *Byt, kul'tura, natsional'nye traditsii i verovaniia naseleniia Checheno-Ingushskoi ASSR* (Groznyi: Checheno-Ingushskoe knizhnoe izdatel'stvo, 1971); Viktor Pivovarov, *Na etapakh sotsiologicheskogo issledovaniia: Teoriia i praktika sotsiologicheskikh issledovanii problem ateizma i religii* (Groznyi: Checheno-Ingushskoe knizhnoe izdatel'stvo, 1974); Viktor Pivovarov, *Religioznost': Opyt i problemy izucheniia* (Ioshkar-Ola: Mariiskoe knizhnoe izdatel'stvo, 1976), 34.

54. Iurii V. Arutiunian et al., *Russkie: etnosotsiologicheskie ocherki* (Moscow: Nauka, 1992); see also Viktor Yelensky, "The Revival before the Revival: Popular and Institutionalized Religion in Ukraine on the Eve of the Collapse of Communism," in *State Secularism and Lived Religion in Soviet Russia and Ukraine*, ed. Catherine Wanner (New York: Oxford University Press, 2012), 302–30.

55. Judith Pallot, "Living in the Soviet Countryside," in *Russian Housing in the Modern Age: Design and Social History*, ed. William Craft Brumfield and Blair Ruble (Cambridge: Cambridge University Press, 1993), 211–31; Christopher Ward, *Brezhnev's Folly: The Building of*

BAM and Late Soviet Socialism (Pittsburgh: Pittsburgh University Press, 2009).

56. For more on Solov'ev's career and intellectual trajectory, see Sonja Luehrmann, "A Multireligious Region in an Atheist State: Unionwide Policies Meet Communal Distinctions in the Postwar Mari Republic," in *State Secularism and Lived Religion in Soviet Russia and Ukraine*, ed. C. Wanner (New York: Oxford University Press, 2012), 272–301.

57. GARME, f. P-1, op. 37, d. 29, l. 6, Minutes of May 10, 1972.

58. Viktor Solov'ev, *Sotsiologicheskoe issledovanie—v praktiku ideologicheskoi raboty: Nekotorye itogi izucheniia problem byta, kul'tury, natsional'nykh traditsii, ateizma i verovanii naseleniia Mariiskoi ASSR* (Ioshkar-Ola: Mariiskoe knizhnoe izdatel'stvo, 1977), 41–42; Viktor Solov'ev, personal communication, 2005.

59. "Kak zhivesh', tovarishch?," *Mariiskaia Pravda*, August 2, 1972, 2–3; Viktor Pivovarov and Viktor Solov'ev, *Kak zhivesh', tovarishch? Konkretno-sotsiologicheskoe izuchenie byta, kul'tury, traditsii i verovanii naseleniia Mariiskoi ASSR* (Ioshkar-Ola: Mariiskoe knizhnoe izdatel'stvo, 1973).

60. Viktor Solov'ev, *Po puti dukhovnogo progressa: Nekotorye itogi povtornogo sotsiologicheskogo issledovaniia problem byta, kul'tury, natsional'nykh traditsii, ateizma i verovanii naseleniia Mariiskoi ASSR* (Ioshkar-Ola: Mariiskoe knizhnoe izdatel'stvo, 1987); V. I. Shabykov, S. N. Isanbaev, and E. A. Ozhiganova, *Religioznoe soznanie naseleniia respubliki Marii El: Materialy sotsiologicheskikh issledovanii 1994 i 2004 godov* (Ioshkar-Ola: MarNIII, 2005).

61. Solov'ev, *Sotsiologicheskoe issledovanie*, 13.

62. Pivovarov, *Na etapakh sotsiologicheskogo issledovaniia*, 191–207; Solov'ev, *Sotsiologicheskoe issledovanie*, 22, 92–94.

63. Iulian Bromley, *Etnos i etnografiia* (Moscow: Nauka, 1973); Sergei Sokolovskii, "Men'shinstva v rossiiskikh regionakh: Otechestvennaia etnografiia i politicheskaia praktika," *Etnometodologiia* 4 (1997): 82–100; Tamara Dragadze, "Soviet Ethnography: Structure and Sentiment," in *Exploring the Edge of Empire: Soviet Era Anthropology in the Caucasus and Central Asia*, ed. Florian Mühlfried and Sergey Sokolovskiy (Münster: LIT, 2011), 21–34.

64. GARME, f. P-1, op. 37, d. 29, l. 6.

65. Solov'ev, *Po puti dukhovnogo progressa*, 15.

66. Solov'ev, *Po puti dukhovnogo progressa*, 118; Shabykov, *Religioznoe soznanie naseleniia*, 346.

67. Dragadze, "Soviet Ethnography," 29.

68. Raufa K. Urazmanova, *Byt neftiannikov-tatar iugo-vostoka Tatarstana (1950–1960e gg.)* (Al'met'evsk: Al'met'evskaia entsiklopediia, 2000).

69. Ravil' Gubaidullovich Baltanov, *Sotsiologicheskie problemy v sisteme nauchno-ateisticheskogo vospitaniia: Problemy konkretno-sotsiologicheskogo analiza religii i ateizma v SSSR* (Kazan: Izdatel'stvo Kazanskogo universiteta, 1973).

70. Glaeser, *Political Epistemics*, 24.

71. Solov'ev, *Sotsiologicheskie issledovaniia*, 100; *Po puti dukhovnogo progressa*, 144–45. On secular cultural institutions and expressions of inter-ethnic tolerance as features of Soviet modernity, see Bruce Grant, *In the Soviet House of Culture: A Century of Perestroikas* (Princeton, NJ: Princeton University Press, 1995); Brian Donahoe and Joachim Otto Habeck, eds., *Reconstructing the House of Culture: Community, Self, and the Makings of Culture in Russia and Beyond* (New York: Berghahn, 2011).

72. Sofronov, *Ateisticheskoe vospitanie*; Solov'ev, *Sotsiologicheskie issledovaniia*, 73–74.

73. GARME, f. P-1, op. 41, d. 27, l. 38, Stenographic transcript of the 7th Plenum of the Mari regional committee, July 25, 1972.

74. GARME, f. P-1, op. 41, d. 27, l. 3.

75. Slava Gerovitch, *From Newspeak to Cyberspeak: A History of Soviet Cybernetics* (Cambridge, MA: MIT Press, 2002), chapter 6.

76. GARME, f. P-1, op. 41, d. 27, l. 32.

77. GARME, f. P-1, op. 41, d. 27, l. 73.

78. GARME, f. P-1, op. 41, d. 27, l. 73.

79. GARME, f. P-1, op. 41, d. 27, l. 37.

80. Glaeser, *Political Epistemics*; Katherine Verdery, *Secrets and Truths: Ethnography in the Archive of Romania's Secret Police* (Budapest: CEU Press, 2014).

81. Gerovitch, *From Newspeak to Cyberspeak*; Loren Graham, *Science, Philosophy, and Human Behavior in the Soviet Union* (New York: Columbia University Press, 1987).

82. David Engerman, *Know Your Enemy: The Rise and Fall of America's Soviet Experts* (New York: Oxford University Press, 2009).

83. See Heather Coleman, "Atheism versus Secularization? Religion in Soviet Russia, 1917–1961," *Kritika* 1:3 (2000): 557–568; Sonja Luehrmann, "Antagonistic Insights: Evolving Soviet Atheist Critiques of Religion and Why They Matter for Anthropology," *Social Analysis* 59:2 (2015). On themes of gender, family, and finite social and individual life in the study of secularism see Callum Brown, *Religion and the Demographic Revolution: Women and Secularization in Canada, Ireland, UK and USA since the 1960s* (Woodbridge: Boydell, 2012); Linell Cady and Tracy Fessenden, eds., *Religion, the Secular, and the Politics of Sexual Difference* (New York: Columbia University Press,

2013); Abou Farman, "Speculative Matter: Secular Bodies, Minds, and Persons," *Cultural Anthropology* 28:4 (2013): 737–59.

Chapter 4: Counter-Archives

1. James Faubion, *Shadows and Lights of Waco: Millenialism Today* (Princeton, NJ: Princeton University Press, 2001).
2. Russell Zanca, *Life in a Muslim Uzbek Village: Cotton Farming after Communism* (Belmont, CA: Wadsworth, 2011).
3. "Biographical note," in William Cowper Brann Collection Finding Aid, Texas Collection and University Archives, Baylor University Library, http://www.baylor.edu/lib/texas/index.php?id=55863 (accessed March 6, 2014).
4. *Keston College—The First 20 Years*. Print brochure, 1988, 2. Keston Archive (KA).
5. *Keston College—The First 20 Years*, 3.
6. *Keston College—The First 20 Years*, 11.
7. On identity archives, see Francis Blouin and William Rosenberg, *Processing the Past: Contesting Authority in History and the Archives* (New York: Oxford University Press, 2011), 132–35; Randall Jimerson, *Archives Power: Memory, Accountability, and Social Justice* (Chicago: Society of American Archivists, 2009). For uses of the term "counter-archives," see Adalaine Holton, "Decolonizing History: Arthur Schomburg's Afrodiasporic Archive," *Journal of African American History* 92:2 (2007): 218–38; Tony Ballantine, "Paper, Pen, and Print: The Transformation of the Kai Tahu Knowledge Order," *Comparative Studies in Society and History* 53:2 (2011): 232–60; P. Gabrielle Forman, "Reading/Photographs: Emma Dunham Kelley-Hawkins's Four Girls at Cottage City, Victoria Earle Matthews, and the Woman's Era," *Legacy* 24:2 (2007): 248–77.
8. Terry Cook, "The Concept of the Archival Fonds in the Post-Custodial Era: Theory, Problems and Solutions," *Archivaria* 35 (1993): 24–37.
9. Joan Kelly-Gadol, "The Social Relations of the Sexes: Methodological Implications of Women's History," *Signs* 1:4 (1976): 809–23; Patricia Galloway, "Introduction: How Deep Is (Ethno-)History? Archives, Written History, Oral Tradition," in her *Practicing Ethnohistory: Mining Archives, Hearing Testimony, Constructing Narrative* (Lincoln: University of Nebraska Press, 2006), 1–30; Bernadine Dodge, "Across the Great Divide: Archival Discourse and the (Re)presentations of the Past in Late-Modern Society," *Archivaria* 53 (2002): 17–30.

10. I am inspired here by Michael Warner's notion of counter-publics. These are groups that do not simply stand in political opposition to mainstream public opinion but are held together through different social practices than reading and debating print media. See Michael Warner, *Publics and Counterpublics* (New York: Zone Books, 2002).

11. Blouin and Rosenberg, *Processing the Past*, 212. On provenance and digital collections, see also Emily Ballantyne and Zailig Pollock, "*Respect des fonds* and the Digital Page," in *Archival Narratives for Canada: Re-Telling Stories in a Changing Landscape*, ed. Kathleen Garay and Christl Verduyn (Halifax: Fernwood, 2011), 184–201; Dodge, "Across the Great Divide," 21–24.

12. Parallel Archive, www.parallelarchive.org (accessed March 21, 2014); Soviet Samizdat Periodicals: Uncensored Texts of the Late Soviet Era, samizdat.library.utoronto.ca (accessed April 4, 2014). For an interactive site under construction, see International Samizdat [Research] Association, www.samizdatportal.org (accessed March 21, 2014).

13. Olga Zaslavskaya, "From Dispersed to Distributed Archives: The Past and the Present of Samizdat Material," *Poetics Today* 29:4 (2008): 669–712. See also Jochen Hellbeck's account of the "People's Archive" in Moscow, a collection of personal documents grown out of the same sense of having to safeguard a history that will not be preserved by the state. Jochen Hellbeck, *Revolution on My Mind: Writing a Diary under Stalin* (Cambridge, MA: Harvard University Press, 2006), ix–x.

14. Keston Newsletter 3 (2007), 5, http://www.keston.org.uk/newsletter.php (accessed March 28, 2014).

15. *Keston College—The First Twenty Years*, 6. For an example of Walter Kolarz's work, see his *Religion in the Soviet Union* (New York: St. Martin's Press, 1962).

16. Holton, "Decolonizing History," 220.

17. V. Mikhailov, "Starshii brat," *Izvestiia*, January 17, 1976, 5. KA SU 12/6.33.

18. Typewritten note attached to the article. KA SU 12/6.33.

19. "Foreign speech" (*chuzhaia rech'*) is literally what Voloshinov calls reported speech in Russian. Valentin Voloshinov, *Marksizm i filosofiia iazyka: Osnovnye problemy sotsiologicheskogo metoda v nauke o iazyke* (Moscow: Labirint, 1993 [1929]), 131.

20. On Eshliman and Iakunin, see Nickolas Lupinin, "The Russian Orthodox Church," in *Eastern Christianity and the Cold War, 1945–91*, ed. Lucian Leustean (London: Routledge, 2010), 19–39, esp. 29.

21. Michael Bourdeaux, "Obituary for Boris Talantov," *Church Times*, May 7, 1971. Newspaper clippling without page number, KA SU/Ort

2/Talantov. See also Aleksandr G. Balyberdin, *Bezumie: Khrushchevskie goneniia na Viatskoi zemle* (Viatka: Bukvitsa, 2006), 222–25.

22. Heinz-Jürgen Joppien, *Der ökumenische Rat der Kirchen in den Konflikten des kalten Krieges: Kontexte, Kompromisse, Konkretionen* (Frankfurt: Lembeck, 2000); Lucian Leustean, ed., *Eastern Christianity and the Cold War* (London: Routledge, 2010).

23. Maurice Latey, "The Churches in Russia," European Services News Talk, December 8, 1966. Typescript, KA SU/Ort 2/Talantov.

24. Possev News Service, "Boris Talantov Sentenced," October 23, 1969. Typescript. V. Burov and V. Chernov, "Pod togoi religioznosti," typed text of article from *Prizyv*, December 27, 1967. KA SU/Ort 2/Talantov.

25. Cristina Vatulescu, *Police Aesthetics: Literature, Film and the Secret Police in Soviet Times* (Stanford, CA: Stanford University Press, 2010), 192.

26. Balyberdin, *Bezumie*, 222.

27. Oxana Antic, "Religious Belief and Atheist Propaganda in Kirov," Radio Liberty research, January 2, 1984. KA SU/Ort 2/Talantov.

28. Open letter to His Holiness the Patriarch of Moscow and All Russia Aleksii, from the faithful of the Kirov diocese, June 1966, 2. KA SU/Ort 2/Talantov.

29. Open letter, 12.

30. Open letter, 13.

31. Open letter, 3.

32. Kathy Hillman and Larisa Seago, "The Keston Center for Religion, Politics and Society Library and Archives: Alive and Available at Baylor University in Waco, Texas," *Christian Librarian*, forthcoming.

33. Ann Komaromi, "Samizdat as Extra-Gutenberg Phenomenon," *Poetics Today* 29:4 (2008): 629–67.

34. Samisdat-Archiv, *Sobranie dokumentov samizdata*, 30 vols. (Munich: Samizdat Archive Association, 1968-1978). This collection is now housed in Budapest at the Open Society Archive, Central European University. See also Zaslavskaya, "From Dispersed to Distributed Archives."

35. KA SU/Ort (S[amizdat]), notes on "Historical-Theological Document," 1971.

36. KA SU/Ort 3 (S), notes on "Russia and the Church Today," ca. 1970/71. Emphasis in the original.

37. KA SU/Ort 3 (S), "Russia and the Church Today," 4.

38. Michael Bourdeaux, *Patriarch and Prophets: Persecution of the Russian Orthodox Church Today* (New York: Praeger, 1970), 15.

39. Ian Jones, "The Clergy, the Cold War, and the Local Church; England ca. 1945–60," in *Religion and the Cold War*, ed. Dianne Kirby (Basingstoke: Palgrave Macmillan, 2003), 188–99, quote 193.

40. Viktor Yelensky, "The Revival before the Revival: Popular and Institutionalized Religion in Ukraine on the Eve of the Collapse of Communism," in *State Secularism and Lived Religion in Soviet Russia and Ukraine*, ed. Catherine Wanner (New York: Oxford University Press), 302–30. For a critical discussion, see Sonja Luehrmann, "The Spirit of Late Socialism and the Value of Transformation: Brezhnevism through the Lens of Post-Soviet Religious Revival," *Cahiers du monde russe* 54:3–4 (2013): 543–64.

41. KA SU 4/11.21/1 (S); Liudmila Alekseeva, *Istoriia inakomysliia v SSSR: Noveishii period* (Benson, Vt: Khronika, 1984); Rebecca Reich, "Inside the Psychiatric Word: Diagnosis and Self-Definition in the Late Soviet Period," *Slavic Review* 73:3 (2014): 563–84.

42. Semën Gluzman, "Krest'ianin, syn krest'ianina: Pis'mo datchanke." Typescript, 1976. KA SU/Lut 2/Gluzman (S).

43. The contrast between the forced compliance of the church hierarchy and the dissident spirit of ordinary believers lay behind the title of Bourdeaux's book on Soviet Orthodoxy, *Patriarch and Prophets*. In addition to the articles on Talantov, see also "The 'Xerox' Case," Index of Censorship, Briefing Paper 144, April 12, 1984. KA SU 12/11.27.

44. G. M. Manevich, "Obrashchenie k Glavnomu Ravvinu Moskovskoi Evreiskoi religioznoi obshchiny Rabbi D. I. Levinu." Typescript, March 31, 1971. KA SU/Jew (S). For an approach to cataloging samizdat that is not based on religious confession or political issue, but organized according to people and institutions that collected unofficial publications, see the online finding aid of the Archive of the History of Dissidence in the USSR, maintained by the Memorial Society in Moscow: http://www.memo.ru/d/225.html, accessed April 29, 2014.

45. Ann Komaromi, "The Material Existence of Soviet Samizdat," *Slavic Review* 63: 3 (2004): 597–618; Serguei Oushakine, "The Terrifying Mimicry of Samizdat," *Public Culture* 13:2 (2001): 191–214; Reich, "Inside the Psychiatric Word."

46. Samuel Moyn, *The Last Utopia: Human Rights in History* (Cambridge, MA: Belknap, 2012); Winnifred Fallers Sullivan, Elizabeth Shakman Hurd, Saba Mahmood, and Peter Danchin, eds, *Politics of Religious Freedom* (Chicago: University of Chicago Press, 2015).

47. Bourdeaux, *Patriarch and Prophets*, 11.

48. Winnifred Fallers Sullivan, "Religion Naturalized: The New Establishment," in *After Pluralism: Reimagining Religious Engagement*, edited by Courtney Bender and Pamela Klassen (New York: Columbia University Press, 2010), 82–97.

49. Cook, "The Concept of the Archival Fonds," 26.

50. Peter Novick, *That Noble Dream: The 'Objectivity Question' and the American Historical Profession* (Cambridge: Cambridge University Press, 1988); Blouin and Rosenberg, *Processing the Past*, 29.

51. "The 'Xerox' Case," KA SU 12/11.27; Zaslavskaya, "From Dispersed to Distributed Archives," 694–95.

52. D.O.S., "Dopolnenie k obshchemu molitvenniku," received at Keston April 7, 1975; "Kratkoe opisanie Pskovo-Pecherskogo monastyria: Otvet drugu na pis'mennuiu pros'bu," n.d., ca. 1973. Bound, typed books. KA SU/Ort (S). On relationships between respected monks and their spiritual "children" before and during the Soviet period, see Irina Paert, *Spiritual Elders: Charisma and Tradition in Russian Orthodoxy* (DeKalb: Northern Illinois University Press, 2010).

53. Geoffrey Yeo, "Custodial History, Provenance, and the Description of Personal Records," *Libraries and the Cultural Record* 44:1 (2009): 50–64; Laura Millar, "The Death of the Fonds and the Resurrection of Provenance: Archival Context in Space and Time," *Archivaria* 53 (2002): 1–15.

54. Benjamin Nathans, "The Disenchantment of Socialism: Soviet Dissidents, Human Rights, and the New Global Morality," in *The Breakthrough: Human Rights in the 1970s*, ed. Jan Eckel and Samuel Moyn (Philadelphia: University of Pennsylvania Press, 2014), 33–49. On the role of Western endorsement for the reception of samizdat by Soviet publics, see Ann Komaromi, "Samizdat and Soviet Dissident Publics," *Slavic Review* 71:1 (2012): 70–90.

55. Komaromi, "The Material Existence," 600.

56. Mikhail Epshtein, *Novoe sektantstvo: Tipy religiozno-filosofskikh umonastroenii v Rossii, 70e-80e gody XX veka* (Holyoke, MA: New England Publishing, 1993). On similarities between samizdat and official publications, see also Serguei Oushakine, "The Terrifying Mimicry."

57. Komaromi, "The Material Existence," 615.

58. "List of temples in Moscow as of July 27, 1972," KA SU Ort 3/5.1 (S). The word "temples" (*khramy*) used in the heading suggests that the list was obtained from diocesan rather than state offices, where the term would have been "churches" or "worship buildings" (*tserkvi, kul'tovye zdaniia*).

59. Andreas Glaeser, *Political Epistemics: The Secret Police, the Opposition, and the End of East German Socialism* (Chicago: University of Chicago Press, 2011), 50; Katherine Verdery, *Secrets and Truth: Ethnography in the Archive of Romania's Secret Police* (Budapest: CEU Press, 2014).

60. KA SU 12.33/33 (S).

61. Keston Institute Archive and Library, http://www.keston.org.uk/archive.php, accessed April 10, 2014.

62. Vatulescu, *Police Aesthetics*; Boris Ananich, "The Historian and the Source: Problems of Reliability and Ethics," in *Archives, Documentation, and Institutions of Social Memory*, ed. Francis Blouin and William Rosenberg (Ann Arbor: University of Michigan Press, 2006), 490–96.

63. Ballantyne and Pollock, "Respect des fonds."

64. Komaromi, "Samizdat as Extra-Gutenberg Phenomenon," 632.

65. David Engerman, *Know Your Enemy: The Rise and Fall of America's Soviet Experts* (New York: Oxford University Press, 2009), 333–35.

66. Philip Walters, "Editorial," *Religion, State and Society* 20: 1 (1992): 3–4; Michael Bourdeaux, ed., *The Politics of Religion in Russia and the New States of Eurasia* (Armonk, NY: Sharpe, 1995); Sergei Filatov, ed., *Religiia i rossiiskoe mnogoobrazie* (Moscow: Letnii sad, 2011).

67. Hannah Arendt, *Elemente und Ursprünge totaler Herrschaft: Antisemitismus, Imperialismus, totale Herrschaft* (Munich: Piper, 1986 [1955]), 770.

Epilogue

1. I analyze these cultural shifts in more detail in Sonja Luehrmann, *Secularism Soviet Style: Teaching Atheism and Religion in a Volga Republic* (Bloomington: Indiana University Press, 2011), 122–25.

2. Michel-Rolph Trouillot, *Silencing the Past: Power and the Production of History* (Boston: Beacon, 1995), 29–30.

3. Robert J. Donia, "The New Masters of Memory: Libraries, Archives, and Museums in Postcommunist Bosnia-Hercegovina," in *Archives, Documentation, and Institutions of Social Memory*, ed. William Rosenberg and Francis Blouin (Ann Arbor: University of Michigan Press, 2006), 393–401; Kirsten Weld, *Paper Cadavers: The Archives of Dictatorship in Guatemala* (Durham, N.C.: Duke University Press, 2014); Peter G. Stone and Joanne Farchakh Bajjaly, eds., *The Destruction of Cultural Heritage in Iraq* (Woodbridge: Boydell Press, 2008).

Bibliography

1. Archival collections

State Archive of the Russian Federation, Moscow (GARF)
A-561, Knowledge Society of the Russian Soviet Federal Socialist Republic (RSFSR).
R-6991, Council for Religious Affairs of the USSR.
R-9547, Knowledge Society of the USSR.

State Archive of the Republic of Marii El, Ioshkar-Ola (GARME)
P-1, Mari Regional Committee of the Communist Party (*Obkom*).
P-14, Novyj Tor"ial District Committee of the Communist Party.
R-737, Knowledge Society, Mari republican division.
R-836, Commissioner for Religious Affairs in the Mari Autonomous Soviet Socialist Republic (ASSR).

National Archive of the Republic of Tatarstan, Kazan (NART)
R-873, Commissioner for Religious Affairs in the Tatar ASSR.

Keston Archive and Library, Baylor University, Waco, Texas (KA)
SU, Soviet Union
(S) Samizdat, sorted by denomination and/or author

2. Published sources

Abramzon, Saul M. "Opyt etnograficheskogo izucheniia kirgizskogo kolhoza." *Sovetskaia etnografiia* 3 (1953): 38–60.
Akhmerov, Z. S. "Problemy nauchno-ateisticheskogo vospitaniia v natsional'noi shkole." In *Tezisy dokladov na nauchno-pedagogicheskoi*

konferentsii po voprosam kommunisticheskogo vospitaniia v natsional'noi shkole, edited by Nauchno-issledovatel'skii institut natsional'nykh shkol, 22–24. Maikop: Adygeiskii oblastnoi otdel narodnogo obrazovaniia, 1965.

Alekseeva, Liudmila. *Istoriia inakomysliia v SSSR: Noveishii period*. Benson, VT: Khronika, 1984.

Allworth, Edward, ed. *The Nationality Question in Soviet Central Asia*. New York: Praeger, 1973.

Ananich, Boris V. "The Historian and the Source: Problems of Reliability and Ethics." In *Archives, Documentation, and Institutions of Social Memory*, edited by William Rosenberg and Francis Blouin, 490–496. Ann Arbor: University of Michigan Press, 2006.

Andrews, James T. *Science for the Masses: The Bolshevik State, Public Science, and the Popular Imagination in Soviet Russia, 1917–1934*. College Station: Texas A&M University Press, 2003.

Anokhina, Liudmila, and Margarita Shmeleva. *Kul'tura i byt kolkhoznikov Kalininskoi oblasti*. Moscow: Nauka, 1964.

Appadurai, Arjun. "Number in the Colonial Imagination." In *Orientalism and the Postcolonial Predicament: Perspectives from South Asia*, edited by Carol Breckenridge and Peter van der Veer, 314–339. Philadelphia: University of Pennsylvania Press, 1993.

Appadurai, Arjun. "The Past as a Scarce Resource." *Man* 16:2, n.s. (1981): 201–219.

Arendt, Hannah. *Elemente und Ursprünge totaler Herrschaft: Antisemitismus, Imperialismus, totale Herrschaft*. Munich: Piper, 1986 [1955].

Arutiunian, Iurii V., L. M. Drobizheva, M. N. Kuz'min, N. S. Polishchuk, and S. S. Savoskul. *Russkie: etnosotsiologicheskie ocherki*. Moscow: Nauka, 1992.

Asad, Talal. *Formations of the Secular: Christianity, Islam, Modernity*. Stanford, CA: Stanford University Press, 2003.

Asad, Talal. "Trying to Understand French Secularism." In *Political Theologies: Public Religions in a Post-Secular World*, edited by Hent de Vries and Lawrence Sullivan, 494–526. New York: Fordham University Press, 2006.

Austin, John. *How to Do Things with Words*. New York: Oxford University Press, 1965.

Bakhtin, Mikhail. "Epic and Novel: Toward a Methodology for the Study of the Novel." In *The Dialogic Imagination: Four Essays*, by M. M. Bakhtin, edited by Michael Holquist, 4–40. Austin: University of Texas Press, 1981.

Bakhtin, Mikhail. "Problema rechevykh zhanrov." In *Sobranie sochinenii*, vol. 5, 159–206. Moscow: Russkie slovari, 1996.

Ballantine, Tony. "Paper, Pen, and Print: The Transformation of the Kai Tahu Knowledge Order." *Comparative Studies in Society and History* 53:2 (2011): 232–260.

Ballantyne, Emily, and Zailig Pollock. "*Respect des fonds* and the Digital Page." In *Archival Narratives for Canada: Re-Telling Stories in a Changing Landscape*, edited by Kathleen Garay and Christl Verduyn, 184–201. Halifax, NS: Fernwood, 2011.

Baltanov, Ravil' Gubaidullovich. *Sotsiologicheskie problemy v sisteme nauchno-ateisticheskogo vospitaniia: Problemy konkretno-sotsiologicheskogo analiza religii i ateizma v SSSR*. Kazan: Izdatel'stvo Kazanskogo universiteta, 1973.

Balyberdin, Aleksandr G. *Bezumie: Khrushchevskie goneniia na viatskoi zemle*. Viatka: Bukvitsa, 2006.

Balzer, Marjorie Mandelstam. *The Tenacity of Ethnicity: A Siberian Saga in Global Perspective*. Princeton, NJ: Princeton University Press, 1999.

Baran, Emily. *Dissent on the Margins: How Soviet Jehovah's Witnesses Defied Communism and Lived to Preach about It*. New York: Oxford University Press, 2014.

Barberowski, Jörg. "Arbeit an der Geschichte: Vom Umgang mit den Archiven." *Jahrbücher für Geschichte Osteuropas* 51:1 (2003): 36–56.

Baubérot, Jean. *Laïcité 1905–2005, entre passion et raison*. Paris: Seuil, 2004.

Beglov, Aleksei. *V poiskakh bezgreshnykh katakomb: Tserkovnoe podpol'e v SSSR*. Moscow: Arefa, 2008.

Benet, Sula, ed. *The Village of Viriatino: An Ethnographic Study of a Russian Village from Before the Revolution to the Present*. Translated by Sula Benet. Garden City, NY: Anchor Books, 1970.

Bennigsen, Alexandre, and Marie Broxup. *The Islamic Threat to the Soviet State*. London: Croom Helm, 1983.

Bennigsen, Alexandre, and Chantal Lemercier-Quelquejay. *L'Islam en Union soviétique*. Paris: Payot, 1968.

Bernstein, Anya. "An Inadvertent Sacrifice: Body Politics and Sovereign Power in the Pussy Riot Affair," *Critical Inquiry* 40:1 (2013): 220–241.

Blinova, Elena. *Religiia i zhenshchina*. Moscow: Znanie, 1976.

Blouin, Francis Jr., and William Rosenberg. *Processing the Past: Contesting Authority in History and the Archives*. New York: Oxford University Press, 2011.

Bociurkiw, Bohdan, and John W. Strong. *Religion and Atheism in the USSR and Eastern Europe*. Toronto: University of Toronto Press, 1975.

Bourdeaux, Michael. *Patriarch and Prophets: Persecution of the Russian Orthodox Church Today*. New York: Praeger, 1970.

Bourdeaux, Michael, ed. *The Politics of Religion in Russia and the New States of Eurasia*. Armonk, NY: Sharpe, 1995.

Boyer, Dominic, and Alexei Yurchak. "American Stiob: Or, What Late-Socialist Aesthetics of Parody Reveal about Contemporary Political Culture in the West." *Cultural Anthropology* 25:2 (2010): 179–221.

Braudel, Fernand. "Histoire et sciences sociales: La longue durée." *Annales* 13:4 (1958): 725–753.

Bromley, Iulian. *Etnos i etnografiia*. Moscow: Nauka, 1973.

Brown, Callum. *The Death of Christian Britain: Understanding Secularization, 1800–2000*. London: Routledge, 2001.

Brown, Callum. *Religion and the Demographic Revolution: Women and Secularization in Canada, Ireland, UK and USA since the 1960s*. Woodbridge: Boydell, 2012.

Brown, Callum. "The Secularisation Decade: What the 1960s Have Done to the Study of Religious History." In *The Decline of Christendom in Western Europe, 1750–2000*, edited by Hugh McLeod and Werner Ustorf, 29–46. Cambridge: Cambridge University Press, 2003.

Brown, Kate. *Plutopia: Nuclear Families, Atomic Cities, and the Great Soviet and American Plutonium Disasters*. New York: Oxford University Press, 2013.

Brown, Wendy. *Regulating Aversion: Tolerance in the Age of Identity and Empire*. Princeton, NJ: Princeton University Press, 2008.

Bruce, Steve. *God Is Dead: Secularization in the West*. Oxford: Blackwell, 2002.

Burns, Kathryn. *Into the Archive: Writing and Power in Colonial Peru*. Durham, NC: Duke University Press, 2010.

Cady, Linell, and Tracy Fessenden, eds. *Religion, the Secular, and the Politics of Sexual Difference*. New York: Columbia University Press, 2013.

Campbell, Craig. *Agitating Images: Photography Against History in Indigenous Siberia*. Minneapolis: University of Minnesota Press, 2014.

Casanova, José. *Public Religions in the Modern World*. Chicago: University of Chicago Press, 1994.

Chakrabarty, Dipesh. *Provincializing Europe: Postcolonial Thought and Historical Difference*. Princeton, NJ: Princeton University Press, 2000.

Chumachenko, Tatiana. *Church and State in Soviet Russia: Russian Orthodoxy from World War II to the Khrushchev Years*. Armonk, NY: Sharpe, 2002.

Clark, Katerina. *The Soviet Novel: History as Ritual*. Chicago: University of Chicago Press, 1981.

Cody, Francis. *The Light of Knowledge: Literacy Activism and the Politics of Writing in South India*. Ithaca, NY: Cornell University Press, 2013.

Cohen, David William, and E. S. Atieno Odhiambo. *The Risks of Knowledge: Investigations into the Death of the Hon. Minister John Robert Ouko in Kenia, 1990.* Athens: Ohio University Press, 2004.

Coleman, Heather. "Atheism versus Secularization? Religion in Soviet Russia, 1917–1961." *Kritika* 1:3 (2000): 557–568.

Coleman, Heather. *Russian Baptists and Spiritual Revolution, 1905–1929.* Bloomington: Indiana University Press, 2005.

Coleman, Simon, and Leslie Carlin, eds. *The Cultures of Creationism: Anti-Evolutionism in English-Speaking Cultures.* Aldershot: Ashgate, 2004.

Cook, Terry. "The Concept of the Archival Fonds in the Post-Custodial Era: Theory, Problems and Solutions." *Archivaria* 35 (1993): 24–37.

Corley, Felix. *Religion in the Soviet Union: An Archival Reader.* Basingstoke: Palgrave, 1996.

Cruikshank, Julie. *The Social Life of Stories: Narrative and Knowledge in the Yukon.* Lincoln: University of Nebraska Press, 1998.

Das, Veena. *Critical Events: An Anthropological Perspective on Contemporary India.* Delhi: Oxford University Press, 1995.

Davis, Natalie Zemon. *Fiction in the Archives: Pardon Tales and Their Tellers in Sixteenth-Century France.* Stanford, CA: Stanford University Press, 1987.

Derrida, Jacques. *Archive Fever: A Freudian Impression.* Chicago: University of Chicago Press, 1996.

DeWeese, Devin. "Islam and the Legacy of Sovietology: A Review Essay on Yaacov Ro'i's *Islam in the Soviet Union*." *Journal of Islamic Studies* 13:3 (2002): 298–330.

DeWeese, Devin. "Survival Strategies: Reflections on the Notion of Religious 'Survivals' in Soviet Ethnographic Studies of Muslim Religious Life in Central Asia." In *Exploring the Edge of Empire: Soviet Era Anthropology in the Caucasus and Central Asia,* edited by Florian Mühlfried and Sergey Sokolovskiy, 35–58. Münster: LIT, 2011.

Dobson, Miriam. "Child Sacrifice in the Soviet Press: Sensationalism and the 'Sectarian' in the Post-Stalin Era." *Russian Review* 73:2 (2014): 237–259.

Dobson, Miriam. *Khrushchev's Cold Summer: Gulag Returnees, Crime, and the Fate of Reform after Stalin.* Ithaca, NY: Cornell University Press, 2009.

Dobson, Miriam. "Letters." In *Reading Primary Sources: The Interpretation of Texts from Nineteenth- and Twentieth-Century History,* edited by Miriam Dobson and Benjamin Ziemann, 57–73. London: Routledge, 2009.

Dodge, Bernadine. "Across the Great Divide: Archival Discourse and the (Re)presentations of the Past in Late-Modern Society." *Archivaria* 53 (2002): 17–30.

Donahoe, Brian, and Joachim Otto Habeck, eds. *Reconstructing the House of Culture: Community, Self, and the Makings of Culture in Russia and Beyond.* New York: Berghahn, 2011.

Donia, Rober J. "The New Masters of Memory: Libraries, Archives, and Museums in Postcommunist Bosnia-Hercegovina." In *Archives, Documentation, and Institutions of Social Memory,* edited by William Rosenberg and Francis Blouin, 393–401. Ann Arbor: University of Michigan Press, 2006.

Dragadze, Tamara. "The Domestication of Religion under Soviet Communism." In *Socialism: Ideals, Ideologies, and Local Practice,* edited by Chris Hann, 148–156. London: Routledge, 1993.

Dragadze, Tamara. "Soviet Ethnography: Structure and Sentiment." In *Exploring the Edge of Empire: Soviet Era Anthropology in the Caucasus and Central Asia,* edited by Florian Mühlfried and Sergey Sokolovskiy, 21–34. Münster: LIT, 2011.

Dunn, Ethel. "Review of *Kul'tura i byt kolkhoznikov Kalininskoi oblasti* by L. A. Anokhina and M. N. Shmeleva." *American Anthropologist* 67:4 (1965): 1031–1033.

Dunn, Stephen, and Ethel Dunn. "Talks with Soviet Ethnographers and Some Reflections." *American Anthropologist* 67:4 (1965): 985–997.

Dunn, Stephen, and Ethel Dunn. *The Peasants of Central Russia.* New York: Holt, Rinehart and Winston, 1967.

Dunn, Stephen, and Ethel Dunn. *The Study of the Soviet Family in the USSR and in the West.* Columbus, OH: American Association for the Advancement of Slavic Studies, 1977.

Eiss, Paul. "Notes on the Difficulty of Studying *el Pueblo.*" In *Anthrohistory: Unsettling Knowledge, Questioning Discipline,* edited by Edward Murphy et al., 37–47. Ann Arbor: University of Michigan Press, 2011.

Eley, Geoff. *A Crooked Line: From Cultural History to the History of Society.* Ann Arbor: University of Michigan Press, 2005.

Engelke, Matthew. *God's Agents: Biblical Publicity in Contemporary England.* Berkeley: University of California Press, 2013.

Engelstein, Laura. *Castration and the Heavenly Kingdom: A Russian Folktale.* Ithaca, NY: Cornell University Press, 2003.

Engelstein, Laura. "The Archives Talk Back: Unofficial Collections in Imperial, Soviet and Post-Soviet Russia." *Jahrbücher für Geschichte Osteuropas* 51:1 (2003): 70–76.

Engerman, David. *Know Your Enemy: The Rise and Fall of America's Soviet Experts.* New York: Oxford University Press, 2009.

Epshtein, Mikhail. *Novoe sektantstvo: Tipy religiozno-filosofskikh umonastroenii v Rossii, 70e-80e gody XX veka.* Holyoke: New England Publishing, 1993.

Ershov, N. N. et al. *Kul'tura i byt tadzhikskogo kolkhoznogo krest'ianstva.* Moscow: Izdatel'stvo Akademii nauk SSSR, 1954.

Ewing, Katherine. "Dreams from a Saint: Anthropological Atheism and the Temptation to Believe." *American Anthropologist* 96:3 (1994): 571–583.

Faller, Helen. *Nation, Language, Islam: Tatarstan's Sovereignty Movement.* Budapest: Central European University Press, 2011.

Farman, Abou. "Speculative Matter: Secular Bodies, Minds, and Persons." *Cultural Anthropology* 28:4 (2013): 737–759.

Faubion, James. *Shadows and Lights of Waco: Millenialism Today.* Princeton, NJ: Princeton University Press, 2001.

Field, Deborah. *Private Life and Communist Morality in Khrushchev's Russia.* New York: Peter Lang, 2007.

Fienup-Riordan, Ann. *Yup'ik Elders in the Ethnologisches Museum Berlin: Fieldwork Turned on Its Head.* Seattle: University of Washington Press, 2005.

Filatov, Sergei, ed. *Religiia i rossiiskoe mnogoobrazie.* Moscow: Letnii sad, 2011.

Filatov Sergei, and Roman Lunkin. "Statistics on Religion in Russia: The Reality behind the Figures." *Religion, State and Society* 34:1 (2006): 33–49.

Fitzpatrick, Sheila. *Education and Social Mobility in the Soviet Union, 1921–1934.* Cambridge: Cambridge University Press, 1979.

Fitzpatrick, Sheila. "Signals from Below: Soviet Letters of Denunciation of the 1930s." *Journal of Modern History* 68:4 (1996): 831–866.

Fitzpatrick, Sheila. "Social Parasites: How Tramps, Idle Youth and Busy Entrepreneurs Impeded the Soviet March to Communism." *Cahiers du monde russe* 47:1–2 (2006): 377–408.

Fitzpatrick, Sheila. "Supplicants and Citizens: Public Letter-Writing in Soviet Russia in the 1930s." *Slavic Review* 55:1 (1996): 78–105.

Fitzpatrick, Sheila. *Tear off the Masks! Identity and Imposture in Twentieth-Century Russia.* Princeton, NJ: Princeton University Press, 2005.

Forman, P. Gabrielle. "Reading/Photographs: Emma Dunham Kelley-Hawkins's Four Girls at Cottage City, Victoria Earle Matthews, and the Woman's Era." *Legacy* 24:2 (2007): 248–277.

Foucault, Michel. *L'archéologie du savoir.* Paris: Gallimard, 1969.

Frank, Allen. "Traditional Religion in the Volga-Ural Region: 1960–1987." *Ural-Altaische Jahrbücher* 63 (1991): 167–184.

Freeze, Gregory. *The Russian Levites: Parish Clergy in the Eighteenth Century*. Cambridge, MA: Harvard University Press, 1977.

Froese, Paul. *The Plot to Kill God: Findings from the Soviet Experiment in Secularization*. Berkeley: University of California Press, 2008.

Froggatt, Michael. "Renouncing Dogma, Teaching Utopia: Science in Schools under Khrushchev." In *The Dilemmas of De-Stalinization: Negotiating Cultural and Social Change in the Khrushchev Era*, edited by Polly Jones, 250–266. London: Routledge, 2006.

Furman, Dmitrii, and Kimmo Kaariainen. *Religioznost' v Rossii v 90e gody XX—nachale XXI veka*. Moscow: OGNI TD, 2006.

Gal, Susan. "Language and the 'Arts of Resistance'." *Cultural Anthropology* 10:3 (1995): 407–424.

Galloway, Patricia. "Introduction: How Deep Is (Ethno-)History? Archives, Written History, Oral Tradition." In *Practicing Ethnohistory: Mining Archives, Hearing Testimony, Constructing Narrative*, by Patricia Galloway, 1–30. Lincoln: University of Nebraska Press, 2006.

Garrard, John, and Carol Garrard. *Russian Orthodoxy Resurgent: Faith and Power in the New Russia*. Princeton, NJ: Princeton University Press, 2008.

Geertz, Clifford. *The Interpretation of Cultures*. New York: Basic Books, 1973.

Geraci, Robert. *Window on the East: National and Imperial Identities in Late Tsarist Russia*. Ithaca, NY: Cornell University Press, 2001.

Gerovitch, Slava. *From Newspeak to Cyberspeak: A History of Soviet Cybernetics*. Cambridge, MA: MIT Press, 2002.

Ginzburg, Carlo. *The Cheese and the Worms: The Cosmos of a Sixteenth-Century Miller*. Translated by Anne and John Tedeschi. Baltimore, MD: Johns Hopkins University Press, 1980.

Glaeser, Andreas. *Political Epistemics: The Secret Police, the Opposition, and the End of East German Socialism*. Chicago: University of Chicago Press, 2011.

Goffman, Erving. "Felicity's Condition." *American Journal of Sociology* 89:1 (1983): 1–53.

Goldstein, Diane. "The Secularization of Religious Ethnography and Narrative Competence in a Discourse of Faith." *Western Folklore* 54 (1995): 23–36.

Goody, Jack. *The Logic of Writing and the Organization of Society*. Cambridge: Cambridge University Press, 1986.

Gorlizki, Yoram. "Political Reform and Local Party Interventions under Khrushchev." In *Reforming Justice in Russia, 1864–1996: Power, Culture, and the Limits of the Legal Order*, edited by Peter H. Solomon, 256–281. Armonk, NY: Sharpe, 1997.

Gorlizki, Yoram, and Oleg Khlevniuk. *Cold Peace: Stalin and the Soviet Ruling Circle, 1945–1953.* New York: Oxford University Press, 2004.

Gorsuch, Anne. *Youth in Revolutionary Russia: Enthusiasts, Bohemians, Delinquents.* Bloomington: Indiana University Press, 2000.

Graham, Loren. *Science, Philosophy, and Human Behavior in the Soviet Union.* New York: Columbia University Press, 1987.

Grant, Bruce. *In the Soviet House of Culture: A Century of Perestroikas.* Princeton, NJ: Princeton University Press, 1995.

Grant, Bruce. "Shrines and Sovereigns: Life, Death, and Religion in Rural Azerbaidjan." *Comparative Studies in Society and History* 53:3 (2011): 654–681.

Greene, Robert H. *Bodies like Bright Stars: Saints and Relics in Orthodox Russia.* DeKalb: Northern Illinois University Press, 2010.

Grossman, Gregory. "The 'Second Economy' of the USSR." *Problems of Communism* 26:5 (1977): 25–40.

Guha, Ranajit. "The Prose of Counter-Insurgency." In *Selected Subaltern Studies,* edited by Ranajit Guha and Gayatri Spivak, 45–86. New York: Oxford University Press, 1988.

Hacking, Ian. *The Taming of Chance.* Cambridge: Cambridge University Press, 1990.

Halfin, Igal. "Poetics in the Archives: The Quest for 'True' Bolshevik Documents." *Jahrbücher für Geschichte Osteuropas* 51:1 (2003): 84–89.

Halfin, Igal. *Red Autobiographies: Initiating the Bolshevik Self.* Seattle: University of Washington Press, 2011.

Harding, Susan. "Representing Fundamentalism: The Problem of the Repugnant Cultural Other." *Social Research* 58:2 (1991): 373–393.

Hellbeck, Jochen. *Revolution on My Mind: Writing a Diary under Stalin.* Cambridge, MA: Harvard University Press, 2006.

Hillman, Kathy, and Larisa Seago. "The Keston Center for Religion, Politics and Society Library and Archives: Alive and Available at Baylor University in Waco, Texas." *Christian Librarian,* forthcoming.

Hirsch, Francine. *Empire of Nations: Ethnographic Knowledge and the Making of the Soviet Union.* Ithaca, NY: Cornell University Press, 2005.

Höhn, Hans-Joachim. *Postsäkular: Gesellschaft im Umbruch, Religion im Wandel.* Paderborn: Schöningh, 2007.

Holquist, Peter. "'Information Is the Alpha and Omega of Our Work': Bolshevik Surveillance in Its Pan-European Perspective." *Journal of Modern History* 69:3 (1997): 415–450.

Holquist, Peter. "To Count, to Extract, to Exterminate: Population Statistics and Population Politics in Late Imperial and Soviet Russia." In *A State of Nations: Empire and Nation-Making in the Age of Lenin and Stalin,* edited by Terry Martin and Ron Suny, 111–144. New York: Oxford University Press, 2001.

Holton, Adalaine. "Decolonizing History: Arthur Schomburg's Afrodiasporic Archive." *Journal of African American History* 92:2 (2007): 218–238.

Huhn, Ulrike. *Glaube und Eigensinn. Volksfrömmigkeit zwischen orthodoxer Kirche und sowjetischem Staat 1941 bis 1960.* Wiesbaden: Harrassowitz, 2014.

Hull, Matthew. *Government of Paper: The Materiality of Bureaucracy in Urban Pakistan.* Berkeley: University of California Press, 2012.

Hull, Matthew. "The File: Agency, Authority, and Autography in an Islamabad Bureaucracy." *Language and Communication* 23:3–4 (2003): 287–314.

Humphrey, Caroline. "'Janus-Faced Signs': The Political Language of a Soviet Minority before *Glasnost'*." In *Social Anthropology and the Politics of Language,* edited by Ralph Grillo, 145–175. London: Routledge, 1989.

Humphrey, Caroline. *Marx Went Away but Karl Stayed Behind.* Ann Arbor: University of Michigan Press, 1998.

Husband, William. *"Godless Communists": Atheism and Society in Soviet Russia, 1917–1932.* DeKalb: Northern Illinois University Press, 2000.

Iarygin, Nikolai. *Evangel'skoe dvizhenie v Volgo-viatskom regione.* Moscow: Akademicheskii proekt, 2004.

Ibragim, Taufik, Farit Sultanov, and Aidar Iuzeev. *Tatarskaia religiozno-filosofskaia mysl' v obshchemusul'manskom kontekste.* Kazan: Tatarskoe knizhnoe izdatel'stvo, 2002.

Isakova, Elena V., and Mikhail V. Shkarovskii. *Voskresenskii Novodevichii Monastyr'.* Edited by Igumenia Sofiia [Silina]. St. Petersburg: Art Deko, 2007.

Izmozik, Vladlen, and Nataliia Lebina. *Peterburg sovetskii: "Novyi chelovek" v starom prostranstve, 1920–1930e gody.* St. Petersburg: Kriga, 2010.

Jimerson, Randall. *Archives Power: Memory, Accountability, and Social Justice.* Chicago: Society of American Archivists, 2009.

Jones, Ian. "The Clergy, the Cold War, and the Local Church; England ca. 1945–60." In *Religion and the Cold War,* edited by Dianne Kirby, 188–199. Basingstoke: Palgrave Macmillan, 2003.

Jones, Polly, ed. *The Dilemmas of De-Stalinization: Negotiating Cultural and Social Change in the Khrushchev Era.* London: Routledge, 2006.

Joppien, Heinz-Jürgen. *Der ökumenische Rat der Kirchen in den Konflikten des kalten Krieges: Kontexte, Kompromisse, Konkretionen.* Frankfurt: Lembeck, 2000.

Kalinina, Ol'ga, ed. *Kalendarnye prazdniki i obriady mariitsev.* Ioshkar-Ola: Mariiskii nauchno-issledovatel'skii institut, 2003.

Kamp, Marianne. *The New Woman in Uzbekistan: Islam, Modernity, and Unveiling under Communism.* Seattle: University of Washington Press, 2006.

Kamp, Marianne. "Three Lives of Saodat: Communist, Uzbek, Survivor." *Oral History Review* 28:2 (2001): 28–51.

Kan, Sergei. *Lev Shternberg: Anthropologist, Russian Socialist, Jewish Activist.* Lincoln: University of Nebraska Press, 2009.

Kappeler, Andreas. *Russlands erste Nationalitäten: Das Zarenreich und die Völker der mittleren Volga vom 16. bis 19. Jahrhundert.* Cologne: Böhlau, 1982.

Kelly, Catriona. "From 'counter-revolutionary monuments' to 'national heritage': The preservation of Leningrad churches, 1964-1982." *Cahiers du monde russe* 54:1-2 (2013): 131–64.

Kelly-Gadol, Joan. "The Social Relations of the Sexes: Methodological Implications of Women's History." *Signs* 1:4 (1976): 809–823.

Kenworthy, Scott. *The Heart of Russia: Trinity-Sergius, Monasticism, and Society after 1825.* New York: Oxford University Press, 2010.

Keston Archive. *Keston College—The First 20 Years.* Print brochure, 1988.

Khalid, Adeeb. "Backwardness and the Quest for Civilization: Early Soviet Central Asia in Comparative Perspective." *Slavic Review* 65:2 (2006): 231–251.

Khalid, Adeeb. *Islam after Communism: Religion and Politics in Central Asia.* Berkeley: University of California Press, 2007.

Khlevniuk, Oleg. *Master of the House: Stalin and His Inner Circle.* New Haven, CT: Yale University Press, 2009.

Khorkhordina, Tat'iana, and Tamara Volkova. *Rossiiskie arkhivy: istoriia i sovremennost'.* Moscow: Rossiiskii Gosudarstvennyi Gumanitarnyi Universitet, 2012.

Kirschenbaum, Lisa. *Small Comrades: Revolutionizing Childhood in Soviet Russia, 1917–1932.* New York: Routledge Falmer, 2000.

Kizenko, Nadieszda. "Sacramental Confession in Modern Russia and Ukraine." In *State Secularism and Lived Religion in Soviet Russia and Ukraine,* edited by Catherine Wanner, 190–217. New York: Oxford University Press, 2012.

Kligman, Gail. *The Wedding of the Dead: Ritual, Poetics, and Popular Culture in Transylvania.* Berkeley: University of California Press, 1988.

Kligman, Gail, and Katherine Verdery. *Peasants under Siege: The Collectivization of Romanian Agriculture, 1949–1962.* Princeton, NJ: Princeton University Press, 2011.

Kolarz, Walter. *Religion in the Soviet Union.* New York: St. Martin's Press, 1962.

Koleva, Daniela. "Memories of the War and the War of Memories in Post-Communist Bulgaria." *Oral History* 34:2 (2006): 44–55.

Kolymagin, Boris. *Krymskaia ekumena: Religioznaia zhizn' poslevoennogo Kryma*. St. Petersburg: Aleteiia, 2004.

Komaromi, Ann. "The Material Existence of Soviet Samizdat." *Slavic Review* 63:3 (2004): 597–618.

Komaromi, Ann. "Samizdat and Soviet Dissident Publics." *Slavic Review* 71:1 (2012): 70–90.

Komaromi, Ann. "Samizdat as Extra-Gutenberg Phenomenon." *Poetics Today* 29:4 (2008): 629–667.

Kormina, Jeanne. "Pilgrims, Priest and Local Religion in Contemporary Russia: Contested Religious Discourses," *Folklore* 28 (2004): 26–40.

Koselleck, Reinhart. *Vergangene Zukunft: Zur Semantik geschichtlicher Zeiten*. Frankfurt: Suhrkamp, 1979.

Kotkin, Stephen. "The State—Is It Us? Memoirs, Archives, and Kremlinologists." *Russian Review* 61 (2002): 35–51.

Kozlov, Denis. *The Readers of Novyi Mir: Coming to Terms with the Stalinist Past*. Cambridge, MA: Harvard University Press, 2013.

Kulasalu, Kaisa. "Immoral Obscenity: Censorship of Folklore Manuscript Collections in Late Stalinist Estonia." *Journal of Ethnology and Folkloristics* 7:1 (2013): 65–81.

Kushner, I. P., ed. *Selo Viriatino v proshlom i nastoiashchem: Opyt etnograficheskogo izucheniia russkoi kolkhoznoi derevni*. Moscow: Izdatel'stvo Akademii nauk SSSR, 1958.

Lane, Christel. *Christian Religion in the Soviet Union: A Sociological Study*. London: George Allen and Unwin, 1978.

Lane, Christel. *The Rites of Rulers: Ritual in Industrial Society—The Soviet Case*. Cambridge: Cambridge University Press, 1981.

Lane, Christopher. *The Age of Doubt: Tracing the Roots of Our Religious Uncertainty*. New Haven, CT: Yale University Press, 2011.

LaPierre, Brian. *Hooliganism in Khrushchev's Russia: Defining, Policing, and Producing Deviance during the Thaw*. Madison: University of Wisconsin Press, 2012.

Lassiter, Luke Eric. *The Chicago Guide to Collaborative Ethnography*. Chicago: University of Chicago Press, 2005.

LeGoff, Jacques. *Histoire et mémoire*. Paris: Gallimard, 1988.

Leustean, Lucian, ed. *Eastern Christianity and the Cold War*. London: Routledge, 2010.

Levkievskaia, Elena. "The Silent People? Soviet Militant Atheism through the Eyes of the Russian Peasant." *Russian Studies in History* 38: 4 (2000): 33–52.

Lewis, Bernard. *The Emergence of Modern Turkey*. London: Oxford University Press, 1961.

Lim, Chaeyoon, Carol Ann MacGregor, and Robert Putnam. "Secular and Liminal: Discovering Heterogeneity among Religious Nones." *Journal for the Scientific Study of Religion* 49: 4 (2010): 596–618.

Lincoln, Bruce. *Holy Terrors: Thinking about Religion after September 11.* Chicago: University of Chicago Press, 2006.

Lindenberger, Thomas, Michael Wildt, Lyndal Roper, and Martin Chalmers. "Radical Plurality: History Workshops as a Practical Critique of Knowledge." *History Workshop* 33 (1992): 73–99.

Liubimova, Galina V. *Ocherki istorii vzaimodeistviia sel'skogo naseleniia Sibiri s prirodnoi sredoi.* Novosibirsk: Izdatel'stvo Instituta arkheologii i etnografii Sibirskogo otdeleniia RAN, 2012.

Lonsdale, Richard E., and John H. Thompson. "A Map of the USSR's Manufacturing." *Economic Geography* 30:1 (1960): 36–52.

Luckmann, Thomas. *Die unsichtbare Religion.* Frankfurt: Suhrkamp, 1991.

Luehrmann, Sonja. "Antagonistic Insights: Evolving Soviet Atheist Critiques of Religion and Why They Matter for Anthropology." *Social Analysis* 59:2 (2015).

Luehrmann, Sonja. "Chto my mozhem znat' o religioznoi zhizni sovetskogo perioda? Sopostavlenie arkhivnykh i ustnykh istochnikov iz poslevoennogo Povolzh'ia." *Gosudarstvo Religiia Tserkov'* 30:3–4 (2012): 485–504.

Luehrmann, Sonja. "The Magic of Others: Mari Witchcraft Reputations and Interethnic Relations in the Volga Region." *Russian History* 40:3–4 (2013): 469–487.

Luehrmann, Sonja. "A Multireligious Region in an Atheist State: Unionwide Policies Meet Communal Distinctions in the Postwar Mari Republic." In *State Secularism and Lived Religion in Soviet Russia and Ukraine*, edited by Catherine Wanner, 272–301. New York: Oxford University Press, 2012.

Luehrmann, Sonja. "On the Importance of Having a Method, or What Does Archival Work on Soviet Atheism Have to Do with Ethnography of Post-Soviet Religion?" In *Anthrohistory: Unsettling Knowledge, Questioning Discipline*, edited by Edward Murphy, David William Cohen, Chandra Bhimull, Fernando Coronil, Monica Patterson, and Julie Skurski, 273–285. Ann Arbor: University of Michigan Press, 2011.

Luehrmann, Sonja. "Recycling Cultural Construction: Desecularisation in Post-Soviet Mari El." *Religion, State and Society* 33:1 (2005): 35–56.

Luehrmann, Sonja. *Secularism Soviet Style: Teaching Atheism and Religion in a Volga Republic.* Bloomington: Indiana University Press, 2011.

Luehrmann, Sonja. "The Spirit of Late Socialism and the Value of Transformation: Brezhnevism through the Lens of Post-Soviet Religious Revival." *Cahiers du monde russe* 54:3–4 (2013): 543–564.

Lupinin, Nickolas. "The Russian Orthodox Church." In *Eastern Christianity and the Cold War, 1945–91*, edited by Lucian Leustean, 19–39. London: Routledge, 2010.

Mahmood, Saba. *Politics of Piety: The Islamic Revival and the Feminist Subject.* Princeton, NJ: Princeton University Press, 2005.

Markwick, Roger. *Rewriting History in Soviet Russia: The Politics of Revisionist Historiography, 1956–1974.* New York: Palgrave Macmillan, 2001.

Martin, Terry. *The Affirmative Action Empire: Nations and Nationalism in the Soviet Union, 1923–1939.* Ithaca, NY: Cornell University Press, 2001.

Martin, Terry. "Interpreting the New Archival Signals: Nationalities Policy and the Nature of the Soviet Bureaucracy." *Cahiers du monde russe* 40:1–2 (1999): 113–124.

Marx, Karl. "Contribution to the Critique of Hegel's Philosophy of Law: Introduction." In *The Collected Works of Karl Marx and Frederick Engels*, vol. 3, 175–187. New York: International Publishers, 1975.

Masco, Joseph. *The Nuclear Borderlands: The Manhattan Project in Post–Cold War New Mexico.* Princeton, NJ: Princeton University Press, 2006.

McLeod, Hugh. *Class and Religion in the Late Victorian City.* Hamden, CT: Archon Books, 1974.

McLeod, Hugh. *European Religion in the Age of the Great Cities, 1830–1930.* London: Routledge, 1995.

Millar, Laura. "The Death of the Fonds and the Resurrection of Provenance: Archival Context in Space and Time." *Archivaria* 53 (2002): 1–15.

Minnullin, Il'nur. *Musul'manskoe dukhovenstvo i vlast' v Tatarstane (1920–1930e gg.).* Kazan: Akademiia nauk Respubliki Tatarstan, 2006.

Mitrofanov, Georgii. *Istoriia Russkoi Pravoslavnoi Tserkvi, 1900–1927.* Moscow: Novoe literaturnoe obozrenie, 2002.

Mitrokhin, Nikolai. *Russkaia Pravoslavnaia Tserkov': Sovremennoe sostoianie i aktual'nye problemy.* Moscow: Novoe Literaturnoe Obozrenie, 2004.

Moyn, Samuel. *The Last Utopia: Human Rights in History.* Cambridge, MA: Belknap, 2012.

Mrázek, Rudolf. *A Certain Age: Colonial Jakarta through the Memories of Its Intellectuals.* Durham, NC: Duke University Press, 2010.

Nathans, Benjamin. "The Disenchantment of Socialism: Soviet Dissidents, Human Rights, and the New Global Morality." In *The Breakthrough: Human Rights in the 1970s*, edited by Jan Eckel and Samuel Moyn, 33–49. Philadelphia: University of Pennsylvania Press, 2014.

Naumescu, Vlad. *Modes of Religiosity in Eastern Christianity: Religious Processes and Social Change in Ukraine*. Berlin: Lit, 2007.

Nekhoroshkov, Mikhail. *Sem'ia i religiia*. Ioshkar-Ola: Mariiskoe knizhnoe izdatel'stvo, 1967.

Niethammer, Lutz, and Wilhelm Trapp. *Lebenserfahrung und kollektives Gedächtnis: die Praxis der Oral History*. Frankfurt: Syndikat, 1980.

Northrop, Douglas. *Veiled Empire: Gender and Power in Stalinist Central Asia*. Ithaca, NY: Cornell University Press, 2004.

Novick, Peter. *That Noble Dream: The 'Objectivity Question' and the American Historical Profession*. Cambridge: Cambridge University Press, 1988.

Oushakine, Serguei. "The Terrifying Mimicry of Samizdat." *Public Culture* 13:2 (2001): 191–214.

Paert, Irina. "Demystifying the Heavens: Women, Religion, and Khrushchev's Anti-Religious Campaign, 1954–64." In *Women in the Khrushchev Era*, edited by Melanie Ilič, Susan Reid, and Lynne Attwood, 203–221. Basingstoke: Palgrave Macmillan, 2004.

Paert, Irina. *Spiritual Elders: Charisma and Tradition in Russian Orthodoxy*. DeKalb: Northern Illinois University Press, 2010.

Pallot, Judith. "Living in the Soviet Countryside." In *Russian Housing in the Modern Age: Design and Social History*, edited by William Craft Brumfield and Blair Ruble, 211–231. Cambridge: Cambridge University Press, 1993.

Panych, Olena. "A Time and Space of Suffering: Reflections of the Soviet Past in the Memoirs and Narratives of the Evangelical Christians-Baptists." In *State Secularism and Lived Religion in Soviet Russia and Ukraine*, edited by Catherine Wanner, 218–243. New York: Oxford University Press, 2012.

Papkova, Irina. *The Orthodox Church and Russian Politics*. New York: Oxford University Press, 2011.

Pelkmans, Mathijs, ed. *Conversion after Socialism: Disruptions, Modernism, and Technologies of Faith in the Former Soviet Union*. New York: Berghahn, 2009.

Peris, Daniel. *Storming the Heavens: The Soviet League of the Militant Godless*. Ithaca, NY: Cornell University Press, 1998.

Pickel, Gert. "Areligiosität, Antireligiosität, Religiosität: Ostdeutschland als Sonderfall niedriger Religiosität im osteuropäischen Rahmen?" In *Atheismus und religiöse Indifferenz*, edited by Christel Gärtner, Detlef Pollack, and Monika Wohlrab-Sahr, 247–269. Opladen: Leske & Budrich, 2003.

Pivovarov, Viktor. *Byt, kul'tura, natsional'nye traditsii i verovaniia naseleniia Checheno-Ingushskoi ASSR.* Groznyi: Checheno-Ingushskoe knizhnoe izdatel'stvo, 1971.

Pivovarov, Viktor. *Na etapakh sotsiologicheskogo issledovaniia: Teoriia i praktika sotsiologicheskikh issledovanii problem ateizma i religii.* Groznyi: Checheno-Ingushskoe knizhnoe izdatel'stvo, 1974.

Pivovarov, Viktor. *Religioznost': Opyt i problemy izucheniia.* Ioshkar-Ola: Mariiskoe knizhnoe izdatel'stvo, 1976.

Pivovarov, Viktor, and Viktor Solov'ev. *Kak zhivesh', tovarishch? Konkretno-sotsiologicheskoe izuchenie byta, kul'tury, traditsii i verovanii naseleniia Mariiskoi ASSR.* Ioshkar-Ola: Mariiskoe knizhnoe izdatel'stvo, 1973.

Plamper, Jan. "Archival Revolution or Illusion? Historicizing Russian Archives and Our Work in Them." *Jahrbücher für Geschichte Osteuropas* 51:1 (2003): 57–69.

Pollack, Detlef. *Säkularisierung—ein moderner Mythos? Studien zum religiösen Wandel in Deutschland.* Tübingen: Mohr-Siebeck, 2003.

Pollack, Detlef, Irena Borowik, and Wolfgang Jagodzinski, eds. *Religiöser Wandel in den postkommunistischen Ländern Ost- und Mitteleuropas.* Würzburg: Ergon, 1998.

Popov, Nikandr. "Na mariiskom iazycheskom molenii." *Etnograficheskoe obozrenie* 3 (1996): 130–145.

Porter-Szűcs, Brian. "Introduction: Christianity, Christians, and the Story of Modernity in Eastern Europe." In *Christianity and Modernity in Eastern Europe,* edited by Bruce Berglund and Brian Porter-Szűcs, 1–34. Budapest: Central European University Press, 2010.

Powell, David. *Antireligious Propaganda in the Soviet Union: A Study of Mass Persuasion.* Cambridge, MA: MIT Press, 1975.

Quijada, Justine. "What if We Don't Know Our Clan? The City Tailgan as New Ritual Form in Buriatiia." *Sibirica* 7:1 (2008): 1–22.

Raleigh, Donald J. "Doing Soviet History: The Impact of the Archival Revolution." *Russian Review* 61:1 (2002): 16–24.

Raleigh, Donald J. *Russia's Sputnik Generation: Soviet Baby Boomers Talk about Their Lives.* Bloomington: Indiana University Press, 2006.

Raleigh, Donald J. *Soviet Baby Boomers: An Oral History of Russia's Cold War Generation.* New York: Oxford University Press, 2012.

Ransel, David. *Village Mothers: Three Generations of Change in Russia and Tataria.* Bloomington: Indiana University Press, 2000.

Reed, Adam. "Documents Unfolding." In *Documents: Artifacts of Modern Knowledge,* edited by Annelise Riles, 158–177. Ann Arbor: University of Michigan Press, 2006.

Reich, Rebecca. "Inside the Psychiatric Word: Diagnosis and Self-Definition in the Late Soviet Period." *Slavic Review* 73:3 (2014): 563–584.

Riles, Annelise, ed. *Documents: Artifacts of Modern Knowledge*. Ann Arbor: University of Michigan Press, 2006.

Robertson, Leslie, and the Kwaguł Gixsam Clan. *Standing up with Ga'axsta'las: Jane Constance Cook and the Politics of Memory, Church, and Custom*. Vancouver: University of British Columbia Press, 2012.

Rock, Stella. " 'They Burned the Pine, but the Place Remains All the Same': Pilgrimage in the Changing Landscape of Soviet Russia." In *State Secularism and Lived Religion in Soviet Russia and Ukraine*, edited by Catherine Wanner, 159–189. New York: Oxford University Press, 2012.

Rogers, Douglas. *The Old Faith and the Russian Land. A Historical Ethnography of Ethics in the Urals*. Ithaca, NY: Cornell University Press, 2009.

Ro'i, Yaacov. *Islam in the Soviet Union: From the Second World War to Gorbachev*. New York: Columbia University Press, 2000.

Rosenblum, Karen E. "The In-Depth Interview: Between Science and Sociability." *Sociological Forum* 2:2 (1987): 388–400.

Sal'nikova, Alla. *Rossiiskoe detstvo v XX veke: Istoriia, teoriia i praktika issledovaniia*. Kazan: Kazanskii gosudarstvennyi universitet, 2007.

Schmidt-Lux, Thomas. "Das helle Licht der Wissenschaft: Die Urania, der organisierte Szientismus und der ostdeutsche Säkularisierungsprozess." *Geschichte und Gesellschaft* 34:1 (2008): 41–72.

Scott, James. *Domination and the Arts of Resistance: Hidden Transcripts*. New Haven, CT: Yale University Press, 1992.

Scott, James. *Seeing like a State: How Certain Schemes to Improve the Human Condition Have Failed*. New Haven, CT: Yale University Press, 1998.

Semenenko-Basin, Ilia Viktorovich. *Sviatost' v russkoi pravoslavnoi kul'ture XX veka: istoriia personifikatsii*. Moscow: RGGU, 2010.

Shabykov, V. I., S. N. Isanbaev, and E. A. Ozhiganova. *Religioznoe soznanie naseleniia respubliki Marii El: Materialy sotsiologicheskikh issledovanii 1994 i 2004 godov*. Ioshkar-Ola: MarNIII, 2005.

Shakhnovich, Marianna. *Ocherki po istorii religiovedeniia*. St. Petersburg: Izdatel'stvo Sankt-Peterburgskogo universiteta, 2006.

Shkarovskii, Mikhail V. *Russkaia pravoslavnaia tserkov' i sovetskoe gosudarstvo v 1943–1964 gg.: ot peremiriia k novoi voine*. St. Petersburg: DEAN-ADIA-M, 1995.

Shlapentokh, Vladimir. *The Politics of Sociology in the Soviet Union*. Boulder: University of Colorado Press, 1987.

Shlikhta, Nataliia. "Ot traditsii k sovremennosti: Pravoslavnaia obriad-
    nost' i prazdniki v usloviiakh antireligioznoi bor'by (na materialakh
    USSR, 1950e-1960e gody)." *Gosudarstvo, Religiia, Tserkov'* 30:3–4
    (2012): 379–406.
Shtyrkov, Sergei. "Prakticheskoe religiovedenie vremen Nikity
    Khrushcheva: respublikanskaia gazeta v bor'be s 'religioznymi
    perezhitkami' (na primere Severo-Osetinskoi ASSR)." In *Traditsii
    narodov Kavkaza v meniaiushchemsia mire: Preemstvennost' i razryvy v
    sotsiokul'turnykh praktikakh*, edited by Iurii Karpov, 306–343. St.
    Petersburg: Peterburgskoe Vostokovedenie, 2010.
Siegelbaum, Louis. "Production Collectives and Communes and the
    'Imperatives' of Soviet Industrialization, 1929–1931." *Slavic Review* 45:1
    (1986): 65–84.
Silverblatt, Irene. "New Christians and New World Fears in Seventeenth-
    Century Peru." In *From the Margins: Historical Anthropology and its
    Futures*, edited by Brian Keith Axel, 95–121. Durham: Duke University
    Press, 2002.
Slezkine, Yuri. *Arctic Mirrors: Russia and the Small Peoples of the North.*
    Ithaca, NY: Cornell University Press, 1994.
Slezkine, Yuri. "The Fall of Soviet Ethnography, 1928–1938." *Current
    Anthropology* 32:4 (1991): 476–484.
Slezkine, Yuri. *The Jewish Century*. Princeton, NJ: Princeton University
    Press, 2004.
Smith, Christian. "Introduction: Rethinking the Secularization of
    American Public Life." In *The Secular Revolution: Power, Interests, and
    Conflict in the Secularization of American Public Life*, edited by Christian
    Smith, 1–96. Berkeley: University of California Press, 2003.
Smolkin, Viktoria. "Sviato mesto pusto ne byvaet: Ateisticheskoe
    vospitanie v Sovetskom Soiuze, 1964–1968." *Neprikosnovennyi zapas*
    65:3 (2009): 36–52.
Smolkin-Rothrock, Victoria. "The Confession of an Atheist Who
    Became a Scholar of Religion: Nikolai Semenovich Gordienko's Last
    Interview." *Kritika* 15:3 (2014): 597–620.
Smolkin-Rothrock, Victoria. "Cosmic Enlightenment: Scientific Atheism
    and the Soviet Conquest of Space." In *Into the Cosmos: Space Exploration
    and Soviet Culture in Post-Stalinist Russia*, edited by James T. Andrews
    and Asif A. Siddiqi, 159–194. Pittsburgh, PA: University of Pittsburgh
    Press, 2011.
Smolkin-Rothrock, Victoria. "Problema 'obyknovennoi' sovetskoi
    smerti: Material'noe i dukhovnoe v ateisticheskoi kosmologii."
    Gosudarstvo, Religiia, Tserkov' 30:3–4 (2012): 429–462.

Smolkin-Rothrock, Victoria. "A Sacred Space Is Never Empty: Soviet Atheism, 1954–1971." Ph.D. dissertation, University of California, Berkeley, 2010.

Smolkin-Rothrock, Victoria. "The Ticket to the Soviet Soul: Science, Religion, and the Spiritual Crisis of Late Soviet Atheism." *Russian Review* 73:2 (2014): 171–197.

Sofronov, Nikolai. *Ateisticheskoe vospitanie kolkhoznogo krest'ianstva.* Ioshkar-Ola: Mariiskoe knizhnoe izdatel'stvo, 1973.

Sokolovskii, Sergei. "Men'shinstva v rossiiskikh regionakh: Otechestvennaia etnografiia i politicheskaia praktika." *Etnometodologiia* 4 (1997): 82–100.

Solov'ev, Viktor. "Nekotorye osobennosti formirovaniia ateisticheskoi ubezhdennosti cheloveka." In *Ateizm i sotsialisticheskaia kul'tura: Materialy nauchnoi konferentsii,* edited by Viktor Solov'ev, 56–67. Ioshkar-Ola: Mariiskoe knizhnoe izdatel'stvo, 1982.

Solov'ev, Viktor. *Po puti dukhovnogo progressa: Nekotorye itogi povtornogo sotsiologicheskogo issledovaniia problem byta, kul'tury, natsional'nykh traditsii, ateizma i verovanii naseleniia Mariiskoi ASSR.* Ioshkar-Ola: Mariiskoe knizhnoe izdatel'stvo, 1987.

Solov'ev, Viktor. *Sotsiologicheskoe issledovanie—v praktiku ideologicheskoi raboty: Nekotorye itogi izucheniia problem byta, kul'tury, natsional'nykh traditsii, ateizma i verovanii naseleniia Mariiskoi ASSR.* Ioshkar-Ola: Mariiskoe knizhnoe izdatel'stvo, 1977.

Spechler, Dina. *Permitted Dissent in the USSR: Novy Mir and the Soviet Regime.* New York: Praeger, 1982.

Spivak, Gayatri Chakravorty. "Can the Subaltern Speak?" In *Marxism and the Interpretation of Culture,* edited by Cary Nelson and Lawrence Grossberg, 271–313. Urbana: University of Illinois Press, 1988.

Ssorin-Chaikov, Nikolai. *The Social Life of the State in Subarctic Siberia.* Stanford, CA: Stanford University Press, 2003.

Stark, Rodney. "Secularization: RIP." *Sociology of Religion* 60:3 (1999): 249–273.

Stepanian, Tsolak A., ed. *Stroitel'stvo kommunizma i dukhovnyi mir cheloveka.* Moscow: Nauka, 1966.

Stephan, Anke, and Julia Obertreis, eds. *Oral History und (post)sozialistische Gesellschaften.* Essen: Klartext, 2009.

Stocking, George W., ed. *Colonial Situations: Essays on the Contextualization of Ethnographic Knowledge.* Madison: University of Wisconsin Press, 1991.

Stoler, Ann Laura. *Along the Archival Grain: Epistemic Anxieties and Colonial Common Sense.* Princeton, NJ: Princeton University Press, 2009.

Stoler, Ann Laura. *Race and the Education of Desire: Foucault's* History of Sexuality *and the Colonial Order of Things.* Durham, NC: Duke University Press, 1995.

Stoler, Ann Laura. "Rethinking Colonial Categories: European Communities and the Boundaries of Rule." *Comparative Studies in Society and History* 31:1 (1989): 134–161.

Stoler, Ann, and Karen Strassler, "Castings for the Colonial: Memory Work in 'New Order' Java." *Comparative Studies in Society and History* 42:1 (2000): 4–48.

Stone, Andrew. "Overcoming Peasant Backwardness: The Khrushchev Anti-Religious Campaign in the Rural Soviet Union." *Russian Review* 67:2 (2008): 296–320.

Stone, Peter G., and Joanne Farchakh Bajjaly, eds. *The Destruction of Cultural Heritage in Iraq.* Woodbridge: Boydell Press, 2008.

Stronski, Paul. *Tashkent: Forging a Soviet City, 1930–1966.* Pittsburgh: University of Pittsburgh Press, 2010.

Sullivan, Winnifred Fallers. *The Impossibility of Religious Freedom.* Princeton, NJ: Princeton University Press, 2005.

Sullivan, Winnifred Fallers. "Religion Naturalized: The New Establishment." In *After Pluralism: Reimagining Religious Engagement,* edited by Courtney Bender and Pamela Klassen, 82–97. New York: Columbia University Press, 2010.

Sullivan, Winnifred Fallers, Elizabeth Shakman Hurd, Saba Mahmood, and Peter Danchin, eds. *Politics of Religious Freedom.* Chicago: University of Chicago Press, 2015.

Takahashi, Sanami. "Religion as an Object of Science in Atheistic Society: The Function of the Historical Museum of Religion and Atheism in Late Socialist Russia." In *India, Russia, China: Comparative Studies on Eurasian Culture and Society,* edited by Tetsuo Mochizuki and Shiho Maeda, 11–19. Sapporo: Slavic Research Center, 2012.

Taubman, William. *Khrushchev: The Man and His Era.* New York: Norton, 2003.

Taylor, Charles. *A Secular Age.* Cambridge, MA: Belknap, 2007.

Thompson, E. P. *The Making of the English Working Class.* New York: Vintage, 1966.

Tolcheva, Detelina. "An Ethos of Relatedness: Foreign Aid and Grassroots Charities in Two Orthodox Parishes in North-Western Russia." In *Multiple Moralities and Religions in Post-Soviet Russia,* edited by Jarrett Zigon, 67–91. New York: Berghahn, 2011.

Trotsky, Leon. "Culture and Socialism" (1926). In *Problems of Everyday Life: Creating the Foundations for a New Society in Revolutionary Russia,* 281–308. New York: Pathfinder Press, 1973.

Trouillot, Michel-Rolph. *Silencing the Past: Power and the Production of History*. Boston: Beacon, 1995.

Urazmanova, Raufa. *Byt neftiannikov-tatar iugo-vostoka Tatarstana (1950–1960e gg.): Etnosotsiologicheskoe issledovanie*. Al'met'evsk: Al'met'evskaia entsiklopediia, 2000.

Urazmanova, Raufa. " 'Musul'manskie' obriady v bytu tatar." *Etnograficheskoe obozrenie* 1 (2009): 13–26.

Vatulescu, Cristina. *Police Aesthetics: Literature, Film and the Secret Police in Soviet Times*. Stanford, CA: Stanford University Press, 2010.

Verdery, Katherine. *Secrets and Truths: Ethnography in the Archive of Romania's Secret Police*. Budapest: CEU Press, 2014.

Verdery, Katherine. *What Was Socialism and What Comes Next?* Princeton, NJ: Princeton University Press, 1996.

Voloshinov, Valentin. *Marxism and the Philosophy of Language*. Translated by Ladislav Matejka and I. R. Titunik. New York: Seminar Press, 1973.

Voloshinov, Valentin. *Marksizm i filosofiia iazyka: Osnovnye problemy sotsiologicheskogo metoda v nauke o iazyke*. Moscow: Labirint, 1993 [1929].

Vucinich, Alexander. "Marx and Parsons in Soviet Sociology." *Russian Review* 33:1 (1974): 1–19.

Walters, Philip. "Editorial." *Religion, State and Society* 20: 1 (1992): 3–4.

Wanner, Catherine. *Communities of the Converted: Ukrainians and Global Evangelism*. Ithaca, NY: Cornell University Press, 2007.

Wanner, Catherine, ed. *State Secularism and Lived Religion in Russia and Ukraine*. New York: Oxford University Press, 2012.

Ward, Christopher. *Brezhnev's Folly: The Building of BAM and Late Soviet Socialism*. Pittsburgh: Pittsburgh University Press, 2009.

Warner, Michael. *Publics and Counterpublics*. New York: Zone Books, 2002.

Watson, Rubie. "Memory, History, and Opposition under State Socialism: An Introduction." In *Memory, History, and Opposition under State Socialism*, edited by Rubie Watson, 1–21. Santa Fe, NM: School of American Research Press, 1994.

Weiss, Claudia. *Wie Sibirien 'unser' wurde: Die Russische Geographische Gesellschaft und ihr Einfluss auf die Bilder und Vorstellungen von Sibirien im 19. Jahrhundert*. Göttingen: V & R Unipress, 2007.

Weld, Kirsten. *Paper Cadavers: The Archives of Dictatorship in Guatemala*. Durham, N.C.: Duke University Press, 2014.

Werth, Paul. *At the Margins of Orthodoxy: Mission, Governance, and Confessional Politics in Russia's Volga-Kama Region, 1827–1905*. Ithaca, NY: Cornell University Press, 2002.

Werth, Paul. "In the State's Embrace? Civil Acts in an Imperial Order." *Kritika* 7:3 (2006): 433–458.

West, Harry. "Who Rules Us Now? Identity Tokens, Sorcery, and Other Metaphors in the 1994 Mozambican Elections." In *Transparency and Conspiracy: Ethnographies of Suspicion in the New World Order*, edited by Harry West and Todd Sanders, 92–124. Durham, NC: Duke University Press, 2003.

White, Hayden. *Metahistory: The Historical Imagination in Nineteenth-Century Europe.* Baltimore, MD: Johns Hopkins University Press, 1975.

White, Louise, Stephan Miescher, and David William Cohen, eds. *African Worlds, African Voices: Critical Practices in Oral History.* Bloomington: Indiana University Press, 2001.

Wohlrab-Sahr, Monika, Uta Karstein, and Thomas Schmidt-Lux. *Forcierte Säkularität: Religiöser Wandel und Generationendynamik im Osten Deutschlands.* Frankfurt: Campus, 2009.

Yelensky, Viktor. "The Revival before the Revival: Popular and Institutionalized Religion in Ukraine on the Eve of the Collapse of Communism." In *State Secularism and Lived Religion in Soviet Russia and Ukraine*, edited by Catherine Wanner, 302–330. New York: Oxford University Press, 2012.

Yeo, Geoffrey. "Custodial History, Provenance, and the Description of Personal Records." *Libraries and the Cultural Record* 44:1 (2009): 50–64.

Young, Glennys. *Power and the Sacred in Revolutionary Russia: Religious Activists in the Village.* University Park: Pennsylvania State University Press, 1997.

Yurchak, Alexei. *Everything Was Forever until It Was no More: The Last Soviet Generation.* Princeton, NJ: Princeton University Press, 2006.

Zanca, Russell. *Life in a Muslim Uzbek Village: Cotton Farming after Communism.* Belmont, CA: Wadsworth, 2011.

Zaslavskaya, Olga. "From Dispersed to Distributed Archives: The Past and the Present of Samizdat Material." *Poetics Today* 29:4 (2008): 669–712.

Zhamkov, Aleksei. "Sovet po delam religii: stranitsy proshlogo." Interview with Vladimir Pudov. *Bogoslov.ru*, http://www.bogoslov.ru/text/498829.html (accessed November 16, 2009).

Zhidkova, Elena. "Sovetskaia grazhdanskaia obriadnost' kak al'ternativa obriadnosti religioznoi." *Gosudarstvo, Religiia, Tserkov'* 30:3–4 (2012): 407–428.

Zhuk, Sergei. *Rock and Roll in the Rocket City: The West, Identity, and Ideology in Soviet Dnepropetrovsk, 1960–1985.* Baltimore, MD: Johns Hopkins University Press, 2010.

Zemskov-Züge, Andrea. "Narrating the Siege of Leningrad. Official and Unofficial Practices in the Memorialization of the 'Great

Patriotic War.'" In *Unsettling History: Archiving and Narrating in Historiography*, edited by Alf Lüdtke and Sebastian Jobs, 199–217. Frankfurt: Campus, 2010.

Ziemann, Benjamin, and Miriam Dobson. "Introduction." In *Reading Primary Sources: The Interpretation of Texts from Nineteenth- and Twentieth-Century History*, edited by Miriam Dobson and Benjamin Ziemann, 1–18. London: Routledge, 2009.

Zuckerman, Phil. *Faith No More: Why People Reject Religion*. New York: Oxford, 2012.

The Oxford Series on History and Archives
General Editors: Francis X. Blouin Jr. and
William G. Rosenberg, *University of Michigan*

Processing the Past: Changing Authorities in History and the Archives
Francis X. Blouin Jr. and William G. Rosenberg

*"Collect and Record!": Jewish Holocaust Documentation in
Postwar Europe*
Laura Jockusch

*The Archive Thief: The Man Who Salvaged French Jewish History
in the Wake of the Holocaust*
Lisa Moses Leff

Index